selected pages.

DATE DUE

To Archbishop Desmond Mpilo Tutu,
Freedom Fighter

CHALLENGE TO APARTHEID

Toward a Morally Defensible Strategy

Mokgethi Motlhabi

WILLIAM B. EERDMANS PUBLISHING COMPANY
GRAND RAPIDS, MICHIGAN

Copyright © 1988 by Wm. B. Eerdmans Publishing Co.
255 Jefferson Ave. S.E., Grand Rapids, Mich. 49503

Library of Congress Cataloging-in-Publication Data

Motlhabi, Mokgethi B. G. (Mokgethi Buti George), 1944–
Challenge to apartheid: toward a morally defensible strategy /
Mokgethi B. G. Motlhabi.
p.   cm.
ISBN 0-8028-0347-4
1. Apartheid—South Africa.
2. Government, Resistance to—South Africa.
3. Apartheid—Moral and ethical aspects.
I. Title.
DT763.M69   1988
305.8′00968—dc19   88-7157
                                                              CIP

Contents

Preface vii

Abbreviations xi

Introduction 1

1. GENERAL HISTORICAL OVERVIEW 7
The Setting 9

Forms of Opposition 17

The Consequences of Opposition 29

Summary 35

2. THREE MOMENTS OF RESISTANCE 37
Backgrounds and Origins 39

Long-term and Short-term Goals 43

Practical Implications 58

Government Response 68

Regrouping and Change of Strategies 72

Critical Evaluation 76

3. ALLIANCES OF THE 1980S 79
Origins 82

Black Consciousness Reviewed 86

Long-term and Short-term Goals 87

Practical Implications 99

Government Response 111

Critical Evaluation 114

4. TOWARD A CONCEPTION OF CONTINUITY
   BETWEEN PHILOSOPHICAL AND
   THEOLOGICAL ETHICS   119
   Coherence in Social and General Ethics   120
   The Moral Laws   123
   Practical Implications of Moral Law
   in Christian Social Ethics   130

5. THE MORAL SIGNIFICANCE OF THE SOUTH
   AFRICAN STRUGGLE   133
   Review of Goals   134
   Review of Strategies   141
   Conclusion   163

6. FUTURE ACTION: HOW VIABLE?   165
   Search for Alternative Structures   166
   "Guidelines for Strategy"   176
   Alternative Strategies for the Internal Quest for Change:
   Limited Options   183
   Conclusion   206

   Afterword   209
   Notes   217
   Index   239

Preface

When I was invited to prepare this manuscript for an American edition, I hesitated a little but took it as a challenge. It was an enormous task, and I had little time to carry it out. I realized, however, that to do so would offer me an opportunity to provide the "outside world" with an alternative analysis and interpretation of the South African crucible and its challenge by those it affects directly.

This book originally appeared in South Africa in 1984 under the title *The Theory and Practice of Black Resistance to Apartheid: A Social-Ethical Analysis*. In December 1984 the South African government declared the book undesirable and banned its distribution. The ban was lifted four months later after an appeal by the publisher, who argued that the book was an objective and scholarly work. It was not meant, as the publications control board charged, to incite violence or to encourage currently ongoing unrest in the country.

This present edition is a revised and updated version of that book. The main revision is in the present Chapter 2, an abridgement of three chapters in the original manuscript that examined in some detail the theoretical and practical orientations of three earlier national movements that operated in South Africa. These movements are the African National Congress (ANC), the Pan Africanist Congress (PAC), and the Black Consciousness Movement (BCM). The last was represented chiefly by the South African Students Organization (SASO) and the Black People's Convention (BPC).

In addition to the abridgement, this edition has been edited stylistically for smoother reading. I have elaborated slightly on some statements and have also added minor updates to reflect changed circumstances—where absolutely necessary—between the date of the original publication and the time of the revision. Major discussion of changed circumstances is in the Afterword. Where it has not been possible to reflect such changes either in the relevant part of the text or in the After-word, I have been content to infer the information in a new chapter, which updates the situation.

This main update of the book is found in the new Chapter 3, which examines the activities of three new national movements that have come into being since the BCM was declared illegal in some of its constituent organizations in 1977. The earliest of these is the Azanian People's Organization (AZAPO), followed by the National Forum (NF) and the United Democratic Front (UDF). I have examined these movements in the same light as the earlier ones, emphasizing theory and practice. I have integrated their social-ethical evaluation into Chap-ter 5, which was originally Chapter 6. This approach seemed better to me than to treat them separately and completely afresh, particularly since most of the conclusions regarding the moral standing of the ear-lier movements apply also to them. No doubt by the time this book comes out in print, some changes will have occurred in the situation it discusses. This is the plight of writing in a state of flux.

The present American edition has benefited greatly from the com-ments provided by various people and from my discussions with them. I am particularly grateful to Paul K. Deats, Jr., who has continued to offer me his support and time in spite of his very busy schedule. He patiently read the two new chapters in relation to the original manu-script and offered useful suggestions in rendering the book meaningful for the American reader. Professor Deats continues to follow events in South Africa with concerned interest and welcomes this study as another way of conveying the issues there to the American people. Katherine Demuth, head of the Department of African Languages at Boston University African Studies Center, was kind enough to read the new chapters and to offer suggestions to make them more readable. I am also grateful to two South Africans currently teaching and studying in the United States: Richard Rive, who is a visiting professor at Har-vard University, and Saths Cooper of Boston University. They offered useful comments on aspects of the contents of Chapter 3. If I have not included all of the comments of those who read the new material, it was more for lack of space and because of a particular emphasis than because I found some of their comments valueless. I owe a lasting debt to Wal-ter G. Muelder for allowing me to adopt his "moral laws" to use in eval-uating the resistance movements in South Africa and for other previous assistance.

My publisher, Wm. B. Eerdmans Publishing Co., has been very tolerant with me. This edition was to have appeared as early as the fall of 1985, but I was unable to find the time to work on it. I am very grateful to William Eerdmans himself for still finding some value in the book and for negotiating with the original publisher, Skotaville, to let Eerdmans bring out the American edition.

Needless to say, this entire enterprise would not have been possible without the generous support of the Ford Foundation. A grant from the foundation facilitated my travel to the U.S. and underwrote my living expenses during my six months as a visiting scholar at Boston University. I highly value this undeserved support as well as the hospitality of my alma mater, particularly my contacts at the African Studies Center. Ford Foundation will certainly be remembered when the words of the last judgment are pronounced: "I was hungry [in more than one way], and you fed me." I am only one of many who have benefited and continue to do so from its overwhelming generosity.

Finally, though not least, my heartfelt gratitude goes to the National Council of the Educational Opportunities Council for offering me a six-month sabbatical to enable me to pursue my academic interests. The chair of the Council, the Most Reverend Archbishop Desmond Tutu, has been very encouraging to me and has always lamented the fact that I was being "incapacitated" by a lot of administrative duties, with little time for creative reflection and writing. In fact, it is to Archbishop Tutu that I primarily owe most of what I have been able to accomplish academically, as my acknowledgment in the South African edition fully testifies. None of the above benefactors is in any way implicated in the contents of this book, which are my sole responsibility.

Mokgethi Motlhabi
Boston, Massachusetts

Abbreviations

AAC	All African Convention
ANC	African National Congress
ANCYL	African National Congress Youth League
ARM	African Resistance Movement
ASB	Afrikaanse Studente Bond
ASSECA	Association for Educational and Cultural Advancement of Africans
AZAPO	Azanian People's Organization
AZASM	Azanian Students Movement
AZASO	Azanian Students Organization
BAWU	Black Allied Workers Union
BCM	Black Consciousness Movement
BCP	Black Community Programs
BPA	Black Parents Association
BPC	Black People's Convention
BTP	Black Theology Project
BWP	Black Workers Project
CI	Christian Institute
COD	Congress of Democrats
COSAS	Congress of South African Students
COSATU	Congress of South African Trade Unions
CUSA	Confederation of Unions of South Africa
DRC	Dutch Reformed Church
FOSATU	Federation of South African Trade Unions
FRELIMO	Front for the Liberation of Mozambique
IDAMASA	Interdenominational African Ministers Association of South Africa
NECC	National Education Crisis Committee
NF(C)	National Forum (Committee)

NUSAS	National Union of South African Students
PAC	Pan Africanist Congress
PEYCO	Port Elizabeth Youth Congress
SACC	South African Council of Churches
SACP	South African Communist Party
SACTU	South African Congress of Trade Unions
SANNC	South African Native National Congress
SASM	South African Students Movement
SASO	South African Students Organization
SASOL	South African Coal, Oil and Gas Corporation
SCT	Soweto Committee of Ten
SSRC	Soweto Students Representative Council
UDF	United Democratic Front

Introduction

The purpose of this study is to examine the challenge posed to apartheid by national resistance movements in South Africa. The main aim is to determine the moral significance of this challenge and its implications for future resistance. The examination is limited to those movements that have operated or are now operating legally inside the country and to those movements that resorted to internal underground activity after being declared illegal by the government.

Apartheid was introduced as a government policy in South Africa when the ruling National Party came to power in 1948. Literally, the term *apartheid* means "apartness" or "separateness." Some of its supporters have distinguished its meaning from the term and idea of *segregation,* as they see it as having farther-reaching implications than the latter. According to them, the old practice of segregation still offered black people some hope that through education and adequate assimilation of Western values they could become equals with whites and ultimately share with them in the government of the country. Apartheid, on the other hand, does away with all such "false hopes" through its thoroughness and purposefulness in its concept of separation.

As a government policy, apartheid is a legalized form of racial discrimination. It advocates the separation of people in all levels of society on the basis of color. Through it, South African society is divided hierarchically into four major population groups according to their different shades of skin color. Whites occupy the top rank, followed by "coloureds" and Indians in the middle, with Africans at the bottom of the ladder. The majority among the "non-white" groups do not recognize this differentiation among themselves, however, and prefer to see themselves all as constituting a single black group that is collectively oppressed by whites. Notwithstanding this, the government ensures that they are treated differently from one another on the whole, offer-

1

ing "coloureds" and Indians a slightly better deal than Africans, as their middle status implies.

[In practice, apartheid means that not only can black and white people not live together in the same neighborhood; they may also not participate in the same government, not belong to the same social institutions, not worship together, not share the same syllabi of education, not use similar public facilities, and not be rewarded equally for similar duties and achievements. Yet they all have to pay equal taxes to maintain the system that favors some of the groups above others. [Its supporters believe that it is only through such separation among population groups that harmonious living relations can be achieved and maintained among them. Such a view, however, belies the history of the country, as most of South Africa's racial problems since 1948 can be directly attributed to the inequities of the apartheid policy. Apartheid further ensures, according to them, that the country's ruling minority will not be overwhelmed by the black majority—which can only lead to a black government—through their equal participation in the same political structures.

The ultimate goal of apartheid is to make South Africa a "white man's country."[1] To achieve this purpose, the government has established existing African reserves as permanent "homelands" for the various ethnic groups of the African people and offered them "self-rule" in these "homelands." Some of them have even accepted "full independence" from the South African government. However, all these areas together constitute only 13 percent of the most arid part of South Africa's entire territory. They are meant to accommodate and feed more than 21 million of the country's population, while the remaining 87 percent of the land caters to only slightly more than a quarter of the population.[2]

Recently, the government tried to co-opt the "coloured" and Indian people by offering them some form of representation in government, thus acknowledging their South African citizenship. At the same time, the future of those Africans living in urban areas was left on the balance with regard to their citizenship, since previously it had been legislated that all Africans were citizens of only one or other of the "homelands." The majority of both "coloureds" and Indians rejected their proposed parliamentary representation because it excluded Africans[3] and most Africans themselves refuse to be divided into urban and rural groups—which implies different "rights and privileges," however insignificant—in their own land. Whereas apartheid, therefore, is often portrayed as if it stands only for the separation of people who remain equal in all other respects and may have equal or proportional share of resources, the truth is that it is an instrument of exploitation, domination, and oppression, as the following chapters hope to show.

The black national struggle against white domination in South Africa antedates apartheid and the National Party. It has been manifest in mainly three forms since it began in earnest in the nineteenth century, changing from armed resistance to political journalism and finally to political organization and agitation, with some organizations resorting to the armed struggle once more after being declared illegal by the government. While the original armed struggle was a full-scale war—recorded historically as the eight so-called Kaffir Wars—resort to armed resistance in the 1960s mainly took the form of guerrilla tactics. The first national movement that we will examine here began fighting for black rights—against gradual disinheritance by colonial powers—through political agitation in 1912 and continued doing so after the takeover of the apartheid regime thirty-six years later. It was the first national political organization among blacks. While other national organizations during its time either worked in cooperation with it or had separate agendas, it has been chosen for analysis here because it was the leading organization of its time and played a significant role in the history of black resistance in South Africa. The same applies to the other five movements that will be examined, mainly as far as their impact and historical significance in the struggle for change.

However, we are not concerned solely with what these movements *did* to achieve their goal. This is neither a historical study nor merely an accumulation of facts. While I am concerned to discover and record particular events as they occurred in their historical context, my emphasis is rather on the compatibility of theory and practice and their moral significance in the course of the struggle. I seek to find out the ideas and policies that motivated action as well as how such action measured up to those ideas and policies both in faithfulness to them and in extent. This will be done in the case of each movement examined. Also to be determined will be continuities and discontinuities, similarities and dissimilarities, between successive movements with regard to their theories and practices. Finally, I will evaluate ethically each movement's standpoints on theory and practice to determine their moral worth and significance for ongoing and future challenges to apartheid.

The following is an outline of the book: The next chapter will provide the context for our study by giving the historical background to apartheid and earlier forms of resistance and challenge to it, particularly those forms of resistance not constituting the main subject of this study. This chapter will be followed by two others, each dealing with three movements of the periods it encompasses. Thus the African National Congress (1912–1960), the Pan Africanist Congress (1959–1960), and the Black Consciousness Movement (1969–1977) will be treated in Chapter 2. Chapter 3 will consider the Azanian People's Organization (1978–), the National Forum (1983–), and the United Democratic Front (1983–). As already indicated, the treatment will be selective, focusing on theory and practice. The following chapter will examine and adopt a moral theoretical frame of reference that will be used in the next chapter to evaluate the theories and practices of these movements. Finally, the last chapter will consider alternative structures and strategies for future action, bearing in mind past weaknesses and mishaps and calculated to propose a remedy to them through systematic strategizing.

Because of the study's focus on theory and practice and their moral significance, it is impossible to give detailed treatment to certain important historical events. Some of these events were instrumental in bringing the evil of apartheid forcefully to the attention of the international community. In acknowledgment of their historical significance and import for the struggle, though they contain some detail not immediately relevant for the present study, I have chosen to elaborate a little further on them in the Afterword and to consider their links and significance in the history of resistance in South Africa. It is important to note that these events are not simply bypassed in the main text but are rather given selective treatment in accordance with their relevance for the subject under consideration. Three of these events, the Sharpeville killings, the Soweto student uprising, and the death of Steve Biko, and the impact they all had for the whole country, are discussed briefly in Chapter 2. The last event, the recent school boycotts and renewed student activism, is discussed in the context of the National Education Crisis Committee in Chapter 3.

Some may consider it inappropriate to examine the moral significance of the struggle against apartheid, which is both the ultimate aim of this study and proposed point of departure for any future action. "What has morality to do with it?" they will ask. Besides, "we are fighting against an evil system; why focus on the moral worth of our own activities and not that of the system's itself?" There are two main reasons why this kind of study is considered important. The first is to justify the struggle itself and the methods adopted in carrying it out; the second is to inform action through the adoption of appropriate strategies based on morally sound analysis and guidelines.

Sympathizers and those who wish to understand its cause continually ask the resistance movement to explain its position and to justify its actions. Moreover, its members also need to remind themselves constantly why they are fighting so that they do not lose their orientation and continue to engage in struggle merely for its own sake. Thus they have to keep both the struggle and their actions in it in perspective. On the other hand, it is true that the war against apartheid is war against an evil system. It is quite a patent system to everyone who knows it and thus it does not need any elaborate moral exposition or trite condemnation. Rather, it is for those who wage war against it to ensure the justness of their own cause by avoiding sinking to the level of the perpetrators of this system through sheer greed and selfishness, nurtured by unjustifiable human prejudice. Thus as long as the opponents of apartheid have a moral edge over its advocates, with the methods these advocates employ to implement it, the opponents have sufficient grounds to continue fighting this policy and searching for better ways to bring about its complete elimination. It is not unimportant, therefore, for the movements examined here to continue to justify the uprightness of their cause.

Second, and equally important, morality provides the opportunity to count the cost in all aspects of one's actions and hence to avoid taking unnecessary risks or needlessly exposing others to harm. In the case under consideration, it would advocate careful planning of action and serious weighing of consequences before any actual engagement: advantages and disadvantages of a particular line of action; its implications for the cause; its implications for the participants and other fellow human beings; commensurability of means and ends, etc. With proper planning and judgment, failure comes more as a matter of accident than as a result of willful negligence. Further, by studying past weaknesses and casualties of the struggle, one is able to forestall them for the future. Hence the question of morality here is not to be viewed simply as a matter of purposeless "do's" and "don'ts" but rather as a means of informing action through prior analysis and judgment of the situation before the actual decision to act is taken.

By recommending a moral approach to the struggle against apartheid, therefore, we are attempting to employ a two-edged sword for the challenge. On the one hand, this approach will ensure the moral integrity of the cause by using appropriate, well-examined means to achieve its end. On the other, it will ascertain that a careful study of how to formulate and implement strategy is undertaken before any particular strategy can be put into action. In this way, it will become clear that it is immoral—hence destructive—to use unexamined and morally untested strategies for the purpose of achieving change, particularly if the consequences of such strategies may be harmful to those they are intended to help. It will also become clear that sheer moral pronouncements or expressions of moral outrage in themselves are not strategies for achieving change and thus cannot take the place of careful strategizing. Accordingly, both formulation and implementation of strategy must take morality into account, while morality must, in turn, inspire and inform all meaningful strategy for action.

Chapter 1

General Historical Overview

Three approaches have characterized the resistance of black people to white domination in general in South African history. Two of these, armed resistance and political opposition, are more outstanding than the third, which Karis and Carter have referred to as political journalism.[1] Armed resistance played a greater role in the early confrontation of blacks against whites shortly after the two races had met. This was the result of the latter's attempt to restrict the former to certain borders in the southeastern part of the country.[2] It lasted beyond the so-called Last Kaffir War in 1878, after which there were still isolated attempts at armed struggle, as reflected in the rebellions of Mampuru in the Transvaal in 1881 and of Bambata in Natal in 1906.[3]

During the period between these dates it had already become clear to the Africans that they must seek a different strategy if they were to achieve their goal at all. On the whole, their wars had ended in defeat before the superior might of the settlers. Thus by 1882 the first African political organization was formed in the Transkei, Eastern Cape. Two years later John Tengo Jabavu founded an African newspaper, *Imvo Zabantsundu* (Black Opinion). "At the very start of African political journalism, as throughout the history of subsequent African protests, questions of franchise were central."[4] A number of other groups and associations concerned with this same issue of franchise as well as with other legislation affecting Africans were subsequently formed throughout all the provinces of South Africa.

In a sense, these two latter approaches of resistance were a concession of defeat in the military struggle. They involved the abandonment of the sole claim of the African people to the land. Through them Africans were no longer concerned primarily with reestablishing themselves as masters of their own land. Rather, circumstances forced them to be preoccupied with warding off the gradually increasing discriminatory and oppressive legislation coming their way and threatening to disinherit them completely. This diversion was to constitute the immediate or short-term goal of their resistance throughout history. To a stranger it has often given the impression that mere reformism was the ultimate aim of black protests. In actual fact, however, although this was no longer a question of either/or, on the part of Africans, between black and white claims of ownership of the country, the Africans still kept in the background the long-term goal of equality in a democracy composed of all those who inhabited the land. They were now ready to push historical disputes aside and seek a life of peace with their white neighbors. This sentiment was to be expressed in a variety of ways by subsequent generations. The Freedom Charter adopted in 1955 by the ANC and other groups constituting the Congress Alliance[5] conceded that South Africa belonged to all who lived in it. All were to share equal rights, with no special privileges given to either whites or blacks. The implication of this affirmation—hence the long-term goal of black opposition—was that government should be by the majority (i.e., democratic), without any reference to color, race, or creed.

This long-term goal of black people has been, and remains—in the eyes of the white governments—the stumbling block in South African politics. Because whites have refused to accept it, discriminatory practices and legislation have persisted and intensified through the years, reaching their peak in the present policy of apartheid.

As an introduction to this study, then, it seems fitting to begin by attempting to place this policy in its historical context. This will require tracing its roots not only from the beginning of the present administration. Early historical precedents will help to show why apartheid, with each passing age, has consistently become such a hard nut to crack. It will be impossible to include all its aspects in the given space. The main purpose of this chapter is to provide the thinking behind apartheid—and the various reactions it aroused—rather than to discuss in detail its various forms of implementation. Hence emphasis will be placed on its sociopolitical development rather than on its economic implications and other equally important aspects. The theory regarding the bantustans, though they are seen as indispensable to the functioning of apartheid, will also be merely inferred from the evolution and implementation of this policy.

Apartheid is an imposition of a minority on a majority. In the process of this examination, therefore, we cannot but look at the reactions it has aroused in South African society in general. We will also see how it has justified itself or responded to these reactions. I will include as much detail as possible in these few paragraphs on opposition coming from groups other than those which are the prime focus of this project. The role played by the latter will merely be sketched out here for detailed consideration later.

THE SETTING

The System of Apartheid

The word *apartheid* means separation or apartness. The system of apartheid, therefore, stands for the separation of races. This separation is intended not only physically but also politically, culturally, socioeconomically, and religiously. Hill describes the two pillars of apartheid as the belief of the Afrikaner in the "essential difference of races" and fear of the black peril, leading to the need for self-preservation by white South Africans.[6] Schlemmer has described them as race prejudice and class or economic privilege.[7] Primarily, the separation sought is between blacks and whites. The fear of being overwhelmed by a united black majority, however, makes necessary the strategy of divide and rule. Thus the various black ethnic groups that had already attained "national consciousness" are being forced back into individual group shells, there to develop an exclusive self-consciousness and ethnocentrism. Consequently, prejudice is encouraged among black groups. Whereas blacks are to be separated both from one another and from whites as a group, the whites are to be united as a single group. The result is the subjugation of one divided "race" by another, which is united. One of the reasons for the government's uneasiness with the Black Consciousness Movement was that it rejected this imposed division among blacks. Its primary goal was to meet white domination with black solidarity.[8] A similar uneasiness was surprisingly expressed in 1974 by the minister of justice, Mr. Kruger, against an organization originally founded by Chief Dinizulu of the Zulus and recently revived by Chief Mangosuthu Gatsha Buthelezi—*Inkatha Yenkululeko Yesizwe*—in spite of Buthelezi's association with the government's homeland policy. Mr. Kruger expressed his preparedness to recognize this organization if it were restricted to the Zulus, but threatened trouble if its base was broadened. The chief replied that "while the National Party did not exclude English-speaking South Africans and Jews, in the same way *Inkatha* could not exclude other Africans."[9] Because resistance to this system of racial domination and segregation seems to grow with each new generation, cooperation is guaranteed by a ruthless police force and an omnipresent network of secret police, as well as by a cumulative volume or restrictive legislation.[10]

Although *separation* or *segregation* and *apartheid* are almost synonymous when translated, apartheid is often distinguished from segregation as more effective and far-reaching. Segregation is seen as a "mere stage in the evolution of apartheid." While the former is based on "lip service, compromise," and the like, apartheid is said to have in view "lasting arrangements" of black-white relations in "all spheres of human activity."[11] From this it is obvious that apartheid proper begins only in 1948, when the name was adopted and explicitly used by the present administration in its ascent to power. According to this view, then, the foregoing period would have been characterized by segregation.

Apartheid has also been distinguished from *separate development* as somewhat like a genus to a species. In this view apartheid is general, encompassing all South African life—practices and policies as well as legislation. Separate development, on the other hand, focuses on the ethnic and cultural aspects of apartheid as those aspects of life which justify it or provide rationalization for it.[12]

For the present purpose these distinctions do not have much significance. Rather, separate development is taken as a euphemism for apartheid, which the South African government thinks has been very much misunderstood by the world. Segregation and apartheid are generally used synonymously, though mention of apartheid evokes perhaps more sharply a sense of ruthlessness, police brutality, and intolerance because of the way it has been implemented. Except for the latter's anachronism as legislated segregation, however, there seems to be no compelling reason not to continue to use both words as one.

Historical Basis and Significance

Apartheid is the culmination of the Afrikaner's long quest for self-determination and independence, first from the British administration in South Africa, then—lest he be overwhelmed by their numbers—from the indigenous black population of the country. Both the Dutch and British governments of the early Cape had certain policies with regard to the natives on the frontier. The settlers were to have no contact or intercourse with them. As early as 1788 the Dutch Council of Policy established the Fish River as the border between the settlers and the Cape Africans.[13] This measure was continued by the two British governors, the Earl of McCartney and Governor S. F. Craddock, soon after the first British occupation of the Cape in 1795.[14] It was the beginning of the systematic channeling of Africans into specific areas that would later constitute their so-called homelands. For instance, parts of the area lying between the Fish River—which the Africans were forbidden to cross—and the Kei River now constitute what is known as the Ciskei "homeland." Further channeling of Africans into prescribed areas was carried out in Natal in this early period by Sir Theophilus Shepstone.

Neame has referred to him as "an early creator of Bantustans."[15] It is more accurate to say, however, that he merely gave explicit utterance to what was already being carried out in practice wherever a "native problem" was already perceived to exist in the country. According to him, the natives "were to live in their own areas, governed as far as possible through their own chiefs under Native Law." This principle was supported by the establishment of eight reserves for Africans living in Natal. The present Kwazulu bantustan is composed of a substantial amount of these reserves. By the time South Africa became a union in 1910 nearly three hundred reserves were scattered all over the country.[16] These are the bulk of the so-called Bantu homelands today. Some of these reserves are areas "from which the Africans could not be pushed by the advancing white settlers in the 19th century."[17]

In the Union government segregationist sentiments were expressed within a year of its establishment[18] by its minister of native affairs, J. M. B. Hertzog. He attacked the qualified African franchise still existing then in the Cape as a crime toward whites, "and for the Natives . . . 'a snare and a hypocrisy.'" He introduced a land bill in Parliament "to regulate the residence of the Natives in certain portions of the Union and to prohibit [their] unauthorized settlement on any land."[19] This bill temporarily failed because it involved removals not only of Africans from specified lands but also, for exchanging purposes, of certain whites. It was reintroduced successfully in 1913 by General Hertzog's successor,[20] and became known as the 1913 Land Act.

Sentiments similar to those of General Hertzog were expressed by other ministers as well, including the prime minister, General Botha; the world-acclaimed statesman and liberal, General Jan C. Smuts; and H. W. Sampson. Sampson advocated self-government by the African "by separating from the Whites." Botha qualified this by saying that "self-government" could be meaningful only under white supervision. Smuts expressed the idea as follows in a speech made in London in 1917:

We have realized that political ideas which apply to our white civilization largely do not apply to the administration of Native Affairs. To apply the same institutions on an equal basis to White and Black alike does not lead to the best results, and so a practice has grown in South Africa of creating parallel institutions—giving the Natives their own separate institutions on parallel lines with institutions for Whites . . . We have felt more and more that if we are to solve our Native question it is useless to try to govern Black and White in the same system. . . . They are different not only in color but in mind and in political capacity. . . . Thus in South Africa you will have in the long run large areas cultivated by Blacks and governed by Blacks, where they will look after themselves in all their forms of living and development, while in the rest of the country you will have your White communities, which will govern themselves separately according to the accepted European principles.[21]

On another occasion Smuts affirmed that the ideal of the Union government was to make South Africa a "White man's country."[22] An Afrikaner writer and critic of apartheid has pointed out that if the ideal of apartheid was equivalent to the nineteenth-century American one of "separate but equal," as the above quotation seems to imply, there would, indeed, be some virtue in it—and perhaps even fewer critics. Unfortunately, however, this is hardly the case. "And that is why South Africa runs like a sewer through the conscience of the world."[23] Smuts is also contradicted by his government's 1913 Land Bill. This bill puts aside not "large areas" but less than 7.3 percent of all of South Africa as land reserved for Africans.[24] These observations confirm the earlier remark that the present notion of separate (probably intended to give the impression of "but equal") development is merely a misleading euphemism for apartheid.

Our examination so far seems to lead to the conclusion that, whatever other causes were responsible for segregation in South Africa, land claims were basic. Economic causes were second, especially after the emancipation of slaves in the British empire in 1834. This particular cause was partly responsible for the Great Trek inland from the Cape of the Boer settlers.[25] The end of the wars and the living in close quarters between the two races raised the question of franchise for both. It was in search of a solution to this problem that the question of territorial segregation kept returning throughout South African history until it was considered to be the "only practical solution." In the meantime, control of the Africans was to be achieved through a restrictive pass system first introduced in the Cape in 1809 by the Earl of Caledon, but later abolished. Its aim was to compel the so-called Hottentots to work for the settlers and to regulate their movement in the colony. It was reintroduced in the Transvaal by the Boer Afrikaners in 1859,[26] later adopted in the Orange Free State, and finally throughout the country. While not necessarily basic in these developments, racial bias was an accompanying factor.[27] It increasingly grew in importance until it became a tool in political election campaigns. From here it assumed the appearance of the main issue in South African life and politics. Biko sharply illustrates this point, although he places his emphasis on economic matters rather than land as the chief cause:

In South Africa, after generations of exploitation, white people on the whole have come to believe in the inferiority of the Black man, so much that while the race problem started as an offshoot of the economic greed exhibited by white people, it has now become a serious problem on its own.[28]

Accordingly, it was on the race issue that the National Party campaigned for office in 1948. Apartheid then was a racialistic slogan rather than a method of "respect" for the identities of other racial groups as has often been claimed in its justification. The concept of "separate development" was a later expression, meant to repair the external damage already done by this slogan in the eyes of the world. At the same time there was no change internally. Rather, the situation continued to deteriorate dismally, leading to outbreaks like those of Sharpeville and Soweto.

The prime architect of apartheid was Dr. D. F. Malan. He was the first prime minister of the ruling National Party. In an election campaign speech made on April 20, 1948, Malan asked whether the "European race" in South Africa would in the future successfully maintain its rule, its purity, and its civilization, or would it "float along until it vanishes for ever, without honour, in the Black sea of South Africa's Non-European population." The removal of segregation, he warned, would mean that South Africa would sooner or later have to take its place among the half-caste nations of the world.[29] Malan was the first to extend separation between the Africans and the "coloureds," who until then had lived together and identified with each other. It remained for Dr. Hendrik Verwoerd, the third National Party prime minister, to extend this kind of separation among the African ethnic groups.

The idea of territorial segregation and "self-government," which is now being implemented in South Africa, did not seem to impress Malan very much. He rejected it on economic grounds, pointing out that South African economy was to a large extent dependent on black labor.[30] Nor did he believe that Africans, "primitive" as they were, could exercise human rights responsibly.[31] This meant that he was an advocate of white trusteeship, as Strijdom after him.

Malan resigned from the premiership on November 30, 1954. His successor was J. G. Strijdom, the author of white *baasskap*. According to Strijdom, "either the White man dominates or the Black man takes over. . . . And the only way [the Europeans] can maintain domination is by withholding the vote from the [Africans]." He stated emphatically that it was not possible for blacks in general to take over government, either through merit or otherwise.[32] In spite of these utterances, Strijdom still wanted to convince the blacks that his policy was in their interest as well as that of whites. Unlike Malan, he was sympathetic to the idea of African rights in the reserves as their "homelands," but not as independent states.[33]

Strijdom took some practical steps to implement some of his ideas about apartheid. Among them were the separation of labor unions along ethnic lines, job reservation—setting aside certain job categories for whites only—and the separation of university education for blacks and whites. There were to be separate universities also for Africans, Indians, and "coloureds." In response to criticism the prime minister stated:

> The universities are there to serve the nation and are not apart from and independent of the nation. . . . The nation cannot allow such institutions to spread doctrines that are perilous to the life or future of the White race.[34]

A similar idea was to emerge from Dr. Verwoerd, Strijdom's successor, during the 1958 election campaign. He said that the education of blacks in the Western way of life led them to want to become part and parcel of the white community. The government intended to "put an end to that class of Natives."[35]

Verwoerd was perhaps the last and greatest contributor to the theory of apartheid. What was left after him was mainly its implementation, and it would not be wrong to say that Vorster, his successor, managed to carry this out with full determination and ruthlessness. His main aim was to make South Africa a "White man's land in the true sense of the word." To this end, he continued with new zest his party's policy of *onswarting* (unblackening; i.e., the cities).[36]

Verwoerd became prime minister in 1958. One of his early tasks was to outlaw the use of the word *African* in Parliament, claiming that he knew of no such race.[37] Apparently he was annoyed by the fact that the word *Afrikaner* was, and continues to be, used almost synonymously with "Boer," rather than its proper English translation of "African." Thus, in place of *African* he substituted *Bantu.* Derived from the Zulu or Xhosa *abantu* ("people"), this political use of the word is detested and rejected by Africans as a symbol of political disinheritance.

The new prime minister insisted that apartheid "moves consistently in the direction of separate development with the ideal of total separation in all spheres." His paramount scheme for this separation was expressed in the Promotion of Bantu Self-Government Bill, which implied limited self-government for Africans in 13 percent of South Africa. Not less among his plans was the establishment of a republic (1961) and the promotion of white unity,[38] which was to be achieved at the expense of blacks. As already pointed out, they were to be regarded not as a single group, as in the case of whites, but rather as "separate nations." This has often been justified by the claim that Africans are as separate from each other as Europeans from Asians![39] Consequently, the argument that white South Africans do not belong to the same ethnic group nor share the same culture and language is seen as irrelevant.

The creation of the "homelands" following the self-government bill would mean that the Africans no longer belong to South Africa but to "their" respective government-created "homelands." Those living in urban areas would be regarded as temporary sojourners in the white man's land. Their status would be that of migrant laborers. Unemployed Africans, old and disabled people, and all those who had outgrown their usefulness to the white man would be removed from their homes and acquaintances as "surplus Bantu" into a "homeland" they had never seen. In responding to opposition and criticism against such policies the prime minister retorted:

> We do not accept that the white inhabitants must be satisfied as a
> minority in a multi-racial country to compete with the black
> masses on any equal basis, which in the long run can only mean a
> black government. . . . We will see to it that we remain in power
> in this White South Africa.[40]

When Dr. Verwoerd died, many hoped that his successor might bring some relief for the black population of the country. As already shown, however, each new prime minister seemed to be more determined than his predecessor to prove that he could make apartheid work. "Each leader chosen by the National Party," writes Troup, "had been more uncompromisingly a White supremacist than the last and Vorster was no exception."[41] It seems fair to say that the present state president, P. W. Botha, however, appears less certain about the integrity of the Afrikaner cause than his predecessors. This is so notwithstanding his protestations to the contrary.

Sociopolitical Implications

Even before the introduction of apartheid, some of its implications were already anticipated in earlier segregationist practices and legislation throughout the country. The Cape Province and Natal are the only South African provinces where Africans ever enjoyed the rights of franchise for a while. In the Cape this was more the result of a sense of obligation than of liberalism. To make sure that as few Africans as possible obtained a chance to exercise this right, there was a financial qualification of £25 for registered voters. When this amount did not seem to have the intended effect, it was raised to £75.[42] In Natal the original franchise legislation did not make any provision for discrimination. This did not please many whites, and by 1865 the first "statutory colour bar" came to existence and the Africans were disenfranchised.[43] In the Transvaal and Orange Free State the whites made it clear from the very beginning that they would have no equality with blacks. Even after the annexation of these provinces by the British government and the Treaty of Vereeniging in 1902, the question of franchise for blacks was left pending.[44]

Between the years 1910 to 1948 legislation for blacks increased, providing a basis and precedent for future apartheid legislation. Karis remarks that the United Party government before 1948 was only a lesser evil in comparison with the "continuing threat of the rise of power of a doctrinaire Afrikaner nationalism that would bar all opportunities for African entrance into a common society."[45] The flavor of preapartheid laws makes it clear that apartheid was not so far removed from the practices of other foregoing South African administrations. Nevertheless, it did go a step further in ruthlessness, more elaborate separatism, and determination to achieve its ends without consideration to the means used or the consequences to those affected by the process.

The process of apartheid is well illustrated by the title of Muriel Horrell's book, *Action, Reaction and Counteraction.*[46] It is executed by means of laws. These laws necessarily provoke reaction from those affected by them and their sympathizers, as well as from those who are merely appalled by their insensitivity to morality or justice. Upon this opposition the government responds with punitive measures and more laws to counteract further opposition.

Almost all the laws are directed against blacks, though some of them have repercussions in the private and public lives of whites. The greatest of these repercussions is perhaps what Brink has referred to as "cultural malnutrition," which, though affecting mainly blacks, is greatly felt by some whites. Brink describes in particular how apartheid, especially through its censorship laws, deprives white South Africans of cultural contact not only with black South Africans but with the rest of Africa. While the rest of the world has begun to appreciate African culture and literature, this remains a closed book for white South Africans, although they are an integral part of Africa. Because of apartheid, the rest of Africa frowns upon them; because of censorship, most available African literature—even by fellow South Africans—is unavailable to them.[47]

Some of the consequences of apartheid on black people have been described by Fr. Cosmas Desmond in his book *The Discarded People.*[48]

In it he describes the forceful removals of Africans who lived near certain urban areas that had been declared white. The belongings of those who refused to abandon their homes were loaded in trucks under guard and taken to resettlement areas in the "homelands." Their city homes were than bull-dozed to prevent any lingering around. In the resettlement areas they were provided with tents for temporary shelter while the government still made plans for permanent housing in an as yet undetermined location. There was no store, no clinic, no toilet facilities; a few tents were provided for school classrooms for the children. Because of the distances and costs involved in commuting from these places to their city jobs, most men could not afford to come home daily, making the trip home only once a week or once a month. Nothing could be done, however, since there were no alternative jobs nearby. Skin diseases were common, as most people lived in these conditions for more than ten months, and many children died of malnutrition, kwashiorkor, and related diseases.[49] Such resettlements still take place to this day.

The Nationalist government has accepted no criticism or opposition against its policy. Both Verwoerd and Vorster, and lately Botha, have claimed that all South African blacks—except for a few malcontents and "agitators," as well as the hostile world outside—favor apartheid since they are equally "race conscious."[50] Unless it is true that black people are "mindless savages," it is hard to understand how people can rejoice at their subjugation and dispossession. Suffice it to quote Nelson Mandela in refutation of this allegation:

Since 1912 [even much earlier, as already seen] . . . the African people have discussed the shameful misdeeds of those who rule the country. Year after year they have raised their voices to condemn . . . the inhuman exploitation, and the whole policy of white domination. But instead of more freedom, repression began to grow in volume and intensity and it seemed that all their sacrifices would end in smoke and dust.[51]

FORMS OF OPPOSITION

As Mandela implies, black people have opposed the system not only since 1948 but throughout South African history. In this they have had certain allies—with varying degrees of commitment—within the South African white community. The churches were among their earliest allies, in addition to certain liberal individuals and organizations. In recent years the sincerity of these liberal institutions and individuals has been seriously questioned and reevaluated. Even in the past, however, it has never been uncritically taken for granted by all.

The White Liberals

Even as the first black newspaper made its appearance it was with the financial help of white liberals. Parliamentarians J. W. Sauer and James Rose-Innes worked as Jabavu's allies to bring about modifications of certain drastic legislative measures taken against blacks, such as the Franchise and Ballot Act of 1892.[52] Such alliance often had a negative influence on black resistance, however. For instance, Jabavu himself is said not to have opposed this act much. Further, it is believed that he actually supported Sauer, for old times' sake, against the wishes of his people, in the 1913 Land Bill. Perhaps Smuts spoke for all South African liberals—hard as it may seem to believe—when he said: "There are certain things about which all South Africans [i.e., whites] are agreed, all parties and all sections, except those who are quite mad. The first is that it is a fixed policy to maintain white supremacy in South Africa."[53] This kind of attitude is supported from another angle by Schlemmer:

> Some Whites are less motivated by racial considerations than the majority, but very few of these liberals would be equally accommodating in the class issue if their interests were perceived to be threatened.[54]

Some degree of the truth contained in these statements is confirmed by the fact that even the most liberal political party in South Africa today is hesitant about the question of an unqualified franchise for black people. Only two parties in South African history ever supported the idea of equal voting rights for blacks and whites. One, understandably, was the Communist Party. The other, the Liberal Party, gradually evolved to this ideal and finally decided to dissolve itself when the government introduced a law against mixed political parties.[55] The main opposition party until the late 1970s, the United Party, to which most liberal whites belonged, disagreed with the ruling National Party mainly on tactics. Its leader in 1956, Sir de Villiers Graaf, referred to its policy as follows:

> We believe that the European should, in the interest of Western civilization, retain leadership, but . . . we must get the confidence, goodwill and cooperation of the non-European population. If we deny them their place they may turn their backs on White civilization. Our Policy is not equality. It never has been, is not and never will be our policy.[56]

Toward the end of the decade this party merged with the Progressive Party to form the Progressive Federal Party. Those opposed to the merger remained as the New Republic Party.

After the banning of the Communist Party in 1950, many of its former members helped to form the extraparliamentary white Congress of Democrats (COD). The COD was to be an active supporter of the ANC. It enhanced the policy of universal franchise for all adults irrespective of color. It became a member of the Congress Alliance which included the ANC, the South African Indian Congress (SAIC), and the Coloured People's Organization (SACPO). All cooperated in the drafting of the Freedom Charter in 1955. The Liberal Party's support of organized black resistance came quite late. It suspected communist influence because of the former allegiance of some of the members of the COD. Some of its members later formed the radical underground movement known as the African Resistance Movement (ARM), which corresponded to ANC's *Umkhonto We Sizwe* and the Pan Africanist Congress's *Poqo*. Its members were included in the police raids that ended these two movements in 1964.[57]

Among the well-known liberal organizations are student groups. The most recent among these were the National Union of South African Students (NUSAS) and the University Christian Movement (UCM), the latter of which had a short existence (1968–1972). It was the more sympathetic of the two to black student opinion, winning many defections from NUSAS. NUSAS was criticized for its "dichotomy between principle and practice" by the newly formed South African Students Organization (SASO) toward the end of the 1960s. Its basis of integration was rejected as being based on standards predominantly set by the white society. While NUSAS was considered to be "still worth talking to," unlike the "racially-bigoted organization like the ASB [Afrikaanse Studente Bond]," the commitment of its student members was conceived to be limited to a very few individuals, making its credentials as a "sincere and commited aspirant for change" questionable.[58] The UCM was criticized for being dominated by white opinion and leadership, in spite of its having a majority of black students in it. Nevertheless, it was commended for "having overcome the problems of adjustment to a two-tier society like ours."[59]

On the whole, in addition to double standards, white liberals and their organizations have been accused of encouraging the black person to accept his condition and status in South African society.[60] They have also been accused of intentionally delaying blacks in their determination to achieve their goal in the way they find suitable. From these circles, writes one black leader, the "theory of gradualism emanates and this is what keeps blacks confused." Further, their genuineness is questionable, since, rather than fight racism in their own society, they seem to engage in campaigns to prove to as many blacks as possible that they are liberal.[61] Modisane throws this indictment at their supposed double standards:

> The most articulate critics are the liberals whose remarkable campaign has been matched only by their cause; they compiled statistics which showed a gloomy picture of the poverty of the Africans, but in their own backyards their house servants were not paid much better. But then, of course, conscience is like sleeping with a prostitute, one is filled with revulsion only after the act.[62]

The Churches and their Organizations

The English-speaking churches are counted among the liberal institutions that have acted as allies to blacks. Almost all of these have condemned apartheid in principle at one time or another. Some of their leaders are among some of the victims of the government's wrath expressed through bannings, withdrawal of passports or visas, deportations, and often imprisonment. Although the three Dutch Reformed churches in the country are fully behind—and often responsible for—the government's policy, a few individuals in them have dared to oppose apartheid and suffer for their opposition. It needs to be pointed out, however, that there has not always been consistency between theory and practice in the English-speaking churches. Indeed in this respect they have been outwitted by the DRC's in their negative and destructive approaches. It has been observed[63] that the English-speaking churches never, in fact, spoke out against discrimination until the National Party took over the government in 1948. The reason for this, it seems, was more English mistrust of the Afrikaner government than concern for black human rights. The early departures of Africans from these churches were not only religiously motivated but also politically and culturally.[64] The new African independent churches, however, tended to become more exclusively spiritual in orientation and, through time, paid little or no attention at all to sociopolitical issues. The more vocal blacks in the churches today on social issues are those attending the so-called white established churches.

The history of the Dutch Reformed churches in South Africa shows an evolution from liberalism to conservatism. In the early Cape settlements discrimination in the churches was generally based on faith rather than color.[65] In 1857 the Nederduitse Gereformeerde Kerk yielded to popular pressure and introduced segregation not as a rule, but because of the "weakness of some." By 1957, however, this "weakness" had already been rationalized. Segregation in church was "both necessary and in accordance with our understanding of the nature of the church of the Lord Jesus Christ on earth."[66] Seven years earlier the church's recommendation to the government that "total apartheid" be implemented in the country had been rejected, as already indicated, by the prime minister, Dr. Malan.

The theological position of the Dutch Reformed churches on race is that equality between blacks and whites involves a "misapprehension of the fact that God, in his Providence, made people into different races and nations." Yet the statement goes on to affirm that Africans must be led to independence so that "eventually they will be equal [sic!] to Europeans, but each in their own territory and each serving God in their own fatherland."[67]

At the World Council of Churches' 1954 conference in Evanston, the DRC's South African delegates were the only ones to withhold their assent from the declaration that any form of racial discrimination is contrary to the will of God.[68] Later, in 1960, they dissociated themselves from the Cottesloe Consultation Report, Johannesburg,[69] which affirmed—among other things—that "no one who believed in Jesus Christ should be excluded from any church on the grounds of color or race." In the following year each withdrew its membership from the WCC. This situation in the Dutch Reformed churches shows that, in speaking against apartheid, the English-speaking churches are fighting not only against the government but also against these churches.

The largest English-speaking church in South Africa is the Methodist church (MCSA), which also has the most African members. Like its brother-churches, it has had its ups and downs, experiencing its first black walkouts as early as 1884, 1892, and 1896.[70] Although it has a black majority in its membership, the MCSA has a disproportionate representation of whites in its leadership, as do its fellow-denominations.[71] This is one of its inconsistencies. Another is reported by a former black journalist of the *Drum* magazine. Assigned by his white-owned paper to visit fifteen white churches in Johannesburg and record his experiences on race attitudes, he reports receiving—to his embarrassment and surprise—"equal" admittance in a Presbyterian church; segregated in a Methodist church in the pretext that the main hall of the church was full;[72] and being told to his face in a few Dutch Reformed churches that they did not admit black people in their services as there were black churches. On two occasions the police were called and he was arrested for trespassing on church grounds.

In spite of these shortcomings, the MCSA has been among the most vocal churches in its synods in criticizing apartheid. Its position has not been as conspicuous as that of the Anglican or the Catholic church, probably because it lacks many individual leaders who continually challenge the law unofficially, without authorization by their superiors, and find themselves in trouble for it. At about the time the

Nationalist government took over in South Africa the church defended the principle of human rights for every human being.[73] It protested the government's intention to withdraw the white Native Representatives from Parliament and to remove the "coloured" voters from the common roll.[74] It rejected apartheid in 1952 as impractical and "inconsistent with the highest Christian principles." This was reiterated in the years from 1957 to 1960. The church also joined with various anti-apartheid groups in calling upon the government to convene a National Convention representing all South Africans without giving consideration to color. It resolved to "encourage by every possible means consultations between leaders of all communions willing to cooperate."[75] As the token of its desire for change within its ranks, the church elected its first black president in 1963. This followed the intent expressed two years earlier to remove "racial demarcation from its official records and legislation."[76]

By far the most outspoken of the liberal churches against apartheid is the Church of the Province of South Africa (CPSA, Episcopalian). It does so both officially in its synods and unofficially through its individual leaders. Fr. Trevor Huddleston, Anglican priest at the time, however, has expressed dissatisfaction with the inconsistency of principle and deed in his own church. "Idealism," he warns, "like patriotism, is not enough." Referring to the seriousness of the political situation in South Africa, he observes, "The church is facing a challenge which it must meet now, and which it cannot meet effectively with official pronouncements." His own way of meeting the challenge in the political sphere is to arouse world consciousness to the tragedy of apartheid. To improve its own image internally, the church must stop trying to find excuses for its hypocrisy and remove prejudice, uncharitableness, and sheer blindness from its ranks.[77] Other individual churchmen who have opposed the government publicly include the Rt. Reverend Bishop Ambrose Reeves, Fr. Michael Scott, and more recently the Most Reverend Archbishop Desmond Tutu, and a few others.

Two years after the introduction of apartheid the Provincial Synod of the CPSA condemned its legislation as "inconsistent with the respect for human personality that should be characteristic of a Christian society." The bishops reaffirmed the church's position in November 1963, concluding that "whenever the claims of obedience to the State and God are in conflict, it is to God that our obedience must be given."[78]

Another church worth mentioning in this examination is the Catholic church. Its public reputation is like that of the CPSA, but with fewer spokesmen. Internally, although its bishops have spoken against apartheid, it is one of the most conservative churches politically.

Toward the end of the sixties it was confronted by a group of black priests for being ambiguous in its political positions and for not practicing within itself what it preaches or upholds in theory. During the seventies it closed its only black seminary twice rather than yield to the demands of its black seminarians. Two of the seminary's black lecturers, one the rector, were told that "some Catholic bishops did not like their political stand." The seminary was alleged to have been turned into a revolutionary center, the two priests castigated for having participated in a political demonstration in Johannesburg.[79]

One of the Catholic church's most outspoken leaders, the Most Reverend Archbishop Dennis Hurley of Durban, seems to have recognized the shortcomings of the church in South Africa. According to him the "purity of the faith" here has "been suffocated by identification with certain narrow, cultural national experiences."[80] Fr. Huddleston's criticism against the CPSA is even more applicable to the Catholic church. Thus wherever the church has spoken against apartheid, it has not followed this up with corresponding practical measures to prove its conviction.[81]

Within these limitations, the Southern African Catholic Bishops Conference has progressively condemned apartheid since 1952. In 1957 it declared:

> There must be gradual change . . . for otherwise our country faces a disastrous future. This involves the elaboration of a sensible and just policy enabling any person, irrespective of race, to qualify for the enjoyment of full civil rights.

The 1962 pastoral letter affirmed: "As Christian people we dare not remain silent and passive in the face of the injustices inflicted on members of the unprivileged racial groups." Four years later the bishops based their criticism of apartheid and discrimination in general on Vatican II's Pastoral Constitution on the *Church and the Modern World*.[82]

Since the beginning of 1976 the church has attempted a kind of desegregation of its schools by admitting black students in white schools against the country's regulations. It has received the moral support of the CPSA and the MCSA.[83] It is not clear how effective or meaningful this is, however, especially when one considers how much it must cost to go to these schools and what the wages of blacks in South Africa amount to.[84] To a distant observer, it would appear that either the church must be providing quite substantial amounts to black pupils in bursaries or is admitting only the children of higher income black families.

These three churches sum up the position of the English-speaking churches on the country's racial situation. Others include the Congregational church, the Presbyterian church, and the Lutheran church, the position of which has perhaps been less conspicuous than that of the three discussed. In addition to the churches there are interchurch bodies such as the South African Council of Churches (SACC) and the Christian Institute of South Africa (CI). Both bodies—before the CI was banned in 1977—provided certain essential community services especially among blacks. They also continued to oppose specific legislation as it came. Perhaps in practice these organizations moved a little further than the churches they represented, confirming the claim that the individual congregations are mostly responsible for resisting change in the churches.

The most far-reaching statement to come from the SACC before the turmoil of the 1970s was contained in the "Message to the People of South Africa" in 1968.[85] It condemned apartheid as that which limits the "ability of a person to obey the Gospel's command to love his neighbor as himself." Apartheid had become a false faith, a novel gospel, for many South Africans. Christians were asked to discriminate between Christian discipleship and South African citizenship. "To whom or what are you truly giving your loyalty—to a subsection of mankind, an ethnic group, a human tradition, a political idea, or to Christ?" In the past the council has been very careful not to "over-excite" or antagonize the government. This attitude has undergone drastic change in the last few years.

The Christian Institute attracted very little public attention until it was included in the list of the Schlebusch Commission in 1972.[86] The institute was to be investigated for subversive or communistic activities. Although the commission operated in secret, certain members representing the organization investigated were required to testify before it, without any assurance of receiving a fair hearing. There was also the danger that the CI might be prosecuted without its story having been heard by the public. Led by its director, Dr. Beyers Naudé, the CI's leaders refused to testify and faced various forms of prosecution. Since these proceedings, the CI achieved a new public image and became something of a "radical" body and outspoken critic—at least significantly more than previously—of the government.

The commission—now Schlebusch/LeGrange—presented its report in 1975. It found that the CI "is a danger to the State, that it supported violent change in South Africa and that it was working towards a Black-dominated socialist system achieved by way of race conflict."[87] These allegations were strongly repudiated by the CI, which declared itself to have consistently advocated change by nonviolent means. "[Its] consistent and public standpoint has been to advocate justice through reconciliation." Dr. Naudé and Professor C. Gardner of the institute declared the CI's preparedness to face in an open court any of the allegations.[88]

The Christian Institute was established in August 1963. Its director, Dr. Naudé, had been among the few Afrikaner clergymen who defended the Cottesloe Resolutions. He had been forced to resign from his post as Transvaal moderator of the NGK upon assuming the directorship of the CI. The institute strongly condemned apartheid as inimical to Christian values, and the Dutch Reformed churches' support of apartheid. It envisaged a process toward the granting of full rights to blacks.[89]

The Reverend Mr. Carstens has remarked that the CI was basically conservative (1971) both theologically and politically. It held views, according to him, comparable to those of the Progressive Party or even of some *verligte* ("enlightened") Afrikaner Nationalists.[90] This might well have been the case at some stage. Since its rebirth following its investigation, however, such views apparently underwent a tremendous change—that is, if its being the only white-run organization to be outlawed with about a score of black ones in 1977 might be taken as evidence.[91] By this time it had become very controversial in the eyes of the government.

Black Organizations[92]

After the initial concession of defeat in their claims as the only rightful owners of the land, older Africans began a campaign for "equal rights for every civilized man south of the Zambesi" River.[93] By this they subjected themselves to white standards of judgment (which category of blacks was to be considered civilized and which was to be excluded?) and to white leadership, thus opening themselves to the later charge of reformism as already mentioned above. By 1889 the first delegation against passes to Cape African voters had failed.[94] In the same year as the Bambata Rebellion (1906), African, Indian, and "coloured" groups petitioned the British government. They protested against the infringements of their rights by the Provincial governments, giving particular emphasis to the pass laws.[95] This was to no avail. There had been an earlier protest when the British government made a treaty with the Boers in 1902 after the Anglo-Boer War. In this treaty the question of franchise rights for Africans was shelved until "self-government" (meaning for whites) would have been granted.[96] This had led to the formation of many black organizations at various places to represent their own rights and demands.

In March 1909 the Africans convened a South African Native Convention in Bloemfontein. Its purpose was mainly to oppose the

Draft Act of Union as proposed by the whites in their own convention held earlier. The Draft Act revealed the whites' intention to bar African representation in Parliament permanently and to retain the existing system of discrimination. A multiracial delegation sent to London against this threat was unsuccessful.[97] After the establishment of an all-white union in 1910, Africans protested against their further betrayal by the British government. Demanding "full equal rights," they were led by three ministers and newspaper editors: the Reverends Jabavu (J. T.), Dube, and Rubusana.[98] Two years later the ANC (originally SANNC—South African Native National Congress) was launched with the aim of "creating national unity and defending our rights and privileges."[99]

When the 1913 Land Bill was introduced, the ANC sent a delegation to the prime minister to protest against it. A double blow was dealt to their appeal as, following Botha's rejection of it, it elicited no positive response from the British governor general.[100] In 1946 ANC president Dr. Xuma appealed successfully to the League of Nations against South Africa's intention to incorporate the mandated territory of Namibia.[101]

Independent action was taken by women in 1913 in the first act of passive resistance by Africans. At Bloemfontein, Jagersfontein, and elsewhere they presented themselves before the authorities and discarded their proffered passes, thereby courting arrest and police abuse.[102] The ANC picked up on this in a nonviolent demonstration against passes in 1919. Mounted police charged and rode over the demonstrators, killing some of them and encouraging an attack by white civilians.[103] There was a pass-burning campaign in 1930 when further demands for their repeal were ignored.[104]

The question of franchise has been a perennial problem in black political resistance. In this they were continually rebuffed by the British government, which, in spite of early disappointments, they continued to regard as the defender of the rights of freedom and justice. The ANC finally passed a motion of no confidence in the British as well as the South African government in 1922.[105] An all-African Convention meeting in Bloemfontein in 1935 demanded at least a qualified franchise as a minimum for all Africans. They rejected the Native Representative Council as an unacceptable substitute for the franchise. Protests against the Representation of Natives Bill, which effected this substitute, were all in vain in 1936.[106] A Bill of Rights adopted by the ANC in its 1943 "African Claims in South Africa" called for the "extension to all adults, regardless of race, of the right to vote." This was to be repeated in the Freedom Charter of 1955.[107] Four years after the adoption of the Bill of Rights three men, Xuma of the ANC and Naicker and Dadoo of the Natal and Transvaal Indian Congresses, signed an agreement to work together for "full franchise rights and for equal economic and industrial rights and opportunities as well as other freedoms."[108] This was on the eve of the apartheid regime.

One year following the ascent of the National Party to power, the ANC adopted a Programme of Action. It called for noncooperation with government institutions, boycotts, strikes, and civil disobedience.[109] Its practical implications were expressed in the Defiance Campaign of 1952. Pass laws were defied; public facilities marked "for Whites only" were ignored; no permits were requested for entering prescribed areas. When arrested, they chose to go to jail rather than pay fines.[110]

Women's strikes against passes spread all over the country in 1954 and 1955. About ten thousand women walked to the Union Buildings in Pretoria, daring to request a hearing from the prime minister. The ANC held strikes against the implementation of Bantu Education, and various forms of unrest including work stoppages and bus boycotts were manifest all over the country. Following the adoption of the Freedom Charter in 1955, 156 people were arrested and charged with high treason in 1956. Those committed for trial were later all acquitted, the trial having lasted four years. The climactic highlight of this era was the Sharpeville massacre in 1960 and its aftermath.[111] This led to disillusionment among blacks, whose main organizations were declared illegal following a state of emergency proclamation. They resorted to underground tactics and sabotage, which led to a government repression intensified especially during the years 1963–1965. There followed a relative lull in the country until the beginning of the seventies, when the Black Consciousness Movement began reorganization.

The BCM was a child of SASO—the South African Students Organization. SASO was established in 1969. Partly through its efforts, the Black People's Convention came into being in 1972. Subsequently, other black groups, secular and religious, adopted their ideology of Black Consciousness.[112]

By 1972, following an initial misconceived welcoming, the government had taken its first step against Black Consciousness by banning a former director of the Black Theology Project, Reverend Sabelo Ntwasa. A year later eight other leaders of the movement were similarly restricted. This trend continued until most of the leaders had been silenced and eliminated, the rest left for the post-Soweto detentions and subsequent bannings of key black leaders and their organizations.

The BCM's strategy toward the achievement of a nonracial, egalitarian society was black solidarity. This would lead to the ability to bargain with white people on an equal basis rather than as inferiors—as according to the present state of affairs. While engaged with this intermediate goal of raising consciousness and creating solidarity, they regarded whites and their government as irrelevant. Therefore there was no need for or any attempt at direct confrontation with the government. Crisis leadership was provided when needed but, on the whole, the BCM engaged itself fully with its researches, relief projects, and education. In other words, it addressed itself critically and creatively to the black community, including the bantustan leaders, who were regarded as "sell-outs" of their own people because of their cooperation with the government.[113]

Since "conscientization," theoretically, partly meant exposing the government's policy and "homelands" scheme as fraudulent and exploitative, at least verbal confrontation with the government could not be effectively avoided. That is why the government soon found out how mistaken it had been in its initial rejoicing at the emergence of SASO. This accounts for the continuous persecution of the Black Consciousness Movement that has taken place since 1972.[114]

During the 1970s a new organization came into being which has gradually asserted itself in South Africa and also challenged international opinion. This organization, although primarily a cultural movement, has consistently made claims to being a national liberation movement concerned with the elimination of white domination in the country and the apartheid system. It is called the Inkatha National and Cultural Liberation Movement and is headed by Chief Mangosuthu Buthelezi, the chief minister of the Kwa-Zulu "homeland." Buthelezi's Inkatha is, in fact, said to be a revival of an old Zulu cultural movement bearing the same name, originally established by Zulu king Dinizulu. In spite of its new claims, this organization does not constitute part of our major study in this work for the following reasons:

(a) Its president is also a "homeland" leader, hence Inkatha is seen more as an aspect of "homeland" politics than as a national organization addressing the entire South African political scene;

(b) it is perceived as appealing primarily to a single ethnic group, the Zulus, with the majority of its supporters resident in the "homeland" itself;

(c) it has not displayed a strategy of open defiance or challenge to the government for its policies as the other national political movements chosen for examination in this study have done and continue to do;

(d) the majority of blacks do not perceive it as a liberation movement—indeed, Inkatha seems to have done nothing to prove or convince them that it is working for the elimination of racism and white domination in South Africa as a whole;

(e) it has been involved in a number of "counterrevolutionary" activities that led many to believe that it was more on the side of the establishment than of the black majority, and has proved itself to be ruthless and often violent particularly toward those who dared to disagree with it or its leader; it is also alleged to be concerned more with self-preservation or the preservation of its leader's political leadership than with the issues that concern most blacks in their situation of oppression;

(f) finally, apart from those of its "homeland" supporters, it is able to appeal to the support of liberal white South Africans, particularly the business sector, and some overseas communities because of Buthelezi's rhetoric on nonviolent struggle—as if all other groups support violence—and his campaign against disinvestment, notwithstanding the views of other black leaders in the country.

No doubt, a more detailed and sympathetic, though critical, treatment of Inkatha will have to be provided in the very near future because of the interest (and even support) it inspires, particularly overseas. An example of this kind of support was reflected in Buthelezi's several invitations to the U.S. White House and the VIP treatment he received there in the past few years, as well as in his being awarded an honorary degree in 1986 by Boston University. Many black South Africans think that this show of support is misguided and merely self-serving. It is from people and institutions who see Buthelezi as a kind of compromise between extreme (black) radicalism, particularly that of the ANC, and the ingrained conservatism of the apartheid regime and its staunch supporters. They thus fail to understand the history of black resistance in South Africa and its reasonable, democratic demands made unsuccessfully through the years, as well as its consistently conciliatory approach in its demands for human rights and full constitutional participation. The next two chapters will shed more light on these demands and approaches taken toward their realization. Be that as it may, the kind of detailed treatment proposed for Inkatha will, however, have to be in a different context from the one that occupies us in the present study.

THE CONSEQUENCES OF OPPOSITION

Black people in general, and those who defy the government's policies in particular, have suffered from four types of persecution from the authorities of the country. First, there has been general intimidation—which might be called a "preventive" measure—of black people through raids and arrests for technical offenses as well as on suspicions of subversion and related activities. They have also been subjected to lengthy trials for improperly defined charges, unsubstantiated convictions (see below), banishments and bannings of individuals and organizations, as well as detentions without trial involving torture and often death. The South African laws that prescribe these measures may be described in three ways: regulative, punitive, or preventive. Regulative laws are those that prescribe apartheid—that is to say, those primary laws that are calculated to give direction to what may be called the South African way of life. Punitive laws are those measures taken against those who violate prescribed laws with or without intent. Those who violate them with intent constitute political offenders. Preventive laws are countermeasures that see to it that violation is rendered difficult and costly. This is done through the prescription of heavier and heavier penalties and counteroffensive measures against any violation. Both aspects of deliberate punitive laws and the preventive laws as conceived here would fall under the so-called security laws. Both are directed, where they are meted out against those who violate the regulative laws with intent, against political offenders.

The present South African government has inherited and/or improved upon many regulative laws from previous governments. The security laws, however, are almost completely an original contribution of the National Party government. The first, introduced in 1950 as a measure against communism and the Communist Party of South Africa, as well as against the furtherance of their aims, was the Suppression of Communism Act. In addition to the accustomed definition, this law further defined communism as any

> doctrine which aims at bringing about any political, industrial, social or economic change within the Union by the promotion of disturbances or disorder, by unlawful acts or omissions or by means which include the promotion of disturbance or disorder, or such acts or omissions or threats.[115]

This act, amended and extended many times, was replaced by the Internal Security Act No. 79 (1976). In this form it was further extended. It provided for preventive detention of twelve-month periods, which might be successive and indefinite, and for the detention of potential state witnesses in political trials for up to six months.

Following the Defiance Campaign launched by the ANC and SAIC in 1952, the government introduced the Public Safety Act and the Criminal Law Amendment Act in 1953. The latter prescribed high fines and sentences of up to three years for violation of any law in protest against government policy. The former made a provision for the declaration of a state of emergency by the government when deemed necessary, and the assumption of emergency power by the police if public safety appeared to be threatened.[116] This law was invoked throughout South Africa following the Sharpeville events in 1960. At the same time, the Unlawful Organizations Act was passed to outlaw the ANC and the PAC. Those "furthering their aims" were liable to conviction and sentences of up to ten years' imprisonment.[117]

The General Law Amendment Act of 1963 made possible the continued detention of a person previously sentenced for a political offense at the end of his jail term. This particular clause was applied to only one person in the sixties. Mangaliso R. Sobukwe, PAC president, was sent to Robben Island and detained for an additional six years after he had completed his original sentence in 1963 for incitement.[118]

The most vengeful and most comprehensive of the security laws is the Terrorism Act No. 83 (1967). It is notorious for the indefinite detention without trial for suspected terrorists. In this sense it transcended the "180-day" clause of the Criminal Procedure Act of 1965, which enabled detention for up to 180 days for possible state witnesses in political trials.[119] Terrorism detainees are held until they have replied "satisfactorily" to all questions put to them by their interrogators. Like communism, terrorism is also defined broadly. It includes any activity endangering the maintenance of law and order. Most common among these activities is perhaps the "creation" of "hostility between the whites and other inhabitants of the Republic."[120] Many people in the last decade were brought to trial and convicted for this particular offense. Under the terms of the Terrorism Act the burden of proof is with the accused to prove his innocence rather than with the court to prove his guilt.[121] The minimum sentence in case of conviction is five years. No court of law "can either pronounce upon the validity of any detention order or instruct the authorities to release any particular detainee"[122] while he is still being interrogated or awaiting charges to be brought against him.

Political Trials and Imprisonments

As a result of the security laws, South African courts are subjected to severe restrictions. Through the years they have had to give in to certain laws that deprive them of certain powers and bind them to certain minimum sentences of imprisonment. Some judges have often found these minimum sentences too drastic for offenses committed.[123]

It need hardly be pointed out that, especially since 1956, scores of political trials have taken place each year all over South Africa. While there are many individual trials, it is now very common for group trials involving "conspiracies." Many people have been brought to trial for being members of banned organizations, conspiring against the state, leaving the country illegally to receive military training abroad, causing hostility between the races of South Africa, sabotage and murder, and several other offenses deemed to affect the security of the state. Between 1963 and 1965 about two thousand people, mostly Africans, were convicted for such offenses all over the country.[124] Forty-nine received death sentences, fifteen life imprisonment, and about thirteen hundred received various terms amounting to approximately eight thousand years. Within this period, in 1964, Nelson Mandela and seven of his colleagues were sentenced to life after being convicted under the Sabotage Act.[125] In the period of one year between July 1, 1965, and June 30, 1966, about 547 people were tried and 356 convicted under the Suppression of Communism Act; 87 were tried and 77 convicted under Section 21 of the General Law Amendment Act.[126] Those in prison for violating the security laws by the end of 1967 numbered 1,335.[127] During 1977 a total of 401 people were tried under these laws. One hundred forty-four of them were convicted, while fifty-nine cases were still in progress, and the rest were acquitted.[128] By 1978 more than 450 political prisoners had been convicted under security laws such as the Terrorism, the Internal Security, and the Sabotage acts.[129] Understandably, most of these were Africans, while other black groups and whites were represented. Among those convicted were nine BCM leaders *inter alios,* who had been arrested in 1974 for attending rallies in celebration of Mozambique's independence. They were convicted in 1976 and sentenced to terms of five and six years in jail. Leave of appeal was denied.[130]

One of South Africa's long political trials, involving members of the UDF and other groups, has been in progress since 1985. This trial and other recent ones will be discussed in Chapter 3.

Bannings and Banishments

Since it came into power, the Nationalist government has achieved a similar end of disciplining political offenders by banning or banishing them as it does by jailing them. Banning is one of the instant measures the government has adopted to silence people without giving them a hearing or a chance to defend themselves. In banning eight of the BCM leaders in 1973, the minister of justice, Mr. Pelser, admitted to the press that court proceedings would have given them a "platform"—that is, both to defend and to advertise their cause.[131]

When banning was first introduced under the 1950 Suppression of Communism Act, it was applicable mainly to organizations. Individuals who belonged to these organizations were "listed," thus prohibited from being members or active supporters of any organization deemed to be furthering the aims of communism or declared unlawful.[132] According to the minister of justice, 278 banning orders were issued between 1954–1962. Some of those affected were ordered to resign from political organizations, others were prohibited from attending gatherings for periods of up to five years. In some cases they were also confined to certain magisterial districts. Many of the orders were renewed upon expiration.[133]

Extensive banning orders were issued under the General Law Amendment Acts since 1962. From its enactment until October 1963 a large variety of banning orders were issued to 202 people. They included house arrest for periods varying from twelve to twenty-four hours a day during weekdays and twenty-four hours on weekends.[134] By November 1969, 979 banning orders had been issued since the enactment of the Suppression of Communism Act.[135] Blacks accounted for 853 of these. In July 1971, 274 orders were still in effect, including 30 white people.[136] By the end of November 1977, this number had fluctuated to 168 persons, of whom 49 were white.[137]

Since the middle of 1976 banning orders have been issued under the Internal Security Act, which replaced the Suppression of Communism Act. In addition to individuals banned in 1977 were eighteen black organizations, including SASO and BPC, and one multiracial one, the Christian Institute. Two newspapers and a periodical were also included.[138] While individual banning orders may expire and are renewable at their expiration date, organizations and publications are usually banned indefinitely and may never resume operation. Any violation of a banning order is liable to prosecution.

Banishments were introduced in 1927 under the Native Administration Act.[139] In 1956 the law was amended to prevent interdicts and appeals against banishment orders. Banished people are generally sent to isolated places in rural areas. Conditions here and the consequences of leaving permanent places of residence in urban areas for a specified time often make it difficult for a banished person's family to join him. As a rule, a person's family is not notified of his banishment. Since the introduction of banning orders, fewer people have been banished. However, "the terms of certain banning orders . . . have been so drafted that the individuals concerned have, in effect, been banished."[140]

When the present government took over in 1948, about 7 banishment orders were in force.[141] Of about 156 orders issued between 1948 and 1967, 38 were still in force in the latter year. Apparently, nineteen men and one woman were still living in banishment at the beginning of 1971. Two banishment orders were issued as recently as 1976, but it is not clear how many were still in force then or now.[142]

Detentions and their Implications

One of the most shocking measures the government takes against those who oppose it is detention without trial. Most of the laws mentioned at the beginning of this section provide variously for this measure. In the years following July 1976, it was used very extensively as a result of the threat aroused by the Soweto uprising and related events. Even before this time, however, detention without trial had evoked the condemnation of the world because of its injurious consequences, including the death of detainees.

The Amnesty International report on political imprisonment in South Africa has observed:

> The detention laws are not merely a form of restraint to be used in times of crisis or national emergency; rather, they are for everyday use in shoring up white political control and stifling the emergence of effective black political opposition.[143]

A report by the minister of police in 1977 indicated that 2,430 people had been detained for questioning since June 1976. Of these 817 had been tried and convicted, 118 were still awaiting trial, 372 were still undergoing investigation, and 135 were held in preventive detention under the Internal Security Act. Those detained in 1977 included 150 schoolchildren under the age of sixteen. They had been detained over the previous six months under the security laws—many in solitary confinement. "One lawyer handled cases involving 91 children aged under 16 who had been detained . . ., including 10, 12 and 13-year-olds."[144] "Electric shock treatment, kicking and other assaults were revealed to be the causes of injuries inflicted on one student who was given medical examination immediately after a fourteen-hour interrogation period.[145]

Treatment of detainees often does not end merely with torture. Many deaths have occurred during the detention of persons. Few have been acknowledged by the authorities to be direct results of police treatment of detainees, but many of these deaths occur under suspicious circumstances. An example of these was the well-advertised death of BCM leader, Steve Biko. The minister of justice first attributed his death to a hunger strike, then to brain damage, as the inquest later revealed.[146] The inquest also revealed that the doctors who first examined Biko when his physical condition began to deteriorate had been in league with the police interrogators and deliberately gave falsified reports of his condition.

The minister of police reported that ninety-two deaths occurred in detention in 1975. These cases included twenty-eight suicide or self-inflicted injuries. Their causes are usually given as hanging, falling during showers or down high-story buildings while interrogation is in progress, and knocking one's head against a wall or a chair—mostly accidentally.[147] Also included in the above cases were nine people who allegedly died during escape attempts, one case of death by suffocation, and one by internal injuries. Such incidents have evoked various interpretations from the public.

In most cases magistrates have cleared the police following an inquest. In at least three cases during 1970—not necessarily involving death—the minister of justice is known to have paid damages of up to R3,200,00.[148] Significantly, none of these cases involved Africans. At the time of this action about twenty-two other applications for damages were reported pending.

SUMMARY

At least three points of significance have come to the fore in these pages. One is that the origin of apartheid as a form of racial segregation lies deep in the roots of South African history. Although the word was introduced by the ruling National Party only in 1948, involving farther-reaching implications than before, the way to "apartheid" had been paved throughout the foregoing years by the discriminatory practices and legislation of almost all South African governments, including the early settler regimes of both English and Dutch. The second point is that all forms of segregation, apartheid included, have been opposed from the very beginning by the black inhabitants of the country. As they have moved from early armed resistance to political opposition, they have received varying forms and amounts of support from individual whites as well as liberal organizations. Such organizations extend from radical political movements such as the Congress of Democrats and the African Resistance Movement to churches and religious institutions. The scope of their influence on black politics has varied over the years and has recently been subjected to serious questioning. The result has been more and more polarization between black and white anti-apartheid groups, with the former urging the latter to work for the much needed change within their own communities.

Finally, such opposition to apartheid policy has not gone unheeded by the government. The response it evoked, unfortunately, has been a negative rather than a positive one. Serious repercussions have been experienced and severe measures adopted against those who have as much as uttered the word "change." Thus there has been an increase in laws and their amendments, many imprisonments, restrictions, and

even deaths. At each turning point of the resistance movement there
have been hopes of a "new deal." Such hopes, however, have been shat-
tered almost as soon as they appeared about to reach fulfillment; and
disillusionment has set in.

The following two chapters will show how each of the organizations under consideration represents the beginning of new hopes, and
hence new efforts at working for change. Each, however, has met with
frustrations and some of them have ended in exile. The central question
behind this project is whether—given this state of affairs as well as the
government's continuing intransigence—it is still possible to work for
peaceful change within the country and what new methods can be attempted toward this end.

Chapter 2

Three Moments of Resistance

We are aware that the white man is sitting at our table. We know that he has no right to be there; we want to remove him . . . strip the table of all trappings put on by him, decorate it in true African style, settle down and then ask him to join us on our own terms if he wishes.

Steve Biko, BCM

◆ ◆ ◆

[The struggle will go on] until the day dawns when every person who is in Africa will be an African, and a man's colour will be as irrelevant as the shape of his ears . . . until government of the Africans by the Africans for the Africans is a fait accompli.

Mangaliso Sobukwe, PAC

◆ ◆ ◆

There comes a time, as it came in my life, when a man is denied the right to live a normal life, when he can only live the life of an outlaw because the government has so decreed to use the law to impose a state of outlawry upon him. I was driven to this situation, and I do not regret having taken the decisions that I did take.

Nelson Mandela, ANC

◆ ◆ ◆

When apartheid was introduced as a government policy in 1948, the African National Congress (ANC) had been in existence for more than thirty years. Its original reason for being had been to unite all African organizations then working for change in the country, in opposition to the Union government's policy toward blacks. This unity would, it was hoped, enable blacks to speak with one voice in their demand for rights, which had been systematically eroded from them particularly since the country was declared a Union in 1910. Although the focus of the present study is on black resistance to the policy of apartheid in particular, in examining the role of the ANC it will be necessary to trace its policies beyond the current administration in South Africa from the earlier years of the ANC's existence. In this way we will be able to understand their development and their final implementation in relation to apartheid itself.

Ten years following the implementation of the government's policy, another opposition movement came into being with objectives similar to those of the ANC. It was called the Pan Africanist Congress (PAC) and was the result of a breakaway from the ANC. Those individuals who participated in the formation of the PAC were dissatisfied with the lack of progress in the ANC's struggle against apartheid and white domination in general. As they had failed to influence the activities of the organization from within, they thought they could do so more effectively by forming a separate organization and through its medium attempt to redress perceived shortcomings of the ANC.

Through their agitation and activities both organizations soon fell into disfavor with the government. Following a period of unrest in 1960, during which many people lost their lives at the hands of the police, the government banned them both. In this way they were forced underground and to a violent turn of the struggle, which had hitherto been nonviolent. In the vacuum that ensued, almost eight years elapsed before another organization came into being that restored opposition aboveground. It was a students' organization, but with a very unique character and approach. This organization, called the South African Students' Organization (SASO), later fathered a political organization called the Black People's Convention (BPC) and subsequently became the prime mover of what is now commonly referred to as the Black Consciousness Movement (BCM) in South Africa.

These movements represent for this study the three moments of black resistance to apartheid up to the end of the last decade. The aim of this chapter is to analyze each movement's policies and selected activities with a view to determining their compatibility. Because all three movements addressed themselves to the policy of apartheid, it will also be useful to find out the similarities and/or dissimilarities in their approaches to the problem and whether there were continuities and/or discontinuities in their theories and practices—particularly in the case of earlier and later organizations. The chapter will conclude with a brief assessment, followed by a lengthier social-ethical evaluation in Chapter 5.

BACKGROUNDS AND ORIGINS

The first of the three movements examined, the ANC, was established in 1912. Its name was changed from the South African Native National Congress to the present one in 1925. As already implied, the organization's primary aim was to weld together into one national body the various local and provincial organizations concerned with liberation from white domination. African unity was seen as essential to the gaining of a say and some form of representation in the "whites only" Union of South Africa. It would also be a more effective means of defending African "rights and privileges." According to Pixley ka Isaka Seme, chief among the four founders, the organization was to be an "open body, without sinister motives, seeking to ascertain views and openly submit grievances to the Government for discussion and redress."[1] Its approach to the government would be that of respectful and loyal subjects—"not with assegais but . . . with the intention of airing their grievances and removing the obstacles of poverty, prejudice and discriminatory legislation."[2]

The organization's strategy or *modus operandi,* appearing in its constitution adopted in 1919, shows that the early ANC was more concerned about fighting evil legislation than about the *immediate* representation of Africans in the government of the country. An appropriate method of struggle for the latter goal would be adopted only "when the time is ripe for [it]." In the meantime, resolutions, protests, propaganda, deputations, enquiries, "passive action," education, lectures, and distribution of literature were to constitute the form of action or opposition.[3] The support of sympathetic whites in the quest for change was also deemed desirable.[4]

This mild form of opposition began changing slightly in the early 1940s. Until 1936, when Africans in the Cape still enjoyed some form of qualified franchise, there was apparently some complacency within the ANC. Whatever demands there were of universal franchise for Africans in general were made almost "tongue in cheek." It was not until even this limited franchise was threatened that protests became louder and were joined by other circles.

By 1941 the ANC was speaking explicitly of the right of franchise for all Africans. It also included in its policy the demand for the representation of Africans in all government departments.[5] At this time, the ANC was said to stand for "racial unity and mutual helpfulness, and for the improvement of the African people *politically, economically, socially, educationally,* and *industrially.*" While its ultimate goal was franchise and equal rights for all Africans, as these rights applied to whites, its immediate goal was the removal of "special disabilities"—disabilities made possible by the many discriminatory laws of the country. A distinction was still made regarding the significance of sovereignty with reference to South Africa, on the one hand, and to other parts of Africa, on the other. For the latter it was understood to mean the transference of power to the African majority. For South Africa, however, it was understood to mean simply the recognition of African rights to "full citizenship . . . and participation in all councils of the state."[6] This implied equal opportunity within the country in all spheres, as well as the "repeal of discriminatory clauses in the Constitution of South Africa."[7] Thus, except for its discriminatory practices toward blacks, South Africa was considered to be already a sovereign state.

The organization's revised constitution in 1943 did not mention franchise explicitly in its primary objects. It spoke of the African people's attainment of freedom "from all discriminatory laws whatsoever" and of their "full participation" in the government.[8] The document of African claims appearing at the end of that same year, however, made known "our undisputed claim to full citizenship." It declared that freedom, democracy, Christianity, and human decency could not be attained until all "races" in South Africa participated in them.[9]

It became incumbent upon the youth of the organization, a child of the 1940s, to revise drastically the earlier approach of the ANC and to jettison completely some of its defeatist and apologetic tactics. These were regarded as defective both in form and in matter.[10] Established in 1944, the Congress Youth League (ANCYL) adopted African nationalism as the "national liberatory creed" of Africans. The fundamental aims of this creed were to create a single entity out of the "heterogeneous" groupings of Africans; to free Africa as a whole and South Africa in particular from foreign domination and leadership; and to make it possible for Africa "to make her own contribution to human progress and happiness." The long-term goal of the ANCYL was genuine democracy that guaranteed minority rights in a democratic constitution. The immediate goal of its political action would be "direct representation of Africans in parliament on a democratic basis." It adopted the motto: "Freedom in Our Life Time."

The ANCYL affirmed in no uncertain terms that Africa was a "black man's country." It was thus imperative that the Africans' leader should come "out of their loins."[11] Consequently, they would continue to "suffer oppression and tolerate European domination only as long as they [did not have] the material force to overthrow it." Compromise was not considered possible unless whites abandoned their domination of Africa and assisted in building up a free democracy both in South Africa and throughout the continent. The youth league rejected an African nationalism based on the slogan, "Quit Africa." It favored "inclusive nationalism," in which everyone who paid his full loyalty to Africa and to the principles of democracy would be regarded as an African. The struggle, it was declared, was not directed against whites but against white domination.[12] The league saw African unity and the restoration of African self-confidence as preconditions for interracial cooperation. This was to ensure that Africans were not used by other groups for their own ends.[13] All these policy revisions within the ANC remained on the level of theory throughout the 1940s. Their practical implications were not given expression until the beginning of the following decade.

Although, as we will see later, the ANC did adopt a program of action through which it subsequently began to implement its new standpoint, it was precisely because such implementation was not seen to be far-reaching enough that the PAC came into being. After the ANC's adoption of a Freedom Charter in 1955, two distinct viewpoints gradually began to emerge in the youth league. These viewpoints concerned primarily—though not exclusively—the attitudes of members of the league itself toward the charter. Those members who supported the charter duly came to be known as Charterists; those opposed to it called themselves Africanists and saw themselves as the true representatives of the league and its standpoints. This group led a walkout from the ANC annual conference in 1958 and later formed the PAC.

According to Horrell, the Africanists had been trying before the conference to capture the leadership of the ANC. Their immediate motive was to remove "communist control" of the ANC and other adverse influences allegedly arising from its connection with the Congress Alliance.[14] Failure to win the leadership and to effect the expulsion of communists from the ANC, however, finally led to their breaking away from the organization. In their letter giving notice of dissociation, dated November 2, 1958, the Africanists stated, among other reasons, that the 1955 Freedom Charter was "in irreconcilable conflict" with the organization's program of action, adopted in 1949. The charter, continued the letter, claimed that the land no longer belonged to the African people, but was "auctioned for sale to *all*" who lived in the country. They reaffirmed their commitment to the overthrow of white domination and the restoration of the land to its rightful owners. The letter concluded, "We are launching out openly, on our own, as the custodians of the ANC policy as it was formulated in 1912 and pursued up to the time of the Congress Alliance."[15] They launched the PAC formally on April 5-6, 1959. Mangaliso Sobukwe, lecturer in African studies at the University of Witwatersrand, was elected president. At its first annual conference in December that year, the organization was able to report a successful record of 153 branches with a total of 31,035 members.[16]

The precursor of the third movement under present consideration (the BCM), SASO, was established in 1968, when there was no black national student or political organization operating aboveground. SASO was bound soon to find itself addressing much broader issues in more detail than an ordinary student organization. Thus it originally wore two hats: that of a student body deeply involved in student politics, on the one hand, and that of a "stop-gap" political organization addressing national life issues, on the other. As soon as the opportunity presented itself to do so, it paved the way for the formation of the BPC, which took over the political role.

SASO's establishment followed the demise of a number of African students' organizations that had proliferated on campuses during the 1950s. Some of these had developed, as SASO did itself, as a result of dissatisfaction with the "multiracial" National Union of South African Students (NUSAS). Perhaps the more significant for the present study were the African Students Association (ASA) and the African Students Union of South Africa (ASUSA), student wings of the ANC and the PAC, respectively. Immediately following the outlawing of the two parent bodies, there was little activity among African university students. Organization was left largely to the efforts of NUSAS. This body was prohibited, however, in the newly established university colleges for blacks. Students here were instead encouraged, by their white authorities, to form their own exclusive organizations on the basis of "race." Students from some campuses, however, were still able to attend NUSAS conferences. It was at one such conference that the idea of reviving black student organization began to appeal to some students, irrespective of encouragement from some university authorities.

Events leading to the establishment of SASO are a common occurrence in "mixed" organizations. In short, it was a question of one group perceiving another to live the opposite of what it preached. While NUSAS to some extent advocated an open society, at the same time it felt constrained to abide by most of the segregationist laws of the country on certain matters. Black students could not understand this. Hence when white NUSAS members nodded to the separate accommodation of black members at a NUSAS conference in 1967, some black students decided that they might as well be on their own.[17] However, not until they had attended another conference in the following year—this time of the recently established University Christian Movement (UCM)—did they take the last step. They could not help acknowledging that even in a radical organization like the UCM, with a black majority, the dominant view and leadership were still white. A black student caucus was formed at this conference and ultimately led to the establishment of SASO at a planned black student conference in December 1968.

At the beginning SASO declared itself not to be a rival of NUSAS as a national union of students. What it objected to, its officials said, was the dichotomy between principle and practice among most of NUSAS's members. In considering the kind of relationship it should have with the national union, SASO felt that it could best serve the interests of black students by maintaining only functional rather than structural relations with it and other student bodies—such as UCM. Thus SASO could not affiliate with NUSAS.[18]

Within a few years of its formation SASO had launched a number of student and community development projects. These included literacy campaigns, health services, home study assistant projects, and a number of others.[19] Its message quickly spread through the whole country, eliciting both positive and negative feedback. Despite its relative progress in spreading its philosophy of black identity, solidarity, and self-reliance among students, SASO felt restricted by its nature as a student organization. For its message to reach the wider public, a more inclusive structure would have to be devised. In order to determine such a structure and to work together for its development, several black organizations were approached with which relations had been forged earlier. They included the African Independent Churches' Association (AICA), the Interdenominational African Ministers Association of South Africa (IDAMASA), the Association for Educational and Cultural Advancement of South Africa (ASSECA), and the YMCA. It was from their deliberations and a few others that the BPC originated.[20] Inaugurated in July 1972, it was meant to be a "confederate Black political organization" embracing all the people's mass organizations in South Africa. In the following discussion, unless otherwise indicated, both the BPC and SASO will be taken as the key representatives of the BCM.

LONG-TERM AND SHORT-TERM GOALS

The origin of the PAC was a reflection of growing expectations within the ANC membership that resulted from the influence exerted by the youth league on the overall policy and strategy of the organization. Once some of the members sensed some reluctance on the part of the organization in carrying out the new policies to their logical conclusion and even failed to persuade it to do so, a split was inevitable. This seems to imply that at the time of the breakaway there were more differences than commonalities between the new organization and the old one.

The BCM later, on the other hand, seemed to have more in common with its immediate predecessor than with the ANC, in spite of certain obvious differences it had with both older organizations.

By the end of the 1940s the formulation of ANC policy was almost complete. All that remained was its elaboration and the devising of a suitable strategy to accompany it. Sometimes, perhaps out of custom, the "reformist" language of earlier years was still used. For instance, in a statement following his deposition from the chieftaincy, Chief Albert Luthuli declared that the ANC did not seek to overthrow the "form or machinery of the State." It merely urged the inclusion of all sections of the community in the country's government.[21] Later, however, he wrote:

> Congress is deeply wedded to the ideal of democracy and has at all times expressed its firm and unshakable belief in the need for the *creation of a society in South Africa based on the upholding of democratic values:* values which are today cherished the world over by all civilized people. (Italics mine)[22]

The constitution of the ANC, revised for the second time in 1957, pledged the organization to strive for the attainment of "universal adult suffrage and the creation of a united democratic South Africa on the principles outlined in the [1955] Freedom Charter."[23] Later, at the ANC's treason trial, Mandela stated that what Africans demanded was the extension of the vote to all sections of the population on the basis of one man, one vote.[24] Professor Z. K. Matthews, on the other hand, reassured the whites that Africans were not for domination since they stood for a policy of "full citizenship rights for all."[25] These long-term goals represented a radical shift from the early approach of the ANC. The organization's short-term goals were summed up in its Program of Action as the immediate abolition of "all differential political institutions."[26]

The PAC differed from the ANC in several respects in describing its perception of the goals of the struggle. First and foremost, it believed that it was for the African, both as a South African native and as constituting the majority of the population, to determine the future course of the country. Those other groups in the country who were prepared to regard themselves as African would have an equal say in the affairs of the country—but not special privilege or monopoly. Other differences with the ANC were in the evaluation of the status of South Africa as an independent state, in the definition of the goal of the struggle, and in the tactics to be adopted toward that goal.

The ANC was criticized for regarding the South African government as the rightful government of the land, notwithstanding the exclusion of the majority of the people from the electorate. All that the ANC objected to, it was alleged, were the policies of the government. Its main objective was merely to replace these policies while leaving everything else as it was. "The fact that the Nats are a logical product of past South African history and that what they stand for is approved and supported by the overwhelming majority of whites in the country has apparently escaped the notice of the ANC," was Sobukwe's remark.[27] Because of its preoccupation with merely removing legal restrictions, it was alleged, the ANC saw the foe as the current Nationalist government. Everyone else claiming to be opposed to it was accepted and treated as an ally, regardless of his/her motives and beliefs. Khopung summarizes the ANC's position as follows:

> Before the formation of the Pan Africanist Congress, South Africa had been written off from the list of African countries to be liberated. African leaders themselves [in South Africa] including white communists had made the African masses believe that South Africa was not a colony. It was, therefore, an exception from the rest of Africa. It was an "independent state."

Khopung contends, on the contrary, that to the African people "South Africa was a colony through which the Anglo-Boers had dispossessed them."[28]

As opposed to the view attributed to the ANC, the PAC aimed at the complete overthrow of white domination as represented in the 1909 South Africa Act. The main source of difference between the two organizations was said to stem from the fact that the ANC emphasized solely the democratic aspect of the struggle to the neglect of the nationalistic aspect. Consequently, there were differences in tactics as well.[29] The long-term goal of the PAC was reflected in two slogans of the organization: "Africa for Africans"—which has been greatly distorted from the PAC's own interpretation of it—and *Izwe Lethu* ("Our Land"). Both slogans represented the political goal of a government "of the Africans for the Africans by the Africans." In the new Africa the term "African" would refer to "everybody who owes his loyalty only to Africa and accepts the democratic rule of an African majority."[30] Owing loyalty *only* to Africa seemed to imply less a rejection of dual citizenship than of the perpetuation of colonial times' distinctions between "Europeans" and "Natives." The rule of an African majority gives recognition to the fact that any legitimate government in South Africa is bound to reflect the leanings of the majority of the population. The tendency to substitute "exclusive" for "majority" is, therefore, wrong and was not in accordance with PAC conception. Thus Sobukwe pointed out, "There is no reason why in a free democratic Africa, a predominantly black electorate should not return a white man to Parliament, for colour will count for nothing in a free Africa."[31]

The PAC conceived of the struggle in Pan-Africanist terms rather than as exclusively South African. It envisaged an Africanist Socialist Democracy in a "United States of Africa."[32] The ideal South Africa, and consequently the rest of the continent, would guarantee no minority rights. Individuals rather than groups would be recognized because "we are fighting precisely that group exclusiveness which those who plead for minority rights would like to perpetuate." A guarantee of individual liberties was seen as the highest guarantee necessary.[33] The concept of "multiracialism" was also frowned upon as the opposite extreme of group exclusivism. It was perceived to imply some kind of "democratic apartheid," that is, "racialism multiplied, which is probably what the term connotes."

> Against multi-racialism [wrote the PAC president], we have this objection that the history of South Africa has fostered group prejudices and antagonism, and if we have to maintain the same group exclusiveness, parading under the term of multi-racialism, we shall be transporting to the new Africa those very antagonisms and conflicts. Further, multi-racialism is in fact pandering to European bigotry and arrogance. It is a method of safeguarding white interests irrespective of population figures. In that sense it is a complete negation of democracy.

Rather than multiracialism, the PAC chose the idea or goal of "non-racialism" as more expressive of its ideals. The first step toward this goal was to be the complete removal of the present government and white domination in general within the country. Totalitarianism in any form would not be tolerated. Further, while borrowing "the best" from both the East and the West was considered desirable, the PAC wished to maintain the "distinctive personality" of Africa and refused to be "satraps or stooges of either power bloc."[34]

In theory, the PAC appears to have succeeded in focusing strictly on the long-term goals of the struggle, in accordance with its beliefs. In practice, however, it later engaged in a fateful campaign against passes that led to its downfall. The removal of inconveniences such as passes, *inter alia,* were its undeclared short-term goals. On the whole, it declared itself to be more concerned with removing the source of oppression than dealing with its manifestations or merely alleviating it.

Unlike the PAC and more like the ANC, the BCM was very explicit in the expression of its short-term goals. Its very method of conscientization reflected a major part of these goals, the rest being its implementation. This implementation would, it was hoped, lead to black solidarity and so pave the way toward sociopolitical emancipation.[35] The attainment of psychological liberation and solidarity would create bargaining strength for the pursuance of the movement's ultimate goals: a just, egalitarian society with an equitable economic system based on the principle of equal sharing of the country's wealth. There would be a completely nonracial franchise: "an open society, one man, one vote, no reference to colour."[36] Biko elaborated on these views as follows:

> We see a completely non-racial society. We don't believe, for instance, in the so-called guarantees for minority rights, because guaranteeing minority rights implies the recognition of portions of the community on a race basis. We believe that in our country there shall be no minority; just the people. And those people will have the same status before the law and . . . the same political rights.[37]

The future South Africa would require a completely new constitution, the fruit of mutual interchange between black and white. It would stipulate the role of all South African citizens, including whites, after the transition to a new government. A substantial economic sacrifice would be required on the part of the whites in order to attain equity. The new society would also call for "an injection of new values, of new attitudes and a more compassionate regard for society."[38]

In spite of the envisioned ultimate goals and future society, it was emphasized that the immediate concern was not with the future but with the present. "The future will always be shaped by the sequence of present-day events." The immediate concern was the liberation of blacks:

> We are aware that the white man is sitting at our table. We know he has no right to be there; we want to remove him . . . strip the table of all trappings put on by him, decorate it in true African style, settle down and then ask him to join us on our own terms if he wishes.

Black people were no longer merely interested in reforming the system, the BCM declared. On the contrary, they were intent on transforming it completely into their own ideal society and on attaining the "envisioned self."[39] This was the meaning of liberation for them.

Program of Action

Apart from their expressions by representatives of the organizations, most policy statements of these movements were contained in certain organizational policy documents or formulated at conferences. The ANC had two well-known such documents—the Program of Action, adopted in 1949, and the 1955 Freedom Charter—to which the PAC reacted in various ways. The BCM also employed policy documents and conference resolutions to record its positions on various issues.

In addition to affirming the long-term and short-term goals of the ANC, its Program of Action outlined the means to be employed toward these ends. Included were boycotting all "differential political institutions" and educating the people on the matter as well as the use of such tactics as strikes, civil disobedience, noncooperation, and work stoppages to force a meaningful response from the government. This new program was implemented for the first time in 1952 in what was known as the Defiance Campaign, discussed later in this chapter.

While the PAC welcomed the 1949 Program of Action, it decried the Defiance Campaign as a distortion of the practical demands of the program. It also lamented the involvement of the South African Indian Congress in this implementation. Through the campaign and the ANC's activities of later years, in which it cooperated with several other organizations under what was known as the Congress Alliance, it was felt that the ANC had lost direction. As a result, it no longer had a program of action but was reduced to merely reacting to the political program of the government of the day.[40] Further, some alleged that it emphasized "spectacular activity" instead of principled action. For its part, the PAC favored precisely "principled programmatic action." This meant that Africans should work to fashion a new society through "positive action"; that is, through an "honest and relentless execution of the 1949 program."[41] Ironically, however, the PAC's only campaign in 1960 does not appear to have been in accordance with its interpretation of the Program of Action.

Most of the BCM's own program of action was reflected in its black consciousness approach. SASO defined "black consciousness" as an attitude of mind—a way of life. Through it black people were being motivated to reevaluate their worth as human beings and to reject all value systems that sought to make them accept the status of an alien in their own land. They were to build their own value systems, see themselves as self-defined and not as defined by others. Group cohesion and black solidarity were seen as important aspects of black consciousness. Self-definition meant rejecting white stereotypes of blacks and negative references to them such as "non-whites" or "non-Europeans." The place of these negatives was taken by positive epithets such as "black" to refer to all so-called nonwhite South Africans. Blacks were thus defined as "those who are by law or tradition politically, economically and socially discriminated against as a group in the South African society and identifying themselves as a unit in the struggle towards the realization of their aspirations."

The BCM rejected integration, especially if this was understood to mean assimilation of black people into an already existing white society with preestablished values and norms. The idea that a "settler minority should impose an entire system of values on an indigenous people" was frowned upon. As Steve Biko put it,

> If on the other hand, by integration you mean there shall be free participation by all members of a society, catering for the full expression of the self in a freely changing society, as determined by the will of the people, then I am with you. For one cannot escape the fact that the culture shared by the majority group in any given society must ultimately determine the broad direction taken by the joint culture of that society. This need not cramp the style of those who feel differently but on the whole, a country in Africa, in which the majority of people are African, must inevitably exhibit African values and be truly African in style.[42]

Because it excluded whites, the BCM often had to respond to charges of racism. Its proponents strongly protested against such charges, stating that they were merely responding to the situation in which they found themselves in a way they found most appropriate: "We are collectively segregated against—what can be more logical than for us to respond as a group?" Blacks, it was argued, had suffered enough from white racism to want to turn the tables. They were not out to hate whites but to treat them as people.[43]

There seems to have been some confusion in some of the statements of black consciousness leaders regarding the exact status of their ideology as an operative tool. First, it was recognized that black consciousness as an "approach" would be irrelevent in a colorless and nonexploitative, egalitarian society. Its immediate relevance was said to stem from the belief that the existing "anomalous situation is a deliberate creation of man." Yet the task of black consciousness did not seem to end with the achievement of the ideal society envisaged. Biko stressed that black consciousness was not merely a means to an end. What it sought to do, he said, was "to *produce* at the output end of the process real Black people who do not regard themselves as appendages to white society."[44] Except for his denial, however, his statement still stressed the functional nature of black consciousness. As a means, therefore, its end product did not necessarily elevate it to an end, as Biko seemed to imply.

The Freedom Charter

Another earlier policy document, which did not seem to have parallels in the PAC and the BCM, was the ANC's Freedom Charter. At its appearance this document was controversial not only among white supporters of apartheid but also among some black people. Most of the latter thought it was a weak statement of the goals envisaged in the black struggle for change. It was also thought to be unrealistic—if not contradictory to its aims—in some of its phrasing.[45] Chief Albert Luthuli, president general of the ANC at the time of its adoption, admitted that "the declaration made in the Freedom Charter is uneven—sometimes it goes into unnecessary detail, at other times it is a little vague." He believed, nevertheless, that taken as a whole it was significant to those who aspired for a joint homeland for all South African inhabitants.[46]

The charter was a joint effort of an ad hoc National Action Committee composed of the executives of four organizations: the ANC, the South African Indian Congress (SAIC), the South African Congress of Democrats (COD), and the South African Coloured People's Organization (SACPO). Together they constituted a group called the Congress Alliance. Many groups, as well as some black authors, have questioned the real origin of the charter and the amount of participation in its drafting by the individual congresses. These critics allege that the charter was imposed upon the rest of the Congress Alliance by the "communist-dominated" COD. It is alleged that most of the officials at the Congress of the People—the gathering that adopted the charter—including the ANC itself, saw it for the first time at the congress.[47] The PAC also made similar allegations and this was partly what led to dissociation from the ANC by those who founded it. Perhaps the real origin of the document is less important than its significance for South Africa and the response given to it by its group sponsors and the general public.

The preamble of the charter declared that South Africa belonged to all its inhabitants, black and white, and that no government could justly claim authority unless it was based on the will of the people. "Only a democratic state, " it stated, "based on the will of the people, can secure to all their birthright without distinction of colour, race, sex or belief." Those who adopted the charter were, therefore, "equals, countrymen, and brothers." The charter's ten-point commitment included the following: the people shall govern; all national groups shall have equal rights; the people shall share in the country's wealth; the land shall be shared among those who work it; all shall be equal before the law; all shall enjoy equal human rights; there shall be work and security; the doors of learning and of culture shall be opened; there shall be houses, security, and comfort; there shall be peace and friend-ship.[48]

To the government, this was a communist document. To the Afri-canists or "nationalists" within the ANC it was a "sellout" of the Afri-can's birthright. During the treason trial (1956–1961) involving ANC members and some members of the Congress Alliance, it became the key exhibit. Expert testimony given at the trial on its communist in-spiration concluded, however, that the charter was a "moderately so-cialist program with stress on liberal theses." Nothing in it could com-pel the reader to conclude that it was a communist statement, said Polish professor Joseph Bochenski.[49]

The PAC largely saw the charter as a reformist statement and thus a betrayal of the 1949 Program of Action. It was, according to Leballo, a political bluff, promising a utopia around the corner but not indicat-ing how to reach it. "It is utterly useless," he felt, "to go around shout-ing empty slogans such as 'The people shall govern,' 'The people shall share,' without political steps towards that government." Leballo, secretary of the PAC after its formation, suggested that the ANC was simply being made a tool and a stooge by "interested parties" that were anxious to maintain the status quo.[50] The ANC's alliance with the other congresses was said to constitute an ungodly sacrifice of the African's material interests. It was an alliance of master and slave—the exploiter and exploited, the oppressor and oppressed, the degrader and de-graded.[51] For the PAC such an alliance between unequals was incon-ceivable. What made more sense was for the Africans to work to-gether—by themselves—as the victims of oppression and to fight for their desserts. The Congress Alliance only served to blunt the militancy of the black struggle because the whites in it naturally had a vested in-terest in the status quo, it was felt.

On Apartheid in General

In the course of their deliberations on how to improve the condition of blacks in the country, the three movements addressed themselves to the question of apartheid in general as well as to its specific applications. All three agreed that apartheid had to be replaced by a more representative, democratic government based on the will of all the inhabitants of the country. For the PAC, any suggestion of apartheid, "whether total or partial, social or political, or whether it was called Christian trusteeship, partnership or white leadership with justice," was rejected as a camou-flage for continued oppression, exploitation, and humiliation of black people.[52] The three also rejected the government's division of the country into "homelands" for particular black ethnic groups. They saw this as a weakening technique of the divide-and-rule strategy. Chief Luthuli stated that the government used this technique in approaching individual chiefs of each group to get them to agree to its bantustan policy. Most of them rejected it and those who accepted it did so against the will of their people, he said.[53] Thus "homeland" leaders came to be generally regarded as enemies of the people.

The most tragic aim of the bantustan policy was seen as its intention to "wipe Africans off the South African political map."[54] The BCM also saw the idea as an attempt to divert the energy of black people from the true struggle for liberation to "racialist, tribalist and generally divisive political undertakings which at best keep the real and true goal of liberation out of immediate sight and attention of black people and at worst serve to bolster the white racist regime of those who created [these 'homelands']." Thus, in fact, the whole idea of "homeland" politics was calculated to fragment and weaken the struggle for liberation and had to be totally rejected.[55] Both SASO and BPC also explicitly rejected the idea of fighting the system from within because "the architects of the system know it best." Hence they would always be ahead of any black infiltrators in terms of planning. Any kind of participation in government platforms was thus tantamount to selling the souls of black people.

Response to Specific Legislation

The implementation of apartheid gave rise to certain repressive laws that were of great concern to black people and other opponents of the system. We have already discussed some of these laws in the previous chapter, but need to mention here a few others. Most of them were enacted before 1948, but their issues are recurrent and they are continually amended. They concern the franchise question, the pass system, land, economy and labor, and Bantu education, now known as education and training.

Although all three movements addressed these specific issues, the PAC favored a general condemnation of apartheid rather than its specific manifestations. It was skeptical about singling out specific laws, fearing that this led to preoccupation with the effects rather than the root cause of the problem. When a man's house is flooding, Sobukwe observed, the solution is not to use a bucket to remove the water. The PAC's aim was to close the very source of South Africa's evil legislation. Yet the organization could not completely ignore present realities and the need to record its indignation. Hence its leaders continually found themselves reacting to individual laws and issues. The BCM's attitude in this matter was very similar to that of the PAC except that it thought it important to educate people on these laws and various issues in motivating them for the struggle.

The Franchise

By the time the present administration took over government in 1948, the tiny vestiges of African qualified franchise in the Cape had been abolished for twelve years. The Indian franchise question had been insecure since 1896. An attempt in 1946 by the Smuts government to give the Indians limited voting rights—in which they could choose three whites to represent them in Parliament—was dumped when the National Party came to power two years later.[56] By 1951 the government was able to dispose of "coloured" voting rights.

The leaders of the ANC and the SAIC had made a pact in 1947 in which they pledged themselves to work for "full franchise rights" and other freedoms. The Separate Representation of Voters Act (removing "coloureds" from the common roll) and the Bantu Authorities Act of 1951 were some of the laws the ANC and the SAIC openly challenged by threatening a defiance campaign in 1952. The PAC, about six years later, took the position that it did not recognize the independence of South Africa under its current government. Therefore, there was no question for it about the fact that the recognition of African voting rights would lead to majority rule and thus a predominantly black government. This was the position of the BCM as well, later. The BPC explained its position as that of equal suffrage to all sane adult citizens irrespective of color, race, religion, or any other consideration. It committed itself to observing and respecting the United Nations Universal Declaration of Human Rights.[57]

The Pass System

The black struggle against the pass system in South Africa is almost as old as that for universal franchise. Campaigns against passes abound in the history of this country since the union. In 1952 the new administration passed a law consolidating them, called, ironically, the Natives (Abolition of Passes and Coordination of Documents) Act.[58] Besides intensifying the system, it also extended passes to African women for the first time since the failure of earlier attempts to do so.

From 1955 to 1958 African women, with the support of the ANC, were leading the struggle against passes both in urban and rural areas. It was specifically on the question of pass laws that the PAC apparently deviated from its policy of nonintervention in specific legislation. It decided at its 1959 annual conference to embark on a campaign calling for the "total abolition" of passes. This decision was regarded as "a decisive and final action on pass laws."[59] The PAC's decision coincided with that of the ANC for a similar campaign planned for ten days later. The former's turned out to be the last mass campaign against passes. The BCM did not plan any during its time. In 1986 the government announced that it was finally replacing the pass system with that of a uniform identity document for all South Africans. The significance of this step has not yet been tested.

Land

Land has remained a controversial subject in South African politics since the nineteenth-century colonial wars. The final "deed of disinheritance" of the Africans was completed through the 1936 Land Act. It did not go unchallenged by the people and their organizations. Laws introduced by the present administration, such as the Natives Resettlement Act, Native (Urban Areas) Act, and Promotion of Bantu Self-Government Act deal with the issue of land in various ways.[60] They prohibit African ownership of land and dwelling or sojourning in certain areas, and restrict them to others, primarily to the less than 13 percent of South Africa's land proposed by the 1936 Act. Until recently this 13 percent was meant to be the only permanent "homeland" of all Africans. In 1986 the government indicated its acceptance in principle of the permanence of certain categories of Africans in so-called white South Africa.

All three movements under examination rejected the government's land and "homeland" policy and made commitments to have a fair deal. The ANC's climactic statement on the question was in its Freedom Charter, where it stated that South Africa belonged to all who lived in it. "Restriction of land ownership on a racial basis shall be ended and all the land redivided amongst those who work it." For both the PAC and the BCM the land belonged first and foremost to the black people and had to be restored to them before any kind of negotiation could take place about harmonious living relations.[61] For them South Africa had not yet emerged from its colonial status. At the same time, a SASO Policy Manifesto acknowledged, with the concurrence of the BPC, that "South Africa is a country in which both black and white live and shall continue to live together."[62] Consequently, no single group had the right to partition the land to suit its own interests.

Economy and Labor

Throughout South African history, the depriving of African people of their land always assured "white South Africa" of cheap labor for its economy. Without sufficient land Africans were forced to go to white farms, mines, and factories both to earn their living and to be able to afford livestock taxes imposed on them by colonial law. Even today the so-called homelands are deliberately intended as labor reservoirs for the South African economy. Beyond this purpose, "they serve primarily as dumping grounds for the old, the young, the sick and the unemployed."[63]

Various laws, beside the land acts, contributed to this effect. Chief among them are the pass laws, which were described by Dr. Xuma, one-time ANC president, as "the very foundation of economic exploitation." He saw them as instruments of African demoralization, humiliation, and criminalization.[64] Direct economic laws are those of job reservation and other aspects of economic discrimination. Through them most skilled jobs were preserved for whites only, black wages were kept below subsistence level or, at best, as low as possible, and separate facilities and unequal treatment of blacks and whites at places of employment were guaranteed.

Along with the hated pass system, these discriminatory economic laws were targets of organized opposition by blacks. Often national organizations cooperated with unions in their campaigns, as in the 1946 mine workers' strike and many subsequent ones. A report of the Congress Alliance prepared in 1956 stated that its ultimate economic objective was the smashing up of financial, gold-mining, and farming monopolies and the turning over of the national wealth to the people.[65] The PAC coupled its only anti-pass campaign with the demand for a minimum wage as a short-term objective. As a long-term project, a planned economy and the "most equitable distribution of wealth" were to be aimed at and implemented within the framework of political democracy. Any form of totalitarianism or exploitation was shunned. While capital would be accepted from both the East and the West, Africans would remain very much their own master.[66] The PAC supported the All-Africa Conference's call for economic sanctions against the country in the hope that "the crippling of the monopolistic South African White economy shall have the effect of bringing back some sense to Verwoerd's government of minority rule."[67]

As its predecessors had before it, the BCM believed that sociopolitical change in South Africa would mean little unless there was a corresponding rearrangement in the economic sphere. At the moment there was such ill-distribution of wealth in the country that it was felt that mere change in the color of the government would not necessarily affect the system itself. Its economic policy evolved over a few years and was apparently more thought out than those of the two older organizations. In devising an economic policy for the future the BPC sought to avoid the dilemma of having to choose between capitalism and communism.[68] It opted for a socialist solution that was considered to be "an authentic expression of black communalism." Black communalism was defined as a philosophy of sharing characteristic of black people throughout the world. It was seen as similar in many ways to African Socialism. Though the concept had a "tribal" background, it was meant to accommodate an elaborated present-day economic concept.[69]

The BPC had a thirty-point economic program for a liberated "Azania" (its new name for South Africa). Its main thrust was on the ownership by the state of all land and land-related industry such as mining and forestry. The state was to play a crucial role in the planning and development of industry and commerce, and was to own all those industries whose products were of strategic importance to the nation and its economy. Workers were to be protected by state supervision of industrial enterprises and regular reviewing of salaries and wages. In agriculture, emphasis would be placed on cooperatives. Such cooperatives and villages would receive state assistance in marketing their products for both internal and external consumption. Foreign investment in industry and commerce would be kept to a minimum. All workers would contribute toward the welfare of the handicapped and toward other individual and social disabilities in what would amount to a welfare state arrangement.[70]

During the years 1972–1973 there was much labor unrest among Africans throughout South Africa, largely spontaneous. Although there were a number of unregistered trade unions, most of the strikes did not seem to be organized by any of them. While the BCM had no direct influence on the origin and conduct of these strikes, they later served as a catapult for the movement to begin thinking of organizing in the labor field. The resulting Black Workers' Project was to work for the establishment of a black workers' council that would act as a coordinating body to serve the needs of black workers, to unite and bring solidarity among them, and to create awareness and a sense of obligation in them toward black development. SASO was later joined by the Black Community Programs (BCP) in this undertaking with a joint contribution to its staff.[71] Subsequently a union umbrella body was established, called the Black Allied Workers Union (BAWU).

Foreign Investments

The condition of black workers and the fact that there were foreign companies also employing them and contributing to the economy of the country led to a closer examination of these bodies. This seems to have been more a concern of the BCM than of the other two organizations. It is obvious that these companies treated their employees just as domestic companies did, by apartheid laws and attitudes. They abided strictly by the letter of the law and the discriminatory practices of the country, through which they derived maximum profits in their invest-ments.

SASO adopted its policy on foreign investments in 1971. In view of the foreign companies' acceptance of apartheid, SASO rejected their investment in the country because it was seen to benefit the South African government more than the people who suffered under it. Because they profited from the system, it was believed, they ended up having a vested interest in its maintenance. They made it possible for South Africa to spurn world opinion and maintain its racist regime; they boosted the country's international image and made it an ideal land for investment while the social evils practiced within it were lost sight of; they also gave South Africa an economic stability that enabled it to gain diplomatic and economic acceptance in the international scene.[72] The BPC corroborated this position and further called for the "total with-drawal of foreign investment from South Africa." In adopting its posi-tion on foreign investment, the BCM implicitly hoped that these com-panies would pressure their home governments to apply pressure on South Africa to change its internal policies—or else "they might as well get out."[73]

Bantu Education

One of the ways in which apartheid has been implemented and trans-mitted through the years has been through the system of Bantu educa-tion, which now falls under the Department of Education and Train-ing. A much-quoted statement by Dr. Hendrik Verwoerd, prime minister from 1958–1966 and arch-designer of apartheid, was that "there is no place for the Bantu in European community above the level of certain forms of labour." This became the basis for an inferior system of education for Africans, for

> what is the use of teaching a Bantu child mathematics when it can-not use it in practice? . . . That is absurd. . . . Education must train and teach people in accordance with their opportunities in life. . . . It is therefore necessary that native education should be controlled in such a way that it should be in accordance with the policy of the State.[74]

Accordingly, the old missionary school system, which hitherto had drawn the African "away from his own community and misled him by showing him the green pastures of European society in which he is not allowed to graze," was replaced by Bantu education in 1953. Its im-plementation was to begin in 1955.

Needless to say, Africans and other opponents of apartheid throughout the country loudly condemned this system of education.

Parents, at the same time, were faced with the dilemma of either allowing their children to participate in it, thus appearing to condone the "moral and spiritual enslavement of our children,"[75] or withdrawing their children from school altogether and freeing them for the streets. The latter was a less favorable option.

A boycott of schools called by the ANC at its 1954 conference managed to attract only about seven thousand children. The ANC declared its position to favor full educational opportunities for all African children. Such education had to be free, compulsory, and state financed as was the education of other sections of the South African community. Speaking against the system prior to the PAC breakaway, its president, Sobukwe, asserted that to the African youth education meant service to Africa. It also had to be the "barometer of African thought." To him Fort Hare, the only university for Africans at the time, was to be for the Africans what Stellenbosch and Pretoria were for the Afrikaners.[76] The PAC National Executive Committee expressed anger and frustration in 1959 when the university college was taken over by the government's Department of Bantu Administration and Development.

Most of the BCM supporters, unlike those of the earlier movements, were products of Bantu education and other segregated systems. They believed, however, that the system could be countered only by the recruitment of as many teachers as possible into the black consciousness line of thinking. In this way they would still be in the system, but not entirely for its benefit. Like the older organizations, the BCM rejected Bantu education as "education for domestication" and favored one that would make "millions of downtrodden Blacks self-reliant and free from oppressive strains perpetrated by the racist government of South Africa."[77]

PRACTICAL IMPLICATIONS

The test of any organizational policy is in its implementation, its translation into practice. Too often bodies purporting to work for change or the improvement of living or other social conditions are merely "talk-shops" that specialize mostly in sloganeering and the hurling of "sticks and stones" at the incumbent without any significant action. The theoretical grounding and development of the South African struggle are, indeed, honorable and justifiable. Anyone who still denies the justness of any genuine cause for freedom must be an agent of the Antichrist. The question now confronting us is, To what extent was each of the movements discussed able to carry out in practice what it advocated so faithfully—within its context—in word, and what success, if any, did it have in doing so?

In its earlier years the ANC worked for change mainly on its own or cooperated with other African bodies such as the All-African Convention (AAC). One of its objects, according to its first constitution, had been to "educate Parliament and Provincial Councils, Municipalities other [sic] bodies and the public generally regarding the requirements and aspirations of the native people."[78] In its revised constitutions of 1943 and 1957 the organization had no statement regarding its modus operandi corresponding to the one expressed in the first constitution. However, the mode of action expressed in the Program of Action became normative since 1949. The Program of Action had three practical consequences, only one of which was expressly indicated in it. These were (1) a new approach in communicating with the authorities; (2) more cooperation with other black organizations; and (3) more aggressive campaigning for political and social change.

Only the last of these consequences formed part of the PAC's own agenda of action. The first was entirely excluded: the organization's objective was to wrench power rather than to negotiate with the government for it. It was prepared to cooperate with other black organizations if this was advantageous to it. But there does not seem to be any indication that it ever did so to any significant consequence. The BCM's own attitude was very close to that of the PAC rather than the ANC. However, it was more of a cooperative of black organizations and so involved broader relations with them both inside and outside itself than the PAC had done. Its withdrawal stance meant almost total abstention from open conflict with the powers that be. It was a building-up process in which blacks would concentrate more on strengthening themselves for ultimate, future action than on immediate benefits through a directionless approach. How long it would be before the time was considered ripe for final action was not clear.

Communication with the Authorities

After the adoption of the Program of Action in 1949, the ANC temporarily abandoned its old method of deputations and negotiation, embarking on a policy of noncooperation with the government. As a result, communication between the two bodies degenerated into threats and ultimatums. The ANC still hoped that warning the government about some impending "doom" might bring about the desired effect. However, the government remained as intransigent as ever. In turn, it threatened to make "full use of the machinery at its disposal to quell any planned disturbances."[79]

Such was the communication that preceded the Defiance Campaign of 1952. As a final appeal in good faith to the government, coming after a forty-year attempt "to bring about conditions for genuine progress and true democracy," the ANC wrote to the government requesting the repeal of certain laws. This repeal was to be the government's first step at recognizing Congress's firm belief that

> the freedom of the African people, the elimination of exploitation of man by man and the restitution of democracy, liberty and harmony in South Africa are such vital and fundamental matters that the Government and the Public must know that we are fully resolved to achieve them in our lifetime.[80]

It further recorded its "firm determination to redouble our efforts for the attainment of full citizenship rights." The government refused to yield to these demands, maintaining that the difference between blacks and whites was not man-made.

Despite this breakdown is communication, the ANC made no attempt to deceive or elude the authorities during the Defiance Campaign. The resisters tried to cooperate as fully as possible with them. Letters were written to the magistrates, warning them of what was intended to be done, when and where. The names of relevant leaders were also given in advance.[81] Often their plans were disrupted by the police because of this, and rearrangements were needed. Members of the organization also adopted a policy of addressing the courts when arrested for political infringements, in the hope of reaching both the government itself and the white community. Two further attempts to communicate directly with the government failed in 1957 and 1961.

In accordance with its policy of nonrecognition of and noncooperation with the regime, the PAC did not want to have anything to do with the government directly, least of all communicate with it for concessions. At least once, however, while it was planning its campaign against passes, it was compelled by circumstances to communicate with the authorities. This was more as a question of convenience than an appeal for legal reforms. In a letter to the Commissioner of Police, the PAC president asked him to instruct the police to refrain from actions that might lead to violence during the campaign. He said the people were under strict orders to avoid violence. If told to do so and given time, they would disperse peacefully. "But we cannot be expected to run helter-skelter because a trigger-happy, African-hating young white police officer has given thousands or even hundreds of people three minutes within which to remove their bodies from his immediate environment."[82]

Similarly, the BCM also avoided any direct dealings or communication with the government—which was regarded as irrelevant—

while concentrating mainly on motivating the community. Its policy also was that of "non-cooperation with oppressive structures." True to its policy, on no occason did the BCM attempt to make any direct demands or voluntary protests to the government concerning the black condition. Its condemnation of the regime was largely contained in its policy statements and addresses to the black community rather than to any government department. Such condemnation was meant to keep black people aware of the issues regarding their condition.

Some areas of black life demanded an element of compromise with the "system," however. For instance, BCM members were often forced to negotiate with "homeland" authorities if they wanted to conduct community projects in areas falling under these leaders' jurisdictions, even if they themselves did not recognize these areas as autonomous. Applying for permits was often the only way out for them to render service to their people.[83]

Cooperation with Other Organizations

The earliest cooperation between the ANC and other organizations seems to have been with members of the South African Communist Party. This cooperation was mainly centered on individual communists rather than on the party itself. Some African communists were joint members of the ANC and the Communist Party before the latter was banned in South Africa. Naturally, when the party was outlawed, these people became exclusive members of the ANC unless otherwise affected.

This association with communists was a controversial issue both within the movement and outside it. Within, the ANCYL complained that such groups of people sought "to impose . . . cut-and-dried formulae, which so far from clarifying issues of our struggle, only serve to obscure the fundamental fact that we are oppressed not as a class, but as a people, a Nation." The league rejected "wholesale importation of methods and tactics" that might harm the African's cause of freedom.[84]

Communist presence within the ANC, however, was defended by people such as Professor Matthews and Chief Luthuli. The former referred those who laid such charges to the resolution on dual loyalty, "that anyone who subscribed to the constitution was free to become a member." Those who complained about communists in the organization were to be asked, "Have they gone against any resolution?"[85] Luthuli's position was curt: "The Congress stand is this: our primary concern is liberation, and we are not going to be side-tracked by ideological clashes and witch hunts."[86] The ANC was also part of the All-African Convention, an umbrella African political body in the late 1930s. Later relations with the SAIC and the Franchise Action Committee of the "coloured" community ultimately led to the Congress Alliance. Also included in the alliance were the COD, SACPO, and later the South African Council of Trade Unions (SACTU).

The PAC extended its policy of noncollaboration to its relationship with other organizations. They in turn regarded the PAC as an extremist, "black-racist" organization. Its immediate attitude toward the ANC was one of regret or chagrin rather than hostility. The PAC said that it did not have a common ground with any of the other antiapartheid organizations. It was prepared, however, to cooperate with any of them if it were satisfied that the action would benefit the African cause. Bunting suggests that the PAC actually had strong ties with the Liberal Party. It even had the support of this party's newspaper, *Contact,* whose editor later joined the organization in exile.[87] This association was possible, apparently, because both bodies were strongly anticommunist. The PAC rejected forthright any form of cooperation with communists.

Its difficulty in cooperating with white organizations in particular was the PAC's conviction that they had a stake in the current system of government and hence an interest in maintaining it. Sobukwe concluded that Africans were the only people in the country who, by virtue of their material condition, could wish for a complete overhaul of the current political structure. Indeed, whites could become intellectual converts to the African cause, but they could not completely identify themselves with it.[88]

This rejection of cooperation with whites seems to be one chief point of similarity between the PAC and the BCM. The BCM did condone some form of parasitical relations with white organizations, however, as was perhaps the case between the PAC and the Liberal Party. Beyond this, it retained the prerogative to relate to whatever organization it deemed appropriate in relaying the "true feelings of Blacks in their country to the outside world."[89]

As already indicated and as the name implies, the BCM itself represented a movement of organizations related to one another by their common espousal of the black consciousness approach. This means that there was a substantial amount of sharing in the expounding of this ideology among these organizations. There was also some amount of interorganizational communication, very close in some cases—as in that of SASO and BPC—but not necessarily so in general. The general policy on such relationships was to maintain contacts and to cooperate with other black organizations that worked for the same end of liberation. Organizational initiative and independence were, on the other hand, encouraged. The BCM also recognized the presence within the country of "historical organizations" and committed itself to good relations with them.[90]

Sociopolitical Campaigns

Most important in the practice of the three movements was how they carried out their programs of action with regard to actual engagement in forcing the government to institute change. All three engaged in some activities and campaigns of varying significance. More relevant for our purpose are the ANC's 1952 Defiance Campaign, the PAC's Positive Action Campaign of 1960, and some of the activities of the BCM and its Viva Frelimo Rally in 1974.

The pioneering cooperation between the ANC and the SAIC, which made possible the Congress Alliance, was responsible for carrying out the ANC's 1949 Program of Action. Through it they would jointly plead the cause of their communities. The method proposed by the program was not entirely new to the SAIC. Although its champions called it the Defiance Campaign, rejecting any association of it with passive resistance, Kuper and Fatima Meer identify it simply as passive resistance.[91]

Following the government's refusal to yield to the two Congresses' demands in 1952,[92] two dates were set for alternative types of action. April 6, 1952—Van Riebeeck's three-hundredth anniversary of landing on South African land—was chosen as some sort of "test day" for the government to change its mind. The real day of reckoning, of launching the Defiance Campaign, would be June 26. On Van Riebeeck Day thousands of black people all over the country held demonstrations, joined by some white university students. The highest numbers were in Port Elizabeth and Pretoria, with more than ten thousand people each.[93] However, the demonstrations neither impressed nor bothered the government. Accordingly, the commencement date of the Defiance Campaign, June 26, was confirmed. A target of ten thousand volunteers—people who would participate in the violation of various laws on particular days—was set.[94]

The campaign was preceded by a day of prayer in many townships. The next day, pledged to discipline, the volunteers embarked upon their task of "liberation." They did so by various means: entering an African residential area other than one's own without a required permit; violating curfew laws; neglecting "Europeans only" signs and using seats, waiting rooms, and coaches reserved for whites in the railway stations; and entering the "European" sections in the post offices and demanding service.[95]

On its first day the campaign was launched in the Witwatersrand area in the Transvaal and in Port Elizabeth in the Cape. Those in other big cities throughout the country followed suit. The plan was to involve rural areas last. In all, 8,557 volunteers participated. The Eastern Cape alone accounted for more than half this number. The number of volunteers increased progressively from the last five days of June until the end of October. Upon arrest, they chose imprisonment rather than pay fines imposed when convicted. They also used courtrooms as "platforms" to advance their cause.[96]

Suddenly, in November and December, riots occurred in various parts of the country, resulting in a drop in the number of participants in the campaign. The riots, generally attributed to *agents provocateurs*—for the campaign was "far too orderly and successful for the government's liking"[97]—ended in a total of 23 deaths and 109 people wounded in Port Elizabeth, Denver (near Johannesburg), Kimberley, and East London.[98] The ANC's request for an impartial commission of enquiry by the government was turned down. In the end, the campaign did not reach the rural areas nor achieve its intended goal, but it gained the ANC an increased membership of more than 100,000.[99]

The PAC's Positive Action Campaign represented a hijacking of an earlier planned campaign called the status campaign. The latter was to have involved an assertion of the political, social, and economic status of the African people. It was to have been seen as part of the "unfolding and expanding, dynamic nation-building programme of the PAC" and would have endured

> until the day dawns when every person who is in Africa will be an African, and a man's colour will be as irrelevant as the shape of his ears . . . until government of the Africans by the Africans for the Africans is a *fait accompli.*[100]

Various reasons have been advanced for why the idea of the status campaign was abandoned in favor of the Positive Action Campaign. Perhaps a plausible reason, given plans by the ANC for an anti-pass campaign around the same time, was competition for both effectiveness and attraction of new membership.

The Positive Action Campaign was planned for March 21, 1960. On the date appointed for the campaign men were to leave their passes at home. Under a PAC leader, they would go to the nearest police station and submit themselves for arrest on pass law violations. Those arrested would accept jail terms under the slogan "No bail, no defence, no fine." If not arrested, they were to return later—and again—and offer themselves once more until they were taken in. There was to be absolute nonviolence.[101] The leaders would be the first to turn themselves in, lest they make people into victims of the police while they themselves maintained a safe distance.

The campaign began as planned. At several places around the country the people walked to police stations to carry out their mission. At some places they were taken in, but at others police refused to make arrests. In Johannesburg, PAC president Sobukwe and members of his executive, as well as about two hundred followers, presented themselves successfully for arrest.[102] There were similar arrests in Durban and several other places. The most active area in the country at this time was around the Vaal complex, in the southern Transvaal, where various incidents occurred between the people and the police. The main center of activity, however, became Sharpeville. Its counterpart was the African townships of Cape Town.

In Sharpeville five thousand to twenty thousand people, led by PAC's Nyakane Tsolo, crowded around the main police station and offered themselves for arrest. The police refused to take action. Court evidence later was to demonstrate that although the crowd had been "noisy and excitable," it had been neither hostile nor armed. As the crowd increased, police reinforcements and armoured cars arrived. Ultimately, Tsolo and two of his colleagues were arrested. During the excitement that followed two "unidentified" shots were heard, followed by two more, and the rest of the police opened fire without any verbal warning. By the end of the day 69 people were reported dead and 178 wounded.[103]

Similar incidents at Nyanga in Cape Town left six people dead and forty-seven injured. A stay at home was called here to mourn the dead, followed by an official call by both the PAC and the ANC for a national day of mourning. The stay at home lasted three weeks and, following the day of mourning, spread to other places in the country with high rates of success in key metropolitan areas. However, rioting and arson were employed all over as means to express the people's anger and frustration. A moment of "triumph" was seemingly lost when an "army" of thirty thousand people marched through the center of Cape Town toward the government buildings on March 30, demanding a hearing from the minister of justice. The tense atmosphere was deflated when the crowd, led by PAC member and medical student Philip Kgosana, obeyed a police order to disperse after an assurance that an interview with the minister would be arranged for later that day. On returning to the city at the appointed time, however, Kgosana and his colleagues were instead incarcerated under new emergency regulations.[104]

The BCM, in preparing itself for the "ultimate" bargaining process, addressed itself almost completely to the needs of the black community, regarding the white component of the society as irrelevant for the meantime. Through relevant organizations within the movement it ran a number of community projects, the immediate objective of which was "conscientization," immediate relief from present suffering, and the inculcation of self-reliance in the community. The organizations mainly responsible for these projects were SASO and the Black Community Programs (BCP).

SASO was particularly set on encouraging students to become involved in the political, social, and economic development of black people. With their help, it conducted literacy campaigns, health projects, physical projects—such as the building of schools, clinics, and community centers, especially in rural areas—as well as ran home education schemes for assisting those adults who were interested in furthering their education through extramural studies. SASO also set up commissions on the Black Press, the Black Workers Project, the Free University Scheme, and the Black Bank. The organization's chief instrument of "conscientization" was its monthly newsletter and other publications.[105]

Programs of the BCP included publications such as the annual *Black Review* and the occasional *Black Viewpoint,* youth, church, and educational programs as well as research projects. It also ran literacy classes, leadership training courses, and self-help schemes such as "home industries," that is, economic projects in the form of cottage industries and production of various articles. One of its main achievements was the Zanempilo Clinic in King Williams Town and also mobile clinics in other rural areas.[106] The political significance of the BCP was not immediately visible, except in some of its publications, which analyzed the political state of the country. Its leaders, however, saw great psychological value in its projects, necessarily the first step toward political liberation.

While not seeking confrontation, the BCM also often found itself called upon to challenge the authorities on certain matters, especially those affecting students. Almost all such challenges were directly provoked by the authorities themselves rather than by the movement or its members. One such confrontation was the national student strikes that originated at the University of the North in 1972. The strike there was the result of the university's expulsion of a student, Onkgopotse Ramothibi Tiro, for criticizing treatment of black students and the black community in general at the university's graduation ceremony. In solidarity with Tiro, the students boycotted lectures and were joined by students at other campuses calling for his reinstatement. Representatives at a SASO seminar at Alice, Cape, on May 13, 1972, drew up a document that came to be known as the "Alice Declaration." Part of it proposed that as a sign of protest against the oppressive laws of the country and the racist education given them, students should force their institutions to close down by a mass walkout.[107] Tiro was never reinstated and many other students were not allowed back after the continuous boycotts that followed his expulsion. In February 1974, he was killed by a letter bomb in Botswana, where he and other BCM members had taken refuge from their banning orders.[108]

A directly political activity by the BCM, which later turned into a challenge of government orders, was a series of rallies planned by SASO and the BPC in celebration of Mozambique's independence in 1974. The rallies were inspired by the significance placed on Mozambique's achievement for the South African struggle. Intervention by the government, however, turned it into a sour experience and—as in other similar events—occasioned riots and violence.

On the day before the rallies, a government ban was imposed on all SASO and BPC gatherings from September 24 to October 20, 1974, which included the date of the rally. The next day, the two organizations issued a press statement announcing that the rally would go on that afternoon as scheduled. In Durban alone, "thousands of pamphlets and several bill posters announcing the rally had been posted . . . , so that it was unlikely that SASO and BPC could have prevented the black community from gathering even if they had wanted to do so."[109] This was quite a momentous decision. The movement was faced with the prospect of either letting the people gather—unaware of the ban—and face the wrath of the police alone, or boldly assuming their leadership and facing up to the consequences.

At the rally police charged on the celebrants with their dogs, assaulting them with their swagger sticks. That there was no shooting is obviously because the rally was taking place in town rather than in an African township. Fourteen people were arrested on the spot, while many others were picked up by the police while undergoing treatment in hospitals. About forty BCM leaders were rounded up and arrested throughout the country.[110] In follow-up operations the offices of SASO were raided and property and publications confiscated. Some of the people arrested in these raids were later charged under the Terrorism Act, as explained in the next section.

It is appropriate, in closing this section, to acknowledge that although the Soweto uprising in 1976—which led to countrywide unrest—was not a direct result of organizational planning by the BCM, it was nevertheless an important manifestation of the black consciousness influence. Suffice it, therefore, to quote Biko's interpretation of it. Some time before his death, asked if he could point to any evidence of support for the BPC and black consciousness among the young black generation in South Africa, he replied:

> In one word: Soweto! The boldness, dedication, sense of purpose, and clarity of analysis of the situation—all these things are a direct result of Black Consciousness ideas among the young in Soweto and elsewhere. This is not quantitatively analyzable, for the power of a movement lies in the fact that it can indeed change the habits of people. This change is not the result of force but of dedication, or moral persuasion.[111]

More will be said about the impact of Soweto in the Afterword in the context of proposing a program for the future study of resistance to apartheid.

GOVERNMENT RESPONSE

Police violence and shooting of demonstrators at assertive campaigns was not the government's only reaction to these organizations' activities. As seen in the previous chapter, there was ongoing legislation for purposes of punishng, preventing unwanted acts, and even forestalling possible violations of other laws or government policy. Among the laws and penalties imposed for these purposes were banning orders on individuals, detentions without trial, prosecutions, curfew laws, bans on meetings, and so forth. The ultimate act that could be taken on any organization was its being declared illegal. In the decade from 1950 to 1960 only one, the South African Communist Party, had been so declared. Yet all these movements were to undergo a similar fate at the peak of their opposition to the government. As a result they were forced underground and/or into exile.

Those ANC supporters convicted for defiance in the Defiance Campaign received varying sentences around the country. The prosecutors demanded heavy sentences to serve as a deterrent, but the offenses committed were minor and could not be punished heavily enough to satisfy their demands. Apart from the direct arrest of volunteers in the defiance of specified laws, the government's response to the campaign was largely indirect until the time of the riots.[112]

Not long after the beginning of the campaign the police raided the offices of the ANC and SAIC and the homes of their officials, seeking evidence of incitement or some conspiracy against the state. Those arrested and convicted accordingly received suspended sentences of imprisonment, conditional on their ceasing to engage in further violations—thus depriving the movements of their leaders.[113] Twenty ANC leaders convicted under the Suppression of Communism Act were sentenced to nine-month suspended sentences. The judge conceded, however, that their charge had "nothing to do with communism as it is commonly known." He also accepted the evidence that "you have consistently advised your followers to follow a peaceful course of action and to avoid violence in any shape or form."[114] In addition to such curbs that resulted from the government's counteraction, fifty-two other members were banned and subjected to harsh restrictions, including prohibition of their continued membership with the ANC.[115]

In 1953 the Public Safety Act and the Criminal Law Amendment Act were introduced. The first enabled the government to call a state of emergency whenever it saw this necessary for the safety of the public; the second increased penalties for acts of defiance. The police also took it upon themselves since the Defiance Campaign to crush every meeting or activity of the ANC. Raids and their consequences were the order of the day. Yet some banned leaders like Nelson Mandela and Walter Sisulu—now serving life sentences on Robben Island—continued to defy their banning orders so as to continue their organizational work.[116] Armed policemen attended events such as the Western Areas removal in 1954 and the Congress of the People in 1955. The raids of 1956, referred to in passing in the previous chapter, resulted in the arrest of 156 people who were later brought to trial on charges of high treason. The prosecution's case rested on the ANC's policy between 1952—the year of the Defiance Campaign—and 1956. Of particular significance was the Freedom Charter. The defense contended that it was not the accused who were on trial "but the ideas that they and thousands of others in our land have openly espoused and expressed." Acquitting them all at the end of the trial in 1961, the presiding judge said that there was no evidence that they had become communists or intended the violent overthrow of the state.[117]

After the events of Sharpeville and other related incidents in 1960, there were numerous arrests and detentions of both PAC and ANC members under the imposed state of emergency. A ban on all public gatherings of more than ten people was imposed. As a result of the state of emergency, police assumed wide powers to suppress any strikes. The army was placed on alert. Heavier penalties were imposed for publications deemed to incite or subvert the situation in any way. Thousands of people were arrested and nearly two thousand political activists, including some members of white organizations, were detained under the emergency regulations.[118]

On March 28 the government introduced in Parliament the Unlawful Organizations Bill, which paved the way for the banning of the two current organizations. Not until April 8, however, was the government able to take action against them. Those people suspected of furthering their aims were liable to a prosecution of ten years in jail under the Suppression of Communism Act.[119] In speaking for the bill the minister of justice alleged that the aim of these organizations was "to bring to its knees any White Government in South Africa which stands for White leadership. . . . [They] do not want peace and order; what they want is not £1.00 a day for all the Bantu in South Africa; what they want is our country!"[120] The banning of these organizations was followed by house-to-house police searches and the arrest of people for multiple offenses. By May 16, 18,011 people had been detained. Some of them were charged, others committed to institutions, and at least 978 discharged, while a further 176 had their charges withdrawn.[121]

Sobukwe and 18 other PAC members were convicted on May 4 for inciting people to engage in law violations. The president was sentenced to three years imprisonment while the others received between eighteen-month and two-year jail terms. About 150 others were given an option for a fine of up to £300 or three years in jail. Those who broke their commitment not to appeal were nonetheless denied leave to do so. The minister of justice gave the total number of detentions on May 16 as 1,813 blacks and 94 whites. A number of volunteer groups were set up to assist the families and to provide legal aid for those finally brought to trial.[122]

Following "Sharpeville" and the treason trial of 1956–1961, the year 1963 was one of the climactic years in this period. During this year detentions under the ninety-day law and those falling under the Transkei emergency regulations reached 3,355. Of these people 1,186 were held without trial and 201 were juveniles. One man who died in detention under the ninety-day clause was banned posthumously to prevent his statements being quoted.[123] The major event of the time, however, was the so-called Rivonia Trial, in which nine people, all ANC leaders, were tried under the Sabotage Act. Of the nine, only one was finally acquitted and the rest convicted and sentenced to life imprisonment.[124] Also during this year police "mopping up operations" continued against the banned ANC and PAC members, suspected members, and supporters. The main charges brought against most of them were sabotage and furthering the aims of these organizations. While a general political lull set in among blacks following the government's harsh measures, the government kept its momentum in suppressing all suspected opposition right through the 1970s: sentencing suspects to jail terms, banning suspected "terrorists" and "communists," as well as "disciplining" those supposed to be furthering the aims of unlawful organizations.

Although gradually intensifying in ruthlessness, the government's response toward the BCM was initially one of a sense of achievement. Black consciousness was praised as the most positive step to have come from "black South Africa" thus far. No doubt, this credit was attributed to the "tribal university system" imposed by the government. Black consciousness was apparently seen as nothing but the "tribal consciousness" the government had been trying to impose on black people through its bantustan and Bantu education systems as well as through the entire concept of apartheid. SASO, therefore, had no difficulty in establishing itself in these universities as an alternative to NUSAS and the UCM. Only gradually did the government catch up with the full implications of the movement and begin to realize its blunder. Its initial reaction, though, was cautious.

The government's first "assault" on the BCM was the banning in 1972 of Sabelo Ntwasa, director of UCM's Black Theology Project until 1971. The banning of Dr. Basil Moore of the UCM was partly because of his association with this project. During the same year three SASO officials were denied South African passports, several were arrested or detained for questioning in connection with other members of the movement, and two SASO T-shirts with black consciousness designs were banned.[125] In 1973 BCM leaders representing SASO, BPC, BCP, and BAWU were banned for five-year terms. Among them was Steve Biko. Ten others were restricted two months later. By the end of 1973 alone fifty-four blacks in all were banned, most of them associated with the BCM. There were also ongoing trials involving members of the movement.[126]

The major assault on the movement occurred in 1974 following the rallies in celebration of Mozambique's independence. Of those arrested at this occasion, nine were ultimately charged with terrorism and brought to trial after more than three months' detention. They remained in custody during the entire trial period, which lasted for almost two years, beginning in January 1975.[127] The nine were accused of "endangering the maintenance of law and order" in South Africa or, alternatively, of conspiring to "transform the state by unconstitutional, revolutionary and/or violent means," to foster or create "feelings of racial hatred, hostility and antipathy by Blacks toward Whites," and "to discourage, hamper, deter or prevent foreign investment" in South Africa's economy. The government's case rested principally on the documentary evidence of SASO and BPC policy and speeches as well as writings of individual members and leaders. No overt acts of terrorism were demonstrated.[128]

Before the end of the trial, the media focus on it was diverted by the eruption of Soweto in the middle of 1976. For the next two years the number of arrests, detentions, and deaths in detention rose. The government's wrath culminated in the death of Black Consciousness leader and BPC's honorary president, Steve Biko, and the outlawing in 1977 of nineteen black organizations, at least one sympathetic white organization—the Christian Institute—and its periodical, *Pro Veritate,* and two black newspapers.[129] Since 1976 until the time of Biko's death twenty-two deaths had occurred in detention under security police interrogation. Little publicity had been given to these casualties until Biko's death and the scandal surrounding it. In 1979 the government awarded his family $78,000 as "compensation for his accidental death." By then the truth regarding his death had been exposed and it was obvious that the government's statement was merely face-saving.[130]

Most of the people detained after the outbreak of Soweto and following Biko's death were not released until around the middle of 1978. Some of them were handed five-year banning orders immediately upon their release. By the end of the year a total of 167 restriction orders were in force. In January 1978 there were 440 political prisoners; a year later, with a few releases and 194 new convictions, the total rose to 550. The remaining number of those detained under security laws by the end of 1978 was 150. A substantial number of bannings, trials, and convictions, as well as detentions without trial, continued into 1979 before it began a slight decline. The "Viva Frelimo" defendants were finally given their verdict the week before Christmas, 1976, after more than two years of custody and proceedings. They were all convicted and sentenced to five or six years. Although the presiding judge conceded that the organizations represented in the trial were not revolutionary groups, he nevertheless felt that the emphasis of black consciousness on black solidarity encouraged "feelings of hostility" between the "races" in South Africa.

REGROUPING AND CHANGE OF STRATEGIES

The government's drastic action on black opposition and its organizations left a vacuum in black politics after each banning of the major movements. In the first instance some members of the older organizations were finally driven underground, then forced to flee into exile from where they continue to operate today. In the case of the BCM many also went into exile, some of them joining the already reorganized older organizations there, while others reorganized themselves under the name Black Consciousness Movement of Azania (BCM-Azania). Yet others remained inside the country and later established a new organization called the Azanian People's Organization (AZAPO), discussed in the next chapter. It is not our task in this study, however, to discuss the activities of these movements in their exiled status.

In 1961, after a failed attempt by an All-in African Conference to persuade the government to convene a national convention, a new group called *Umkhonto We Sizwe* was established by some members of the banned ANC. Nelson Mandela, who had been elected secretary of the new All-in African National Action Council, disappeared from the scene after gaining a temporary respite from his incessant banning orders. The police were soon after him. In a press statement on June 26, 1961, he said that it would be "naive and criminal" for him to surrender to them. "We have an important programme before us and it is important to carry it out very seriously without delay," he said.[131]

The formation of *Umkhonto We Sizwe* meant a change of strategy for the ANC from nonviolent to violent opposition. It was a recognition of the fact that the banning of both the ANC and the PAC represented a ban on nonviolence itself as an option. A flyer issued by *Umkhonto* in December 1961 claimed that attacks had been carried out against government installations, especially those directly representing "the policy of apartheid and race discrimination." It said that only two alternatives were now left to the struggle—submitting or fighting. The latter choice had been compelled by the government's intransigence. The government had rejected every "peaceable demand by the people for rights and freedom and answered every such demand with force and more force!" It was still hoped, nevertheless, that the government would allow peaceful change to take its course.[132]

Only in 1963 was *Umkhonto* openly linked to the ANC by exiled ANC leaders. Not until the "Rivonia Trial" was Mandela himself identified as one of its important leaders. At this time he was already serving a prison term for inciting a stay-at-home in May 1961 and for leaving the country illegally in 1962, having been arrested in August of the latter year.[133] Justifying the ANC's resort to violence, Mandela observed that fifty years of nonviolent struggle "had brought the African people nothing but more and more repressive legislation." Later he explained that South African history had conditioned Africans to the fact that if their demands were made strongly enough to have some chance of success, they would be met by force on the part of the government.[134]

In a statement he made at his "Rivonia Trial," Mandela made a distinction between four forms of violence: sabotage, guerrilla warfare, terrorism, and revolution. The course of *Umkhonto* had been to exhaust sabotage before choosing another option. This was because "sabotage did not involve loss of life, and it offered the best hope for future race relations. Bitterness would be kept to the minimum and if the policy bore fruit, democratic government could become a reality."[135] Opposed to *Umkhonto*—"the military wing of the struggle"—the official

ANC, also gone underground, retained its nonviolent policy. It refused, however, to condemn the former. It continued to organize political activities secretly as well as to raise funds for trials and for its victimized members.

The internal, underground operations of *Umkhonto We Sizwe* were short-lived. Within a year and a half of its announced existence its hideout in Rivonia, Johannesburg, was raided by the police. Its leaders, together with piles of evidence in the form of plans for sabotage, were captured. The charge finally brought against them after preparatory examinations was 193 counts of sabotage. The state, however, failed to prove more than twenty which had been conceded by the defense.[136] Before the sentence was passed, two of the accused made significant statements. One, Elias Motsoaledi, declared:

> When I was asked to join Umkhonto we Sizwe it was at a time when it was clear to me that all our years of peaceful struggle had been of no use. *The government would not let us fight peacefully any more, and had blocked all our legal acts* by making them illegal. [Italics mine][137]

The other statement was from Nelson Mandela:

> . . . there comes a time, as it came in my life, when a man is denied the right to live a normal life, when he can only live the life of an outlaw because the government has so decreed to use the law to impose a state of outlawry upon him. I was driven to this situation, and I do not regret having taken the decisions that I did take.
> . . . Whatever sentence Your Worship sees fit to impose upon me . . . when my sentence has been completed I will still be moved . . . to take up again, as best I can, the struggle for the removal of those injustices until they are finally abolished once and for all.[138]

Alas! This was not to be. Mandela, now over sixty-five years old, and his colleagues have been in prison for nearly twenty-five years on life terms. Part of the continuing struggle today is for their release and for the return of all exiles.

Like the ANC, the PAC also resorted to a strategy of violence after it had been outlawed by the government. Apart from the immediate demands of its Positive Action Campaign, it had made no prior commitment to either violence or nonviolence as a suitable form of strategy for its aims. Nevertheless, it certainly had a bias toward nonviolence. At the same time, it felt that conditions in South Africa were such that one could not make a definite commitment to nonviolent struggle.[139]

After government action had suppressed the post-Sharpeville disturbances, there was a lull within PAC quarters for about two years.

Most of its leaders were still serving their prison terms, as were many others who were arrested at this time. Former secretary P. K. Leballo returned from prison in 1962 and immediately retired to Lesotho on voluntary exile. There he began some form of reorganization. In December of that year he declared,

> The African people recognize that to effect change in South Africa the present situation whereby white South Africa holds the monopoly of military power must be changed. This can be changed only by our acquisition of the means of challenging that military power.[140]

At the same time, another independent offshoot of the PAC also took shape in Cape Town. It organized itself into groups or cells. *Poqo,* as this body was known, "succeeded with a minimum of leadership or formal organization to create widespread fear among Whites" throughout the country. They saw it as the local version of the dreaded Mau-Mau of Kenya.[141]

In 1962 seven men were arrested in Paarl, Cape Province, and charged with intimidating and killing eight other black men when these refused to join *Poqo.* A crowd of people marching to the police station to demand their release was intercepted by the police. In the ensuing riot, seven people, including two whites, were killed and many were wounded. *Poqo* was suspected also of being responsible for the killing of three African policemen in Langa, Cape Town, and a white businessman in February 1963. Several attempts made on the lives of bantustan chiefs in the Transkei were suspected to be by the same group. At least one of them and several alleged informers were killed. On February 2, 1963, five whites were killed in a road camp near Bashee River, Cape. Ten Africans suspected to be members of the group and a white policeman died in a clash while the former were traveling from the Western Cape. Other smaller incidents took place in Cape Town, Victoria West, Benoni, East London, Worcester, and elsewhere, although many of them were forestalled by the police.[142]

A one-man commission of enquiry into the Paarl riots recommended swift action against the "menace of *Poqo.*" The government responded with the enactment of the General Law Amendment Act of 1963, which gave the police wide powers of detention without trial or charges for up to ninety days—cumulative "till this side of eternity," according to the minister of justice. It also included the notorious "Sobukwe Clause,"[143] which allowed the continued detention of a person after serving his original jail term. The only person on whom it was applied at this time was Mangaliso Sobukwe, PAC president. By June 1963 the minister of justice, B. J. Vorster, reported that 3,246 *Poqo* or

PAC members were in custody. Of these, 1,162 were already convicted and sentenced; 124 were convicted for murder. By June 1964, according to Strauss, 202 *Poqo* members had been found guilty of murder and 1,724 of lesser crimes.[144]

Between the years 1962–1965 hardly a day passed in the South African scene without a trial taking place involving *Poqo* suspects. The government saw the group as its chief adversary because of the image that it had created for itself. In 1964 the General Law Amendment Act made it an offense to refuse to give evidence for the state. The penalty was twelve months in prison. The General Law Amendment Act of 1965 substituted 180 days for the 90-day detention clause.[145] Numerous trials of *Poqo*-related events were held in Pretoria, Johannesburg, Benoni, Cape Town, King Williamstown, Lady Frere, and Germiston. Sentences ranged from five years to life imprisonment and death. Needless to say, police brutality exceeded proportions and became a pretrial form of sentence for those already "judged" and "convicted." A report by the minister of justice indicated that between 1960 and 1963, 177 policemen and about a similar number of members of the prison department were convicted of irregular treatment of prisoners.[146] In subsequent years such admissions were made impossible by the government's restriction of press exposure of prison conditions.

CRITICAL EVALUATION

The above study clearly reflects a four-stage development process in black resistance to white domination in South Africa since 1912. It also reflects, in Gail Gerhart's words, an "evolution of an ideology," but also an evolution in the practice related to this ideology. The ANC "old guard," the influence of the ANCYL, the PAC, and the BCM represent each stage of this development process. The ANCYL stands as a bridge between the ANC and the PAC, while the BCM both inherits some aspects of the legacy of the PAC and stands on its own.

The policy of the early ANC was certainly not revolutionary either in theory or in practice and has rightly been labeled reformist. In the words of Seme and Dube, the organization merely sought to "submit grievances to the government for discussion and redress" and thus depended on negotiation and moral suasion for the achievement of its limited goals. These goals were chiefly representation in government and the removal of "special [legal] disabilities." Although the organization had somewhat transcended some of its policy limitations by the time of the ANCYL, there is no queston that the latter had a radicalizing role on the organization as a whole, which to some extent guided the ANC's approach in later years. The Youth League strongly insisted on African sovereignty. Recognizing the inanity of the old negotiation strategy, it also fashioned an aggressive program of action for black people to employ in asserting themselves and claiming their birthright. Following on the footsteps of the ANCYL, both the PAC and the BCM adopted its revolutionary theory but were not immediately able to translate this theory into revolutionary practice. The PAC faltered through its Positive Action Campaign while the BCM approached its practice in stride but was never allowed to go beyond the first step.

Any judgment on the activities of the ANC before it was declared an unlawful organization must thus ultimately hang on its response to the influence of the Youth League. Consequently, it must be based on the ANC's interpretation and implementation of the 1949 Program of Action and its resultant Defiance Campaign. In the Program of Action, tactics such as civil disobedience and noncooperation, depending on where they were focused, could have served as weapons for the long-term objectives of the organization, namely, to coerce the government for radical change. While some amount of success in this regard could have been conceivable, it seems unlikely that they could have forced the government to give up power completely, in accordance with the aims of the ANCYL, given its tenacity and fear of the so-called *swart gevaar* (black menace). On the other hand, tactics such as strikes and work stoppages could only have been for the achievement of particular short-term goals.

In the Defiance Campaign the immediate focus of civil disobedience was on specific legislation and so served only a short-term objective. The same can be said of the PAC's Positive Action Campaign eight years later, insofar as its focus was on the abolition of passes. Thus while the PAC was right in taking the ANC to task for concentrating on the manifestation of the problem instead of the problem itself, it did not notice when it fell into the same trap. The main problem here appears to be precisely that of focusing: that is, of not only relating theory to practice in a consistent manner but also of aligning specific tactics to the end in view. If the end sought by the ANC at the time was merely the removal of specific laws (short-term goal), then the tactics adopted in the Defiance Campaign were appropriate whether they were successful or not. But this was precisely what the PAC considered preoccupation with the symptoms and rejected. If, on the other hand, the aim was the removal of apartheid and white domination as the real roots of the problem, then the tactics were incommensurate with the end and, therefore, inconsistent. Our study has shown that the campaign was targeted on particular laws.

Since the PAC was clear on the whole that its end was not the removal of specific legislation but of the reigning power itself, its deciding to campaign for the removal of passes was inconsistent with its own policy. The campaign focused on the short-range rather than the long-range. Consequently, while both organizations could ultimately address their theory to both the short-range and the long-range needs of the struggle, albeit with varying emphases, they both found it easier to direct their practice to the short-term needs than to the long-term ones. Because of the firmness of the PAC's standpoint on the issue of ends (power) and means (program), this organization ended up the more inconsistent not so much because its position was wrong but because it was not implemented as advocated.

The BCM, on the other hand, clearly distinguished its long-term and short-term goals both in theory and in practice. Like its predecessors, in theory it sought the same ends—a nonracial South Africa based on the principle of universal franchise. In practice, it purposefully concentrated on the short-range goal of motivating people for future action and ultimate exercise of power. It was not clear when the transition would occur from concentrating on action for the short-range to action for the long-range. No timetable was set. By sheer tragedy, however, the movement was outlawed before this transition could take place, so that it left behind some unfinished business. While up to the time of its banning, therefore, the BCM was the most consistent of the three movements in relating its theory to practice, there is no way of telling what would have happened—how it would have ended up—had it had an opportunity to carry on with its activities. It should be noted, though, that it remained consistent in its position for almost nine years, while its immediate predecessor became unfaithful to its program in the short space of a little more than a year.

As for the change from nonviolence to violence, we can only say for now that it was quite consistent with the aims of the two older organizations to reassess their strategy after they had been declared unlawful organizations. Whether violence was the answer or not is a question that need not detain us here. We will consider its moral significance in Chapter 5. A violent strategy in this regard could be only for long-term, radical change—which both organizations at this stage recognized. It was the first method of action thus far to be targeted on their long-term aspirations. Given appropriate resources and provided it could pass the moral test, it was also consistent with these aspirations. The questions that will be raised in considering the ethical status of violence as a strategy in this instance will include: its appropriateness at this stage of the struggle; its appropriateness as an ethical option; its chances of success, based on human and material resources; the strength of the opponent; its consequences on human life, for the country, and on those who had been driven to it.

Chapter 3

Alliances of the 1980s

Militant movements that vow to have no truck with apartheid in what
remains the apartheid state tend to be reduced to debating
societies—doomed, it sometimes seems, to reenact perpetually the tactical
and ideological disputes that divided the two congresses in the late 1950s.
Or, in another guise, they become commemorative associations that often,
in the drastically contracted arena of legal black politics, seem to function
like patriotic and veterans' groups in more settled societies, ritualistically
marking the anniversaries of heroic efforts of past generations and the
deaths of martyrs or organizing the funerals of loyalists to their cause.

Joseph Lelyveld

◆ ◆ ◆

The banning of twenty organizations, two newspapers, and a periodical
in South Africa in 1977 naturally raised some concerns about the future
of black opposition for those people who had been involved in some of
these organizations. In the 1960s the government's banning of the
ANC and the PAC had resulted in a prolonged lull in black political activity, lasting for almost five full years from 1963 to 1968. During that
period the government had managed to consolidate its bantustan policy
and to implement it with seemingly little overt resistance from those it
affected. Of course, any information on such resistance was suppressed
to give the impression of its total absence.

This period was the reign of terror of forced removals of people
into remote, arid areas. Those who resisted saw their meager belongings forcefully loaded onto trucks for transporting to their new unwanted homes, and their current abodes flattened by bulldozers. It was
also the "reign of the tent." Seldom had any facilities been constructed
at the sites to which most of the people were being moved. Their new
homes consisted of flat, dry, and rocky open velds, where they were

simply dumped and left with tents to pitch for themselves and to "make themselves at home," if they could. Those chiefs in rural areas who dared to challenge the removal of their communities were merely deposed, often banished to some other area of the country where they were not known. Others, who were more agreeable to the government's policy, were appointed in their places—later to become future "homeland" leaders. Thus they came to be referred to as collaborators and "sellouts"—meaning usurpers of chieftaincies.

Soon after the bannings of 1977, therefore, some members of the Black Consciousness Movement were already thinking about possible future organization. Toward the end of 1978 a group assembled to discuss the formation of a new organization, which became known as the Azanian People's Organization. This group would fill the vacuum left by the banning of the Black People's Convention (BPC), in particular, which had been the political wing of the Black Consciousness Movement (BCM). The group was walking a tightrope in doing this. First, it still hoped to follow the black consciousness approach. Hence, in order to survive, it had to ensure that there was something in its policy and program of action that distinguished it from the BPC itself. It also had to ensure that it was not open to the charge of planning to further the aims of the recently banned organizations. Second, there was no guarantee that it might not meet a fate similar to that of those organizations—and all the sooner—if it were to prove effective in its own challenge of the government.

Even from its very beginning, therefore, the Azanian People's Organization (AZAPO) was fully aware that it was working within a set of constraints that constituted, in effect, a dilemma. Either it "soft-peddled" the government to such an extent that it became virtually ineffective in its challenge of it—thus ensuring its own survival; or it came out in full challenge of government policy, thus risking its own existence. AZAPO was finally launched in 1979. What it committed itself to is part of the subject of this chapter.

While the influence of the 1976 student uprising—which led to the clampdown of 1977—never fully subsided, the 1980s saw a new wave of student unrest and boycotts all over the country. It began in the Western Cape, moving up to Pretoria, then to the Eastern Cape, finally affecting the entire Reef (Witwatersrand) and other parts of the country. The students had many grievances, ranging from their demands for a say in matters of school government that affected them, such as the restoration of abolished student representative councils, age restrictions in the various school grades, and corporal punishment. In 1984 and 1985 students were involved in leading rent boycotts in the

Vaal townships of southern Transvaal, resulting in government intervention and a repetition of the Sharpeville and Soweto killings.

About this period, the government was seeking support from the "coloured" and Indian communities for its new constitutional reforms. These reforms would allow these groups limited participation in government through a tricameral form of Parliament, which would mark a change from the Westminster system of government. Africans, on the other hand, would remain excluded from power-sharing. For urban Africans—since rural Africans were considered to have already been offered "political self-expression" in the "homeland" structure—the government proposed three bills to govern them. These were known as the Black Local Authorities Bill, the Orderly Movement and Settlement of Black Persons Bill, and the Black Community Development Bill.

There was very strong resistance to these government moves among all the affected groups. First, it was felt that the government wanted to consolidate its apartheid policy through the co-opting of the Indians and "coloureds" to its "unholy system." They could then fight side by side with the whites in defending the system and their own stakes in it against the so-called total onslaught of black extremists and their world supporters. Second, the Black Local Authorities Bill was seen as the whitewashing of the community councils, which had never received the support of the people in the first place, and were currently in the middle of rent disputes in various parts of the country. In short, the new legislation was not for the benefit of "coloureds" and Indians, nor for that of Africans. Rather, it represented the government's tactic of delaying response to the urgent need for drastic change by trying to make apartheid more comfortable for some, no matter how oppressive it remained for others. The government was once again, it was seen, up to its tricks.

Two alliances came into being at this time primarily for the purpose of campaigning for common, united action against the government's proposals. The first was called the National Forum (NF) and was originally spearheaded by AZAPO. The second, the United Democratic Front (UDF), apparently originated from a speech by Dr. Allan Boesak at a campaign to protest involvement by the Indian community in the South African Indian Council, which was prepared to give the new government constitution a try.

The purpose of this chapter is to discuss these two alliances and their forerunner, AZAPO, to determine their theory and practice for further assessment later in the book. To do so we will take an analytical and comparative look at them, as we did with the organizations discussed in the previous chapter. Because the NF has certain policy similarities with AZAPO, there will often be an overlap in discussing the two bodies. It must be clear from the onset, however, that although AZAPO has the largest representation in the Forum alliance, the latter is not an alliance of black consciousness organizations, as is often thought. Rather, the alliance has broader perspectives. At the end of the chapter we will briefly evaluate the bodies discussed, leaving a more detailed assessment for Chapter 5.

ORIGINS

Of the NF, the UDF, and AZAPO, only the latter was conceived in accordance with the need for continuing the struggle against the government and working toward ultimate, radical change. In other words, AZAPO was not established for the immediate need of fighting specific new legislation. Rather, it was established to continue the trend of resistance to all that the South African government and its policy of apartheid stood for. The NF and the UDF, on the other hand, were formed as alliances first and foremost for the purpose of protesting against the government's constitutional proposals and the so-called Koornhof Bills, as the three bills governing Africans came to be known. This does not mean that they did not have the end of apartheid in view nor that they were purely ad hoc alliances. They certainly saw their resistance as a continuing one and leading to the eventual fall of the apartheid regime. The fact remains, though, that their emergence was occasioned by the new government legislation.

AZAPO was established in 1978. It saw as one of its early tasks the reorienting of the black consciousness movement by "taking [it] to the broad masses of people."[1] By this it was probably mooting its worker-focus policy, which has been increasingly emphasized since the organization was launched. At its launching in September 1979, AZAPO expressed its understanding of the South African problem as an economic one, racism being used as an instrument of economic exploitation and oppression. Accordingly, it defined the workers as all those who were thus exploited and oppressed, that is, black people. These were the people to be on the vanguard of the liberation struggle.[2]

The structure of AZAPO consisted of a national executive committee and several branches, which constituted regions. In 1985 it was said to have ninety-six branches in all. It was strongest in the Transvaal and the Eastern Cape, "with some good prospects" in Natal.[3] One of the officials of the UDF, "Terror" Lekota, has distinguished AZAPO from UDF by seeing the former as "a first level organization with a political program that it is pursuing." The UDF, on the other hand, is considered to be a second-level organization "with a specific campaign it has launched and is waging."[4] While this distinction seems to shed more light on the distinctive origins of the two bodies, as they were explained above, it does not seem to be very useful in view of the continuing involvement of both in the struggle with long-term goals.

The NF came into being on June 11-12, 1983, followed two months later by the UDF. As already pointed out, each alliance was launched in response to a call for a common front among blacks in fighting the government's constitutional proposals. The call of the NF was made by AZAPO. It was, according to its president, "a response to the crisis facing the oppressed and exploited black masses."[5] Its main purpose was "to map out the bases for a closer working relationship of all organizations notwithstanding their ideological orientation."[6] The one restriction in this alliance, however, was that all participant organizations had to be predominantly black. The NF itself was not a black consciousness alliance, however. It represented "different political tendencies"[7] and claimed to have no problem in accepting affiliate organizations that had white members, nor had it any difficulty in working with individual whites. It would not, however, accept "affiliates" made up of predominantly "ruling class" organizations.[8] The reason for this exclusion of white organizations was the conviction that, "however well-intentioned, [whites, as a class] cannot identify with the class interests of the oppressed Black Masses." Further, there was a stronger need for them to conduct the struggle in their own community.[9]

Apart from its restriction on white organizations, the NF saw itself not as a homogeneous structure—nor was it an affiliate structure—but rather as an alliance of organizations that were, in a "realistic" way, "limited to acting as a catalyst on principled activists to bring people together."[10] All the organizations brought together as such were of the left, being socialist in orientation. It would appear that, except for its not being an affiliate structure and for its focus on only socialist organizations, the NF shared many similarities with the UDF in its structure. As Barrell points out, both alliances brought together a wide variety of predominantly black political, community, labor, student, professional, and pressure groups of varying strengths.[11] Some organizations participated in both.

The UDF was launched on August 20, 1983. Earlier in the year, addressing the anti–South African Indian Council (anti-SAIC) campaign, Dr. Allan Boesak had advocated the "politics of refusal" as the "only dignified response blacks [could] give in this situation"—that is, the attempted co-opting of Indians and "coloureds" through the new constitutional proposals. To succeed in their opposition to this legal imposition, he said, blacks needed a "united front." Such a front implied the uniting of all bodies opposed to the government's tactics and its new legislation, including churches, civic associations, trade unions, student organizations, and sports bodies—all uniting on this issue. It also implied their pooling of resources as well as informing the people of "the fraud that is about to be perpetrated in its [sic] name, and on the day of the election expose these plans for what they are."[12] Whereas on this occasion Boesak spoke about the response to be taken by black people, on the day of the launching of the UDF he advocated the unity of *all* opponents of apartheid, including whites, in the general struggle for change in the country. The struggle could not be determined "by one's skin color but rather by one's commitment to justice, peace, and human liberation." It had to be remembered, Boesak urged, that apartheid did not have the support of all whites in the country and many of them suffered along with blacks in the common struggle for freedom.[13] These remarks were obviously aimed at the NF, which had had its own launching two months earlier and had spelled out its own position on the question of white participation in the struggle. This attitude toward white involvement was to constitute one of the major points of difference between the two alliances.

Thus gathered together in common opposition to the government's proposals, it was said, the people meant further to tell the government that these proposals were inadequate. They did not express the will of the vast majority of South Africans. Boesak continued:

What we are working for is one, undivided South Africa that shall belong to all its people: an open democracy from which no South African shall be excluded; a society in which the human dignity of all shall be respected.[14]

In saying this, he was not expressing a partisan opinion. All opposition groups in South Africa have and do subscribe to this same political goal of one South Africa with equal rights and opportunities for all. It has rightly been observed that the differences among the various black resistance groups in this country are based more on tactics than on principles. That is why it is regrettable that they are often at one another's throats.

The following points were given as reasons why the constitutional proposals had to be opposed:

1. they were an entrenchment of apartheid and white domination;
2. their basic premise was that the government's homeland policy was irreversible;
3. the basic tenets of apartheid remained intact: racial classification, group areas, separate education, and security laws;
4. these laws could not be changed as they fell under the jurisdiction of the white Parliament;

5. they emphasized group interests, inculcating ethnicity and tribalism, black and white;

6. they excluded the majority of South Africans;

7. they were morally wrong and unacceptable.[15]

Since it was established a few years ago, the UDF's own self-perception has apparently changed. Whereas originally it conceived of itself as a front rather than as an organization,[16] it seems to have gradually assumed the role of an organization, with offices and staff. Many of its officials also refer to it, perhaps unwittingly, as an organization. Its structure is divided into six regions composed of local affiliate organizations. According to one source, there are close to six hundred affiliates,[17] ranging from the largest trade union confederation to the most insignificant local club. The regions have their own general council and executive committees, which are all coordinated by the National Executive. The National Executive has the last word on national policy.[18] UDF officials stress, however, that there is more emphasis on "unity in action" than on a "uniform political policy." The latter, it is feared, might "undermine the concept of the Front." Out of common action, however, a common policy is often forged.[19] Most differences on policy matters were originally blurred and began to emerge only "after the euphoria of the Front's formation" had died down. For instance, "you will find groups in [it] who have adopted the Freedom Charter and others who have not reached that point yet."[20] Still, such differences have not yet been to the extent of hindering the UDF in achieving common action from its members.

The second change in the UDF's self-conception is that, with its success in the original aims of its "politics of refusal," it now sees itself working toward broader goals. It did not cease to exist after the "coloured" and Indian elections in 1984. It continued to put pressure on the government in other ways, pushing forward the ultimate demand of a future, nonracial South Africa based on the principle of one man, one vote. This fact applies also to the NF, except that the Forum had always had an open program and never adopted the clearly restricted and time-bound strategy of the "politics of refusal." Our aim will be to analyze the strategies of both alliances toward their goal of a future South Africa.

Except for the minor differences in strategy and affiliation to be discussed later, it seems obvious that the two national alliances have much in common, beginning with their origins. In some ways they also resemble and transcend the Congress Alliance of the 1950s. While concerned about immediate legal obstacles, they look forward to the fall of the current system and, especially the UDF, have outlived their original reason for existence. AZAPO, on the other hand, is an organization unto its own, with a more pointed focus on the ultimate goals of the resistance movement like the organizations discussed in the previous chapter. Further discussions will reveal whether or not this organization has an appropriate strategy to achieve these goals. It is also a major organization in the NF alliance. Given the right direction, AZAPO seems to have far greater potential in its task—if only because it is an organization with a unitary policy, whereas the two alliances are largely heteronomous because of their constitution.

BLACK CONSCIOUSNESS REVIEWED

In many respects, AZAPO's policy has been a continuation of that of the earlier BCM, although there are many points of difference. Hence we cannot simply assume that AZAPO is itself only a continuation of any of the past black consciousness organizations under an assumed name. What AZAPO has mostly in common with the old BCM is the black consciousness approach, with its emphasis on conscientization as a motivating strategy. This philosophy is shared neither by the NF as a whole nor by the UDF. Of the difference between AZAPO and, in particular, the UDF in this respect one South African journalist has observed:

> There are those who think the BC philosophy is still valid but that it has achieved its major objective of politicisation or conscientization, and that blacks are now in a position to reassert themselves. . . . So they support BC but not AZAPO or the National Forum. Like "Terror" Lekota, an ex-BC leader, they are comfortable in the UDF.[21]

This observation implies that the UDF has moved a step further than AZAPO in political assertion toward the stage of openly challenging the government in its policies. This, in turn, implies that AZAPO is itself still concentrating solely on the process of conscientization rather than on open political action. AZAPO leadership does not agree with this assessment.

Although at its inception AZAPO adopted aims and objectives that focused purely on the conscientization strategy, its activities in subsequent years went beyond this "people-centered" approach to posing some challenges to the government. It is true that this was done mostly indirectly, such as by encouraging rent boycotts or campaigning for the isolation of South Africa by the international community. But this was certainly a step beyond self-help projects and other approaches aimed only at motivating the community for action to take place at some later stage. This new direction of AZAPO certainly distinguishes it from the old black consciousness approach. As has been pointed out in the previous chapter, the BCM in the 1970s engaged in confrontational activities with the government only by accident or as an aberration, rather than as a matter of policy. The time of actual confrontation had not yet come. AZAPO's confrontational strategy may have been inadequate, but it, like the UDF, certainly thought that the time for direct action had now arrived.

Insofar as the NF shares the black consciousness philosophy of conscientization, it naturally agrees with AZAPO in the elaboration and interpretation of this philosophy. Both share the view that conscientization "is not a matter of theoretical input only, but involves practical action and a challenge to existing social relations." In this sense consciousness is understood to enable people "to perceive the best strategy needed to realise their objective interests."[22] It may be said that consciousness thus serves to coordinate theory and practice toward the achievement of set goals.

LONG-TERM AND SHORT-TERM GOALS

Using conscientization as the tool of mobilizing the workers, the NF sees as the immediate goal of the liberation struggle in South Africa the "destruction of the system of racial capitalism," of which apartheid is seen as "simply a particular socio-political expression."[23] Although socialism is espoused as an ideal, no particular models of it are adopted or preferred. It seems to be perceived more as an immediate strategy for organizing than as a long-term goal. It has been explained only as "a process of dealing with specific local problems and issues on a principled basis."[24] According to Legum, while the Forum "favours a Marxist interpretation of society," it is nevertheless hostile to the South African Communist Party.[25] Given the apparent vagueness and caution in its approach to socialism, the Forum's general rhetoric on the subject seems to have been an exaggeration. Surely if socialism is taken as a criterion for membership in the alliance, as it is, there should be at least a commonly accepted standard of socialism than its being conceived merely as a "process of dealing with specific local problems . . . on a principled basis."

Although the UDF, like the NF, had as its original aim the campaign against the government's constitutional proposals, it did not cease to exist after succeeding in its campaign. It continued to put pressure on the government for certain demands and even issued a declaration containing short-term and long-term goals. According to one of its spokespersons, it "challenged the state by providing an alternative analysis of what was happening in South Africa."[26] Because the government's objective was to divide people through its apartheid policies, the UDF saw as its immediate goal the uniting of all in a common struggle against the government's intentions.[27] Originally, the UDF admitted that it had no long-range plans precisely because it was formed in reaction to the government's activities and was thus essentially a protest organization. The future of its activities was left to the future itself.[28] Already at its launching, however, some of its long-range goals were mooted and included in its declaration.

In brief, we may say that the two alliances and AZAPO have similar long-term objectives. Insofar as the existence of the two alliances was occasioned by the government's constitutional proposals, their short-term goals differed slightly from those of AZAPO. The latter's were based on a continuing and more sustained need than only that of resisting the government's current proposals. However, with the immediate struggle over, the two have now come to parallel AZAPO in their short-term objectives, which go beyond challenging the government's constitutional proposals. Both these short-term as well as long-term goals are the same as those that were in the agendas of the previous national resistance movements. First, their campaigns are aimed at doing away with apartheid and the effects of its legislation on the lives of black people in general. Second, they are all in support of a future nonracial democracy, where all South Africans will have equal rights and equal participation in the government of the country. As the ANC, the PAC, and the BCM differed, so AZAPO and the two alliances, the NF and the UDF, differ from one another in their strategies toward these goals, with AZAPO sharing most views with the NF. A more detailed examination of these views now follows.

Manifesto of the People of Azania

The key policy document of the NF, adopted also by AZAPO, is called the Manifesto of the People of Azania. The manifesto is socialist and internationalist in orientation, based on four main principles of anti-racism and anti-imperialism; noncollaboration with the oppressor and his political instruments; independent working class organizations; and opposition to all alliances with the ruling class parties.[29]

Seen by some as competing with the ANC's Freedom Charter, the manifesto sees the future of South Africa as that of a "democratic anti-racist and socialist Azania." The struggle toward this goal, according to the manifesto, is to be in the hands of the black working class,[30] who alone know the full meaning of oppression and exploitation in South Africa.

The issue of land is seen as a key one in the struggle. Hence the land, together with all that belongs to it, is to be "wholly owned and controlled by the Azanian People." Further, its use and all that accrues from it "shall be aimed at ending all forms of exploitation of man by man." All the proceeds of labor from the land will be distributed to all on the socialist basis: "from each according to his ability; to each according to his need."[31] The manifesto also advocates popular control of the means of production, free and compulsory education, and state provision of housing and health services, *inter alia*.

Some of the positions taken in the manifesto have been elaborated in statements made by the NF and its individual and organizational representatives. At its founding in 1979 AZAPO had indicated that it was not opposed to private ownership of property but was concerned rather that the wealth of the country be distributed equitably. There is nothing in the manifesto to indicate a change in this position. The anticapitalist and prosocialist position it takes is adopted on the basis of the need for fundamental change in the country's economy for the benefit of the majority. This is opposed to reforms of the capitalist system as it has been experienced so far, with its inherently exploitative tendencies.[32]

In the new South Africa there will be "no power-sharing" in the sense of recognizing group or ethnic quotas in government. This is a position similar to those of the PAC and BCM earlier. In accordance with democratic principles, it is stated, "power can only rest with the majority of the people."[33] This implies majority rule on the basis of one man, one vote. Although the black working class currently constitutes the excluded majority from power, the ultimate goal of the struggle has nothing to do with so-called black majority rule, any more than current, white Western democracies are referred to as "white majority rule" governments. But the current struggle cannot involve all classes, regardless of the groups represented in them. This would be to ignore "the historically evolved differences,"[34] which give some an amount of vested interest in the current system. The NF, it is concluded, is mainly interested in the correct analysis of such trends and tendencies and consequently has no immediate designs of being "any future type of government in the wings."[35]

The UDF Declaration

The UDF's equivalent to the NF's manifesto is its Declaration, which was adopted at the launching of the Front in August, 1983, and seemed to be based largely on the keynote address given by Allan Boesak. Boesak had declared that apartheid was a "thoroughly evil system, and, as such, it [could] not be modified, modernized or streamlined. It [had] to be eradicated irrevocably."[36] He had gone on to urge whites in the country to realize that their destiny was inextricably bound up with that of blacks and that they would never be free until all in South Africa were free.

The Declaration picked up on the mood of Boesak's speech and a substantial number of points made in it. It affirmed the future of a "single non-racial, unfragmented South Africa . . . free of Bantustans and Group Areas."[37] Needless to say, the new South Africa Constitution Bill and the "Koornhof Bills," which were the main targets in the Front's formation, were doubly frowned upon. They were seen as further instruments in the entrenchment of apartheid and white domination. In effect, any change proposed within their framework was rejected: "We are not looking for an extension of rights within the framework of the present system," declared a UDF official, Matthew Morobe, in clarification later. "We're looking for a different system altogether."[38] This different system was that of one man, one vote; and it was seen as a precondition for any negotiation with the government regarding the future of the country.

The UDF's position on negotiation regarding the future of South Africa, often conceived on the basis of a national convention, seems to have undergone a hardening process through the years. The Front's latest position is that it does not recognize the sovereignty of the present government because the majority of the people in the country were not involved in its election. Hence the government has no right to preside over the proceedings of negotiation in a proposed national convention. For change to occur peacefully in the country, therefore, the government has no other option but to surrender power and allow "a democratic process to determine our future."[39] Such a democratic, political process is believed to be "the only guarantor against tyranny," while the continued banning of organizations is the "antithesis of democracy." The UDF denied charges by the government that it sought to make the country ungovernable through its position and activities. On the contrary, "our objective is to make our country governable . . . under majority rule."[40]

Program of Action

Part of the UDF Declaration was given to outlining what amounts to the Front's program of action. In it the UDF commits itself to organize and mobilize all community organizations; to consult with people on their views and aspirations; to build and strengthen all the organizations of the people; to educate all on unity and the dangers of apartheid; and to unite in action against the constitutional proposals. The program reflects the original intention of the UDF, which was focused on the immediate needs of the problem on hand. This was so notwithstanding the fact that some of the goals expressed in the Declaration were long-range.

Both AZAPO and the NF also committed themselves to some form of program of action. AZAPO does not seem to have spent much time formulating any such systematic program, though it engaged in certain activities and abstained from others as a matter of policy. Its major goal in action, insofar as this impinged directly or indirectly on the government, was campaigning for the isolation of South Africa by the international community through sports, cultural, academic, and, where feasible, economic boycotts. It achieved some successes in some of these, particularly in cultural boycotts and, to a limited extent, sports boycotts. For the large part, however, AZAPO's program has been "inward-looking," urging black self-help activity much as the original BCM used to do.

At the beginning of 1981, about a year and a half after it had been launched, AZAPO committed itself to begin organizing rural and urban workers. It also said that it would cooperate with other organizations in implementing community development projects, literacy classes, and courses on labor relations. In 1986 it supported the NF's call for an "aggressive program of action coupled with a campaign to 'internationalise its socialist position in Southern Africa, Africa and the rest of the world.'"[41] Both AZAPO and the NF were cautious, however, in instigating any activities that might lead to direct confrontation with the state—such as marching to John Vorster Square in protest or to make a demand.

The position taken by AZAPO and the NF on mass action in general seems to have differed from that of the UDF. They seemed to have become wary of turning people into "canon fodder," as Sobukwe had advised against doing more than twenty years ago. By implication, they felt that some of the UDF's tactics were not well thought out. Because of insufficient preparation, it was thought, the UDF often invited adventurism by outsiders who often preyed on the ignorance and innocence of the people. Hence the NF committed itself to involvement in tactics such as consumer boycotts and stayaways only after sufficient consultation with the community, "thereby eliminating the emergence of faceless committees who have no mandate from the community."[42] In addition to consultations with the community, AZAPO felt it was important to do away with confusion regarding what such tactics were intended to achieve and thus to "clarify the demands, and to have clear, realizable goals and objectives."[43]

Clearly expressing dissatisfaction with the way some of the current boycotts have been carried out, AZAPO's one-time president, Ishmael Mkhabela, said that AZAPO believed it could achieve its own objectives "only through sustained and disciplined and democratic struggle," and not through the "political adventurism" of some of the other organizations involved in the struggle.[44] Tactics such as stayaways had to be used wisely, he said, because they called for "risk, sacrifice and suffering" on the part of the people who supported them.

> And if preparation is inadequate, if people are not well canvassed and prepared for any eventuality beforehand, the establishment can afterwards exploit their pain and losses to turn them against the campaign.[45]

Therefore, AZAPO was not opposed to stayaways and other forms of boycotts "as weapons in the hands of the people." Rather, it subjected them to a "critical evaluation, reflecting on the gains and losses of the communities." In the final analysis, it supported only "genuine and legitimate struggles" of the people.[46]

On Specific Issues

Apartheid and Homelands

Insofar as their views on specific questions were expressed at all, the two alliances and AZAPO were fully agreed in their opposition to apartheid and its homeland policy. As a broader term, apartheid is not only a matter of racial segregation. It has, on the one hand, the Jim Crow aspect of the Group Areas Act and the general inequities and oppression of blacks in urban and rural areas. On the other hand, it has an added dimension of the denationalization as well as dislocation of Africans, in particular, from the productive parts of South Africa through its bantustan or "homeland" system. The ultimate goal of this system is to make South Africa a white person's land, where Africans would come only to offer their labor.

In its Declaration, the UDF expressed its abhorrence of both aspects of apartheid by advocating a nonracial South Africa, free of bantustans and the group areas. It then went on to describe what was involved in this system, which contributed to make it a "thoroughly evil system." As such, it cannot be reformed but must be completely uprooted. AZAPO, for its part, saw bantustan leaders as being "part of an oppressive system" that enabled them to prey on the misery of their own people. It urged noncooperation with them and nonparticipation in such government-created platforms.[47] The bantustan system was condemned for "depriving Africans of citizenship of South Africa, destroying black unity and facilitating continued economic exploitation of blacks."[48]

One of the achievements of Black Consciousness was to enable Africans, "coloureds," and Indians to see themselves as a single group on the receiving end of apartheid. There was thus some concern when the government in 1983 proposed to loosen its Jim Crow grip on the last two groups by giving them limited power-sharing. This, it was felt, implied making them partners in the "ruling establishment," which—AZAPO threatened—might lead to the reevaluation of their alliance with Africans.[49] Perhaps the more appealing reaction to this attempted alienation of blacks by the government was the UDF's slogan: "APARTHEID DIVIDES—UDF UNITES." Continuation of such unity on the part of blacks, according to the NF, was important because it "held within itself the message of doom for the capitalist apartheid system in this country."[50] That was why the government found its theory of "ethnic groups" to be a superior instrument of its policy than undefined racism, because through it "it could explain and justify even greater fragmentation of the working people." The views expressed by these organizations on apartheid as such were not different from those expressed by the previous organizations. They amounted more to a restatement and elaboration of their abhorrence and opposition to it in general.

Education

AZAPO did not have a definite policy on education until it launched its Black Education Charter in 1984.[51] This is amazing considering that education had been a hot issue in the country since the 1976 student uprising, which was originally caused by educational problems. As mentioned earlier, this issue has never been settled since then and continues to plague black schools to this day. Yet AZAPO's only concern in its early years was with literacy programs and the training of those involved in labor unions, whatever this concern meant in terms of actual practice.

In 1986 AZAPO formed part of the third National Council of the National Forum, which charged the latter to form an education action committee. The purpose of this committee would be to initiate and coordinate "an alternative socialist education program" that was to be conducted nationally. Further, this committee was to embark on "appropriate action" in schools, colleges, technikons, and universities throughout the country from May 1 to 4 and from June 16 to 26, 1986. The nature of "appropriate action" was not explained, but it was apparently some form of education to be carried out through (a) unions, (b) student organizations, through their student representative councils, (c) civics—street committees, (d) alternative education programs, (e) sports organizations, as well as (f) door-to-door campaigns, (g) workshops, and (h) pamphleteering and relevant media.[52]

The 1986 Council of the Forum met concurrently with the National Education Crisis Committee (NECC), which had been established the previous December to look into the crisis of school boycotts in the county. The NF had not been invited to send representatives to this meeting, apparently because of differences of opinion. The NF, however, offered its conditional support to the decisions of the committee, if they were not in conflict with its own strategy. It also resolved to encourage all sectors of the community to "strike together even if they march separately."[53] For this reason it expressed regret at the partisan way in which it felt the NECC had organized the conference and at the "mockery" that had apparently been made of the crisis itself. The NF said it viewed the education crisis with utmost seriousness and would have wished to participate in the deliberations of the NECC conference.

The idea that led to the establishment of the NECC had come up at a meeting called toward the end of 1985 by then bishop of Johannesburg, Dr. Desmond Tutu, and director of the SACHED Trust, Mr. John Samuel. The meeting had ended with the appointment of a small committee to prepare recommendations for another meeting, which would in turn authorize a national conference on the current education crisis. Some confusion had ensued in the process and the contemplated follow-up meeting before the national conference apparently never took place—at least not under the original leadership. In the end, the national conference was organized under the auspices of some UDF affiliates. It was at this conference that the NECC was formed, becoming a UDF affiliate itself.

Even prior to the establishment of the NECC the UDF had not had any direct involvement in campaigning on educational issues. Some of its affiliates, the Azanian Students Organization (AZASO), the Congress of South African Students (COSAS), the National Union of South African Students (NUSAS), and the National Education Union of South Africa (NEUSA), had launched a campaign for an Education Charter. The UDF had gone only as far as urging its other affiliates to support this charter. It called on them to "set up structures to ensure adult participation in educational issues, and to encourage formation of progressive teachers' organizations."[54] With the organizations behind the Education Charter Campaign, however, and later with the educational campaigns of the NECC, there was seemingly no need for the UDF to have its own "central policy" on education.

Labor

Both AZAPO and the UDF have campaigned in various ways to organize labor through trade union movements, while the NF also claims to
be involved in some ways with unions. The NF has also engaged in
much rhetoric about the working class and its role in the struggle for
change. A number of trade unions are affiliated with the UDF either in-
dependently or through the Congress of South African Trade Unions
(COSATU), considered to be the largest confederation of trade unions
in South Africa. Some unions, however, originally rejected membership in the UDF fearing that their policies and focus on purely labor issues might be compromised by such an involvement. Among these
were the Federation of South African Trade Unions (FOSATU), the
General Workers' Union (GWU), and the food and canning unions.[55]

AZAPO stated at its launching in 1979 that it envisaged "a persis-
tently militant system of trade unions which [would] challenge the discriminatory labour laws of the white minority government and thereby
bring about change."[56] As we saw above, some of its education policies
involved having an impact on the trade union movement and in particular on workers involved in it. In October 1986 two trade union bodies
related to AZAPO—the Council of Unions of South Africa (CUSA)
and the Azanian Confederation of Trade Unions (AZACTU)—merged
and launched a "super-federation." This new federation was said to
have a signed-up membership of 420,000, whereas UDF-affiliated CO-
SATU was believed to have a paid-up membership of 450,000.[57]

The NF, for its part, allocates the central role of the resistance
movement to the black working class and its organizations. Because the
national resistance is perceived to be not only a class struggle but one
against racial oppression as well, it cannot be placed under the command of the working class in general but under that of the black working class.[58] This view seems to be opposed to that of the UDF, which
sees the working class generally as the "backbone and nucleus" of the
resistance struggle, with other sections of the community playing a supportive role.[59] According to one of the chief theorists of the NF, Dr.
Neville Alexander, "class, colour and nation converge in the national
liberation movement."[60] As such, all blacks are understood to constitute
the working class. "The idea of a single nation is [seen to be] vital because it represents the real interest of the working class and therefore of
the future socialist Azania." Although the struggle is to be under the
sole leadership of the black working class, this group is charged,
nevertheless, to work for the democratization of all. For the working
class alone can, first, "unite the oppressed and exploited classes. . . . It
has [also] to redefine the nation and abolish the reactionary definitions

of the bourgeoisie." Consequently, the entire system is to be changed if the nation is to be structured in the interests of the black working class.[61]

Most of the position taken by the NF was contained in Alexander's speech at the launching of the Forum in 1983. Nothing definite seems to have come out of it since then in terms of direct organization of the workers. As AZAPO is a key member of the NF alliance and has itself been involved with workers and the trade union movement, it may be that the Forum has left this responsibility in the hands of AZAPO as the UDF has done with the NECC in the case of education.

Disinvestment

As we saw in the previous chapter, the question of labor in South Africa has for some time now been affected by calls by various organizations and individuals for the disinvestment of foreign holdings in the country. In this section we will restrict our comments to the views of the bodies under discussion.

It is obvious from the general statements made by the three bodies that their position on the question of foreign investment in South Africa is similar to that of the previous organizations, particularly the BCM. The NF's position, adopted at its National Council in 1986, sees any investment in South Africa as furthering the oppression and exploitation of workers in the country. Calling multinationals "agents of imperialism," the council urged the NF to embark on a

> vigorous campaign on disinvestment; to participate in programs aimed at assisting unemployed workers; to advance labor-intensive employment opportunites rather than capital-intensive employment; to establish an international presence to popularise the campaign against investment and the NF's program for a socialist Azania.[62]

One can assume that AZAPO, because of its position in the NF, played a major role in supporting this position.

AZAPO's position was dramatized in 1985 when the members of the organization demonstrated against the visit of Senator Edward Kennedy to South Africa. This visit was at the invitation of the South African Council of Churches, with Bishop Desmond Tutu and Dr. Allan Boesak the main hosts. The senator was first met at the airport by demonstrators carrying anti-American, anti-capitalist, and anti-imperialist placards. He was seen as a symbol of American imperialism and also—unbelievable as it may seem—of the Reagan administration's policy of "constructive engagement." This policy is very unpopular among most blacks in South Africa. AZAPO repeated its demonstration by disrupting a meeting in Soweto later, which was to have been addressed by Senator Kennedy. However, its spokespersons explained afterward that this disruption was not aimed at the senator himself, nor had the group intended him not to be heard, much as it disliked what he "represented." The meeting was disrupted seemingly in reaction to some of the appeals made by the organizers of the meeting, including the bishop himself, before the senator arrived. According to one of AZAPO's top officials, Mr. Ishmael Mkhabela, the appeals implied that AZAPO was allowing itself to be used as an "agent of the system," suggesting infiltration by government agents. This angered members of AZAPO present—who were initially listening quietly to the speakers—and is what subsequently led to the disruption of the meeting.[63]

The UDF is also opposed to foreign investment in South Africa, which it sees as "complicity with apartheid." The Front also believes that foreign investment is not for the benefit of the oppressed and exploited but rather bolsters the apartheid government.[64] Both the UDF and AZAPO have stood behind Archbishop Tutu's call for the economic isolation of South Africa as a means of speeding up change, though their support of the conditions he gives for its relaxation may vary in extent. These conditions resemble to a large extent the Sullivan principles. However, they emphasize especially the contribution that foreign companies can make in the improvement of the lives of blacks outside the work situation, namely, in education and housing. At the same time, all are vehemently opposed to the position taken by Chief Mangosuthu G. Buthelezi, chief minister of Kwa-Zulu, which does not see foreign disinvestment as an appropriate instrument for fighting apartheid.

National Convention

Most black political activity in South Africa thus far has been considered to be the outcome of the government's failure to abandon its policies and to negotiate with blacks on the future of the country. Originally, and until recently, such negotiation was considered possible under the direction of a national convention. All or at least most of the past black political organizations supported the idea of a national convention. Until 1981, AZAPO also still viewed the idea of such a convention positively, given the following conditions:

1. It would have to discuss the transfer of power;
2. political prisoners had to be freed, bans lifted, and all the exiled allowed to return home;
3. structural violence had to be ended;

4. banned national movements would have to be allowed to participate in the proceedings;

5. preemptive strikes by South African troops against neighboring states would have to stop.[65]

The idea of a national convention was also a major item in the campaigns of the UDF, which saw it as an occasion that might provide

> an atmosphere free of racial suspicion and fear of harassment so that the people of our country may, through their acknowledged leaders, hammer out a constitution based on the will of the people and therefore one acceptable to all.[66]

As recently as October 1985 the UDF still believed that there could be meaningful change in the country—consequently a basis for negotiation, by implication—if the government were to meet certain conditions. These conditions largely resembled those laid down by AZAPO, with a few adjustments and additions. They included the unbanning of all organizations, the unconditional release of all detainees and political prisoners, and the scrapping of the "racist constitution," the group areas, and the bantustans. The UDF also stated that "all restrictions on workers' ability to organise themselves" had to be removed.[67]

At the same time, however, almost as a contradiction, a UDF spokesperson went on to reject the state president's authority to govern or to preside over the proceedings of the national convention. The reason given for this rejection was that the present government had not been democratically elected and was, therefore, not representative. This new position of the Front, as was AZAPO's earlier, seemed to have been provoked by the launching of a new alliance early in the year, called the Convention Alliance. This alliance was established at the initiative of the former chairman of the Progressive Federal Party (PFP), Dr. van Zyl Slabbert, who had recently resigned from the party because of irreconcilable differences with the government. The PFP was until May 1987 the main parliamentary opposition party in South Africa. Other members of the new Convention Alliance included Chief Buthelezi's Inkatha and some business establishments.

A few months before the UDF's new position was taken, AZAPO and the NF had announced their own rejection of the convention. They interpreted it as "a deliberate attempt by the ruling class to sidetrack our people." Hence the oppressed and exploited had to be warned against falling into the trap of such "politics of negotiations."[68] In the words of Saths Cooper, first chairman of the NF, the national convention represented a "bourgeois sellout," "intended to dilute revolutionary forces and reproduce them in the image of capital."[69] The champions of the convention failed to realize that the South African people were involved in a "war of liberation" that was not interestd in power sharing: "Power belongs to the working people and will have to be transferred to them at the end of the road or they will simply seize [it]," concluded Cooper.[70] For any negotiation to be possible, therefore, the government had to commit itself to disbanding the present system altogether and negotiate a new one afresh. In this sense the NF was not opposed to negotiated settlement, for negotiation can be in two ways. It can be, first, "for cooptation and more sophisticated repression and exploitation, without the so-called 'ugly face' of apartheid." Or, second, it can be "for empowerment, real empowerment"; and this is what the South African black working class was after.[71]

PRACTICAL IMPLICATIONS

Like the previous organizations, both AZAPO and the UDF have engaged in certain sociopolitical activities to put their beliefs into practice, thus actively expressing their opposition to apartheid, and also to gain the attention of the government and the international community. Some of their actions were initiated by the organizations themselves. In others, however, the organizations only provided crisis leadership after the actions had been started by local groups or had originated spontaneously.

As already indicated, AZAPO seemed to be more cautious in its approach to action than was the UDF. This may have been because the organization wanted to be fully prepared, on the whole, before committing itself irrevocably to confrontation with the government. Yet it is not quite clear what it was doing in practice to bring about such preparation. Hence the impression often gained was that AZAPO was inactive or somehow subdued and had no particular program of action. The UDF, on the other hand, was very active and often provoked criticisms of "political adventurism." There is no doubt, however, that the government viewed it as a greater threat than AZAPO.

In spite of its caution, AZAPO went beyond the strategy of the earlier BCM both in theory and in practice. Whether or not the approach adopted was adequate is another question we cannot consider at this stage. The campaigns of the UDF itself were reminiscent of the ANC activities of the 1950s, particularly following the Defiance Campaign. Both organizations, especially the UDF, would have benefited from the PAC's original criticism of the ANC concerning the need for a rigorous program of action. Such a program, according to the PAC, was necessary if an organization was to go beyond merely reacting to what the government did to actually initiating action for meaningful change. Perhaps the lack of such a program was understandable in the case of the UDF, considering that the origin of the alliance was based on a short-term goal, which was itself a reaction. But this also reflects an inconsistency in the UDF's Declaration, which exceeded the alliance's limited focus in its goal demands. As we saw earlier, these goals went beyond the immediate needs for which the Front was originally established. As for AZAPO, it had a persistent awareness of the need for a sustained program of action but never succeeded in clearly focusing it, let alone acting in accordance with it.

Common Activities

The sociopolitical activities of the two groups in the six years since AZAPO was launched fall into four categories: (1) self-help projects; (2) commemoration services; (3) antigovernment protests; and (4) welfare-centered protests. Only the fourth of these needs to be explained. By welfare-centered protests I mean (a) those protests aimed against particular undertakings, either by the government or by the private sector, calculated to place burdensome demands on already hard-pressed black people; (b) those activities imposed by the people on themselves in order to achieve a particular sociopolitical goal. Two main examples of (a) would be bus boycotts and rent boycotts. Consumer and cultural boycotts would fall under (b). These differ from the former in that they are based on the initiative of those affected rather than being a reaction, except in a most indirect way, to external pressure. In the following discussion I will not try to concentrate on each category of activity but will focus on just some of the activities.

Both AZAPO and the UDF have engaged in various kinds of activity falling under all these categories. AZAPO's campaigns included bus and rent boycotts, cultural boycotts aimed at discouraging overseas performing artists and sports teams from touring South Africa, protests against the government's constitutional reforms, educational and union projects, and other activities. The UDF's activities have included stay-away campaigns, rent and bus boycotts, anticonstitutional reforms, anti–sports tour campaigns, and campaigns for the unbanning of the ANC, for national unity against apartheid and the emergency, and several others.

Since 1980 AZAPO has engaged sporadically in campaigns for bus boycotts and rent boycotts, mostly by providing crisis leadership. In all cases protest was aimed at cost increases, and it often ended in riots. Bus boycotts, directly or indirectly linked to AZAPO, have occurred in Soweto, Seshego, Tembisa, and Kagiso in the Transvaal, as well as in parts of Natal.[72] Before the emergence of the UDF late in 1983, AZAPO was the only political organization involved in providing leadership and crisis leadership where this was needed and possible. Although AZAPO directly organized rent boycotts in Tembisa in 1981,[73] the most far-reaching rent boycotts to hit black South African townships to date started in the Vaal townships in September 1984. They spread to most parts of the country, including Soweto and parts of the Reef, and are continuing up to today. Neither AZAPO nor the UDF were directly responsible for the Vaal boycotts, which resulted in an uprising and thirty-one deaths in three days.[74] Students, who may have belonged to AZAPO- or UDF-related student bodies, were at the forefront of these boycotts.

An AZAPO official, in an interview, attributed the boycotts to "the preeminence of black consciousness among the youth." This, added to the economic situation and the rising cost of living, the recession, and increasing unemployment,[75] contributed to the intolerance of the youth as well as to their realization that their parents were helpless to take any salutary action for themselves. Adding oil to the fire was that the rent increase was imposed by the unwanted community councils, which the government was in the process of rechristening through its "Koornhof Bills." In addition, the impending constitutional reforms excluded Africans from the so-called new deal. At the same time, a spokesperson for the UDF in 1986 also cited the continuing boycotts as "a premier example of local-directed [UDF] anti-apartheid initiatives."[76] While the first of these claims confirms the indirect nature of organizational influence in this instance, the latter is somewhat exaggerated. At most, it can be granted that the Vaal situation offered an opportunity for crisis leadership that has since persisted and turned into other UDF initiatives.

In November 1984 the UDF was involved in supporting a call by the Congress of South African Students and two trade unions for a two-day stayaway. Some of the demands made in this action included the halting of rent and bus-fare increases. Part of the UDF's "hidden agenda" in this was to get the government to "listen to the voice of the people and get rid of apartheid."[77] By the middle of 1986 it was estimated that the ongoing rent boycotts affected thirty-eight black townships all over South Africa and that it was costing the government about 30 million Rand a month.

A major campaign in which both AZAPO and the UDF were involved, but perhaps the UDF to a greater extent, was against the government's constitutional proposals and the related "coloured" and Indian elections. AZAPO decided on this campaign at its 1983 National Council, as did the NF and the UDF at their launching. There seemed to be an unintentional division of labor between itself and the UDF as AZAPO/NF placed its chief focus on the Black Local Authorities Act[78] whereas the UDF concentrated on the "coloured" and Indian elections. However, media coverage was almost entirely limited to the latter campaign, with the UDF later receiving most of the credit.[79] The success of the anti- "coloured" and Indian elections campaign was reflected in their low poll turnout, as it also was with the campaign against the Bantu Local Authorities Act. As is customary in South Africa, however, the government still forged ahead with its plans notwithstanding this overwhelming sign of opposition.

Other Activities of AZAPO/NF

AZAPO's main successes have been in its campaigning against cultural and sporting tours to South Africa by overseas performing artists and sportspersons. This campaign subsequently led to some American and European artists canceling their planned tours to South Africa in sympathy with the cause. AZAPO also approached Equity—the British union of performing artists—at some stage in an effort to organize an international blacklist of artists visiting South Africa. Perhaps not in direct response to AZAPO's campaign, but nevertheless in sympathy with its spirit, the United Nations embarked on its own blacklist of those artists who performed in South Africa in conflict with its recommendations. This blacklist was a source of some controversy in the United States at some stage. AZAPO has also protested against Australian and New Zealand rugby and cricket tours to South Africa, even though these tours continued.

The significance of AZAPO's demonstration against Senator Edward Kennedy's visit in 1985 is difficult to grasp, notwithstanding the organization's anti-imperialist position. Given the pressure Kennedy has continued to put on the U.S. Senate on the South African question even after the embarrassment he suffered from their action, the organization's members must continue to blush in private. It is commonly agreed now that AZAPO's action was a tactical error. Because of its action, it was courted by the government media and favorably quoted by the latter's notorious "Current Affairs." For the first time in years AZAPO found itself being openly endorsed and praised by the government. Alas! This in itself must have shaken AZAPO to the realization that it was on the wrong track. For, as Archbishop Tutu is fond of observing, when the South African government is pleased about something—such as the election of Ronald Reagan as U.S. president—South African blacks have cause to be worried and feel the opposite about it. Because Kennedy's visit made the government uneasy, black people in South Africa were generally jubilant about it and "just knew" that he bore some hope for them—no matter what AZAPO said or did and in spite of the government's protests. AZAPO was thus the odd sheep in the fold and probably still has not recovered from its own embarrassment resulting from the blunder.

On the positive side, the organization claims, through the NF, to have "engaged in practical educational work to instill consciousness, working with student representative councils and parent-teacher associations." The NF also claims to be actively offering "support work for unions," contributing to cultural events, as well as having members directly involved in union organization.[80] Its involvement with student work involves study projects and developing alternative education programs, though it is hampered by limited resources because of the absence of funds.[81] AZAPO once also planned to organize classes to help pupils prepare for school examinations,[82] although there is no indication that it actually did so and, if so, how successful it was.

Often the NF has been vague in its call for action on the part of individuals, although members of the alliance have been critical of a similar vagueness in the UDF because of its implications on the people's safety. One of the resolutions at its National Council in 1986 was to mark the tenth anniversary of the 1976 students' uprising by taking "appropriate action" against oppression. But the form of appropriate action to be taken was to be left with area committees that were yet to be set up. In explaining the vagueness of this resolution, the chairman of the NF said that it was not a call for a boycott but for local organizations to undertake concerted action within their existing programs for the periods in question (May 1-4; June 16-26). "Action," he said, "cannot always be at peak intensity; that is why a period of strongly focused activity is a way of highlighting the power of the people, and at least affecting the government's power base."[83] Considering the state of affairs in the country, however, and the limitations of current resistance strategies, it is difficult to imagine what form of "appropriate action" is possible that is likely to "highlight the power of the people" and "affect the government's power base." Far from offering a clarification of the intended action, therefore, the chairman was simply adding to the mystification of the original statement.

Other UDF Activities

Apart from its own original campaigns against the government's constitutional proposals, the UDF engaged in other campaigns that kept the government on its toes. Alleged to have threatened to make the country ungovernable, it used several methods in its campaigns to reach the people. These included leafletting, "door-to-door" campaigning, as well as public meetings and rallies. Perhaps public meetings and the press coverage they originally generated were the most effective, as there are limits to the extent leafletting and "door-to-door" campaigning can go, particularly in large townships such as Soweto and others of the Transvaal generally, as well as in the Cape and Natal. Besides, it was not always easy to establish the origin of the leaflets, and many people treated them with suspicion.

One of the UDF's early campaigns, which originated from its December 1983 conference in Port Elizabeth, was called the One Million Signature Campaign.[84] This campaign had two main objectives. First, it was the UDF's self-introduction to the public through announcing its cause and requesting the people's support in joining the protest against the constitutional proposals; second, it was a commitment to obtain a target of one million signatures as an endorsement of the rejection of the new constitution, and also as a test of the UDF's strength. This campaign, taking place in January 1984, thus marked the beginning of the main campaign against the government's proposals. The one million signature target was not reached, but UDF officials claimed, nevertheless, that the support received was more than they had hoped for. As the campaign unfolded, it took the normal cause of other planned UDF tactics, described above. The campaign, in which the NF also had a share, was overwhelmingly successful in that only 17.5 percent of the "coloured" people and 15.5 percent of the Indians were later reported to have participated in the elections. The official figures given were 30 percent and 20 percent, respectively.[85]

While AZAPO lost face as a result of its reaction to Senator Kennedy's visit, the UDF gained some "mileage" from it. Although UDF's Transvaal general council had decided "not to be associated with . . . [the] visit in a high-profile manner,"[86] the alliance seems to have been involved later, directly or indirectly, in organizing most of the places where the senator spoke outside Johannesburg, especially in Cape Town. When AZAPO made a fool of itself in Soweto, the UDF members quietly displayed their support of the visit by drawing closer to the people associated with it (i.e., Archbishop Tutu and Dr. Boesak). Shortly after Kennedy's departure, they took advantage of their earned loyalty by offering to organize a rally in honor of the archbishop's receiving of the Nobel Peace Prize. This celebration turned out to be as much a propaganda occasion for the UDF as it was a cojubilation with the man honored and his family. The stadium was bannered with UDF flags and slogans. This is also where Zinzi Mandela read to the public the statement of support for the struggle purportedly from her imprisoned father.

Another UDF-related campaign in 1985 was sponsored jointly with the Black Sash, NUSAS, and the End Conscription Campaign (ECC). Called a "Prescription for Peace," its aim was to obtain signatures to present a petition to the government, demanding: (1) an end to the state of emergency; (2) the release of Nelson Mandela and other political prisoners, and the return of exiles; (3) the unbanning of all political organizations; and (4) the dismantling of apartheid. One may conclude that a campaign of this nature—making a petition—is undertaken more for its propaganda value than with any hope of obtaining results, as few people can be as naive as to expect the government to take it seriously. In this sense it differs from protest actions, which may themselves be indirect appeals, but are only an expression of people's unwillingness to comply with certain legal demand without directly asking for their revocation.

The UDF is also sometimes given credit for instigating the consumer boycott that started in the Eastern Cape in 1985. However, such credit can be only on the initial basis of the Front—through its affiliates—assuming crisis leadership in the course of the boycott rather than actually initiating it. The boycott was calculated to induce the private sector into pressuring the government to give in to certain community demands.[87] It has provided a strategy for the "celebration" of a "Black Christmas" by blacks in most parts of the country. "Black Christmas" has been a kind of self-denial by blacks since the events of 1976. Until 1985, it was limited to abstaining from certain pleasures and activities—e.g., from drinking, from extravagant and showy celebrations, etc.—within the townships. As a result of the Cape consumer boycott, however, white businesses in the cities have been the main target of "Black Christmas" since 1985, when the protest was mostly under the supervision of consumer boycott committees nationally. These did not seem to have any relation to the UDF, judging by the lack of control and courtesy the boycott often displayed in some places.

In 1986 the UDF, COSATU, the NECC, and the South African Council of Churches (SACC) jointly launched what they called "Christmas Against the State of Emergency." They called for the lifting of the state of emergency, the release of detainees and political prisoners, the unbanning of political organizations, the introduction of a "people's education," and other demands.[88] The call was first made in October. When it appeared in the newspapers again just before Christmas, the government prohibited its further publication. One of the issues of the Soweto daily, the *Sowetan,* which continued to carry the call in the form of an advertisement after the prohibition, was seized and withdrawn from the streets. Subsequent court action by the *Sowetan* and another newspaper were unsuccessful.

The activities just described sufficiently indicate the nature and extent of involvement of the bodies under discussion in their struggle against apartheid. Of interest in this examination is not the kinds and number of the activities themselves, but determining the extent to which these activities (practice) complied with the policies (theory) set forth by these bodies for themselves. In other words, my intent is to determine what they hoped to accomplish, how they planned to go about it, and whether or not their approach was appropriate and/or adequate. As explained earlier in this chapter, I will attempt to determine this briefly at the end of the present chapter and in greater detail in a subsequent chapter.

Relationship with One Another and with Other Organizations

Implicit in the strategies of both the NF and the UDF is an alliance of organizations working toward the same ends. Thus, representatives from each organization participate in the decision-making process of each alliance, helping also to plan its activities. AZAPO stands both between the two alliances as an autonomous organization, with its own approach to action and its own relationships, and also within the NF as a major ally, relating to other organizations in the alliance. There are also mutual relations—for good or ill—between, on the one hand, AZAPO and the NF as individual organizations, and, on the other, the UDF.

Shortly after the launching of the UDF in 1983 an AZAPO official, answering a question from a *Sowetan* newspaper reporter, let it be known that AZAPO welcomed consultations with "all organisations of the oppressed and exploited."[89] Later the organization stated that what was important in its relationship with other organizations, including the UDF, was the issue being addressed. Hence AZAPO often rubbed shoulders with the UDF on the understanding that "if an issue affects the whole community, there isn't a UDF zone and an AZAPO zone."[90] On this understanding joint commemoration services are most often held and joint statements often made. For example, the two bodies jointly condemned the killing of five students of the University of Zululand by Inkatha supporters.[91] AZAPO also said that it encouraged its members to play an active role within civic bodies in order to be in touch with the grass roots: "We see it as our duty to infuse political implications and perspectives into civic matters."[92] The organization has also been actively involved with unions, student bodies, and other organizations that serve the community in various ways.

On the wider front, the NF also attempts to move beyond its alliance, when the need demands it, to consult with other organizations and to coordinate action.[93] At its 1986 National Council, the Forum was urged to "take the initiative to establish alliances with other progressive and revolutionary organizations to carry through the Azanian struggle on the basis of anti-collaboration and principled agreement and unity of action."[94]

However open the NF, as well as AZAPO, was to collaboration with other organizations, though, from the very beginning there appeared to be an uneasy kind of relationship between each of them and the UDF. The UDF's own attitude toward them was similarly shaky. For instance, it used to have representatives at the Forum's National Councils but abruptly stopped sending them in March 1985.[95] The NF attributed this termination to the UDF's new conception of itself as having an exclusive authority on the black struggle. Coming at the time it did, however, it can also be attributed to the general tension that pervaded the two alliances in 1985 (see below).

The UDF's own original pledge was to organize, build, and strengthen community organizations, including women's, students', religious, and community organizations in order to unite them in common opposition to the government's attempts at dividing the black community.[96] In doing so, it opened itself—unlike AZAPO and, to a limited extent, the NF—also to white organizations in the belief that "all the oppressed sections of the community had an over-riding interest in the destruction of apartheid."[97] It also indicated that it was not interested whether its affiliates subscribed to black consciousness or to the Freedom Charter.[98] On its relationship to AZAPO, it said: "We feel that the key principle is common opposition to the 'new deal' legislation, and that this is a common feature between UDF and AZAPO." The UDF, however, was unsuccessful in wooing the Forum group of organizations to itself, though it claimed cooperation with them in major campaigns.[99]

The largest support for the UDF was from the Charter group, or the so-called Charterists. These were largely "multiracial" groups that subscribed to the tenets of the 1956 Freedom Charter of the ANC. Because the UDF endorsed the charter, it came to be associated with the ANC and was later charged by the government with being an agent of the latter. These charges were denied, of course, although the UDF welcomed the ANC's expression of support for its activities: "Nor can there be any links [with the ANC] under the present circumstances," said a UDF spokesperson.[100] The reason for this was given as the ANC's illegality in the country because of its strategy of violence. The UDF recognized that to operate aboveground inside South Africa, it had no other option but to commit itself to nonviolence.[101] Nor had it ever considered the alternative of a violent strategy.

Apart from its Charterist alliance, the UDF seemed to be at greater odds with two other organizations than it was with AZAPO/NF. These were Chief Buthelezi's Inkatha movement, especially, and Dr. van Zyl

Slabbert's Convention Alliance. We have already referred to the UDF's attitude toward the national convention as well as to the formation of the Convention Alliance. On this matter its views coincided with those of AZAPO and the NF. In brief, the UDF rejected the Convention Alliance on the grounds that its aim appeared to be a roundtable discussion leading to a "Muzorewa-type of solution" for South Africa—that is, in the person of Mangosuthu Buthelezi. The UDF, however, was not prepared to negotiate on the question of one man, one vote "because that would be to negotiate away a fundamental democratic right."[102]

The UDF and other groups saw Buthelezi as a central figure in the Convention Alliance. Many liberal whites viewed him as a possible solution to the country's problem—a lesser evil than the ANC—if only all the disputants could accept him as a compromise. His Inkatha was also seen as one of the key organizations in the alliance. The UDF rejected Buthelezi's claims of being involved in the struggle against apartheid, however. His organization, it complained, spent its time "attacking other anti-apartheid organizations" and "Inkatha impis violently attack[ed] anyone opposed to Buthelezi in Natal."[103] For the UDF, Inkatha's attitude was rather that of nonviolence toward apartheid while it was one of open aggression toward the people:[104]

> Their energies are directed almost exclusively to attacking (often violently) the UDF and other opponents of apartheid. . . . [T]he complicity which the state appears to give to the rampaging impis should be cause for great disquiet.[105]

A point of major difference between the UDF and AZAPO/NF is that of the participation of white organizations in the national struggle and their view toward ethnic identity/involvement. As already seen, the UDF believes that the black consciousness strategy of "closing ranks" has already served its purpose of conscientization and that the time has now come for all the enemies of apartheid to join hands in a common struggle. Because of AZAPO/NF's criticism of the use of the term *multiracialism,* the UDF has done away with it in favor of *nonracialism.* The former, it acknowledges, retains race as a criterion, while the latter means judging people on merit, not on skin color.[106]

AZAPO continues to insist that in its view, integration belongs to the postliberation era.[107] It rejects, in the interests of black unity or at least of solidarity in struggle, the involvement of whites and "ethnically based organizations" in the fight against apartheid.[108] The NF welcomes in its alliance, however, groups that do not subscribe to black consciousness and that have white members in them. An example of these is the Cape Action League (CAL). The criterion of membership in the alliance is the predominance of black membership in the allied organizations. The main concern here, it is said, is not so much doubt about the commitment of some whites to change in the country and to making personal sacrifices for it, but to ensure that "the leadership of the struggle . . . remain with the black working class."[109] This class alone, with its organizations, is considered to have the "historic task . . . to mobilize the urban and rural poor together with the radical sections of the middle class in order to put an end to the system of oppression and exploitation by the white ruling class."[110] The NF does not find it conceivable that a group "representing the interests of the ruling class" can work for the interests of the black working class. But while it is conceivable that whites can be sympathetic to the cause, as individuals, as a group they are perceived to "generally constitute a problem."[111] Notwithstanding their exclusion, the goal of the struggle is the "development of one national progressive culture" encompassing all the people of South Africa.

The revival of the Transvaal and Natal Indian congresses as instruments of opposing the Indian elections contemplated through the medium of the South African Indian Council (SAIC) came under severe criticism from both AZAPO and the NF. It was, however, welcomed by the UDF as a good gesture that, while recognizing the historically evolved differences, did not condone them and was committed to work for their elimination. For AZAPO, the decision for the revival was a "retrogressive step." It implied that the UDF, which condoned the step, would be a "conglomerate of ethnically oriented groups" whereas "the oppressed should be rallied together in a single organization which is not structured on an ethnic basis."[112] Reservations were also expressed about uncritical support of the Freedom Charter because of its preservation of racial groupings and its recognition of minority rights in its focus. In turn, however, the NF/AZAPO was accused of unnecessarily duplicating the charter through its Manifesto while being deliberately shortsighted on the ethnic issue.[113]

This discussion of organizational relationships would not be complete without reference to the conflicts that have plagued the national struggle inside the country in the last few years. While, as already pointed out, there had always been an uneasy relationship between the Charter group and the Black Consciousness group alliances, this relationship appears to have exacerbated particularly after the Kennedy visit. I do not mean to imply that Kennedy himself was the source of the conflict. Rather, he seems merely to have provided an occasion for its expression. Even then, the conflict actually started at the student level, initially at four notable occasions: (1) when five members of AZASM, AZAPO's student wing, were seriously injured in clashes with COSAS (a UDF affiliate) supporters at the University of the North;[114] (2) when an AZASM representative was forced by COSAS supporters at the University of Natal to affirm—as though in doubt—that Mandela was his leader; (3) when members of the two groups engaged in knife-wielding fights in Tembisa; and (4) when the Port Elizabeth Youth Congress (PEYCO—a UDF affiliate) prevented AZAPO supporters from attending the funeral of victims of the shooting in Uitenhage, Cape.[115]

These conflicts developed into an internecine strife that spread to the larger bodies, particularly in the Eastern Cape. There were cases of house petrol-bombings, the "unholy necklace," kidnappings, and further stabbings, which spilled over to other parts of the country. As the situation went completely out of control, both UDF and AZAPO refused to believe that their members could go so far in brutality and began to see the hand of the "system" in the ongoing conflict. The UDF alleged that "Gestapo tactics" were being used by the state against its opponents.[116] Both bodies condemned the killings and called for peace. A successful service of reconciliation at Regina Mundi Church, Soweto, which included also Inkatha,[117] went unreported by the press in favor of publicity to the continuing feuds in the Eastern Cape. Even after the peace offering, however, isolated incidents continued, resulting in more deaths and bombings. A frustrated AZAPO leader observed that the continuing conflict in some areas, particularly in the Eastern Cape, was "undermining attempts at the constructive resolution of the conflict nationally."[118] By May 1986, members of both groups, especially AZAPO, in Soweto were still actively on the run from mutual manhunts and bombings.

These incidents were very unfortunate, indeed, in view of the minor tactical differences that exist between the two bodies. All of them are agreed that they stand for the same ends and have affirmed that even the racial issue in the membership of some is not a major nor determinative one. Tlholoe offers a good summary of these common standpoints and differences, showing that in view of them the conflict is rather unwarranted and costly:

> The black consciousness organizations and the UDF have more or less the same objectives—they want to see the creation of a non-racial society. They are both vaguely socialist. The major difference comes over tactics. The black consciousness organizations say that all our lives are run by whites—that's the essence of apartheid. . . . Therefore, if we create or own organizations, we should not transfer into them the same structures . . . [T]he UDF position would be that there are some whites who are as committed to black lib-

eration as blacks and we should [recognize this by accepting their role in the struggle and so] anticipate our future.[119]

Hence Akhalwaya has enquired:

> If individuals with differing ideological beliefs can find a home in the National Forum, and organizations with ideological differences can find a home in the UDF, and some are comfortable in both camps, why can't the Forum and the UDF unite?[120]

Or at least display a little more tolerance toward each other! As for their difference over Kennedy's visit, Fr. John Sebidi, the chairperson at Regina Mundi on the day the senator was to have given an address, relates it in the following way:

> Some [AZAPO] were saying, "Kennedy is not going to liberate us," while others [UDF] were saying "O.K., he is not going to liberate us, but he might be useful in internationalizing the struggle." [So, as you can see, it was just a tactical difference.][121]

As explained earlier, however, other intervening factors went beyond this minor difference to create general ill will.

There is no doubt that all the opponents of apartheid in the last few years have agonized over the resolution of these conflicts between AZAPO and the UDF. Like these two bodies, they were only too aware that the government was the only one to gain from this kind of conflict and would do everything it could to keep the situation as it was and to try to sow even greater discord and confusion. In this sense we may not easily dismiss the role of *agents provocateurs* in the conflicts. Indeed, it was even more than probable: how else to gain respite from anti-apartheid agitation than to divert and focus attention on the supposed internecine strife—"black-on-black violence"—of its own opponents? Even as everyone concerned has prayed for peace and reconciliation, the two bodies themselves have never ceased to lick their wounds and to wish for a reversal of the unpleasant, self-destructive events. Former AZAPO president, Ish Mkhabela, was to say in another setting: Even "our revulsion of informers and the acts they perpetrate should not blind us to the fact that in our revolutionary activities we cannot afford to lose our integrity."[122] Both groups, accordingly, devoted themselves to working toward peace and unity among themselves and other opponents of the South African system in 1987.[123]

GOVERNMENT RESPONSE

Whether or not these bodies will succeed in achieving their objective of tolerance, at the least, will depend to a large extent on how much they are still able to function or how free they are to communicate. Since the declaration of the state of emergency in June 1986, the government has detained many of these organizations' leaders, while others have been forced to go into hiding. If those in authority in these organizations are unable to come together and effect the necessary negotiations, it is hardly likely that larger representations from the two groups can meet for more meaningful talks as they were able to do in 1985.

Even before the declaration of the two states of emergency in 1985 and 1986 the government had expressed in various ways its displeasure with the activities of the bodies under discussion and with the unrest that existed throughout the country. Following the crackdowns of 1977, the number of political arrests in the country declined for a brief period. There were ongoing trials of arrested ANC guerrillas who infiltrated the country but failed to carry out their missions without being discovered. After AZAPO had come onto the scene, most of the government's action was directed toward it. Many AZAPO officials were detained during the school boycotts between 1980 and 1982.[124] In July 1980 the organization, in its second year of existence, was accused by the minister of police of furthering the aims of banned organizations. This was generally taken as a threat prefacing the possible banning of AZAPO. Later, as a result of the campaigns against the government's "new deal" proposals in 1983, the number of detentions rose from 772 in 1981—declining to 264 in 1982 and 453 in 1983— to 1,149 in 1984. Those detained in the latter year included both AZAPO and UDF activists as well as officials of trade unions.[125] The government still tried to link AZAPO to banned organizations in 1983, following the launching of the NF. Several AZAPO representatives were questioned by the security police to establish this fact. One official was denied a passport, while another's was seized. In December of the same year AZAPO's offices were raided by the police and documents confiscated in what was regarded as a continuing intimidation campaign by the government.[126]

With the emergence of the UDF, the government turned more of its attention toward it as the press gave it more coverage. By the middle of 1984, the minister of law and order, Mr. Louis LeGrange, accused it of being responsible for the wave of unrest in the country. He concluded that the UDF had the same revolutionary aims as the banned ANC and the SACP and was actively sowing a revolutionary climate.[127] Ongoing detentions during the year, although not limited to UDF supporters, had reached 1,006 by the end of October. Shortly afterward the minister warned the UDF that it was "treading on thin ice." This, as previously in the case of AZAPO, was interpreted as a possible banning threat.

In February 1985 the UDF offices were raided in Johannesburg, Cape Town, and Durban. Police confiscated files and publications and detained thirteen members of the alliance. Six of these were charged with high treason. Eight others had been previously charged.[128] The charge of treason was brought upon sixteen people altogether in July 1985. In accordance with the earlier accusations of the minister of law and order, it was alleged that the sixteen predominantly UDF supporters had identified themselves with the Revolutionary Alliance of the ANC, the SACP, and the South African Congress of Trade Unions (SACTU), thus intending to further their aims.[129] Twelve of the accused were cleared of these charges in December 1985.[130] The other four, who were all union leaders, were finally acquitted on June 23, 1986.[131]

Another treason trial, which for some time ran concurrently with the one just described, arose out of the Vaal uprising in 1984. It involved twenty-two people, most of whom were members of the UDF-affiliated Vaal Civic Association.[132] They were accused of having aimed to overthrow or endanger the state by violence or by the threat of violence, in accordance with the alleged aims of the UDF. The trial was on its seventeenth month in February 1986. Three of the accused were finally acquitted in November of the same year.

Many leaders of the UDF went into hiding after the declaration of the first state of emergency, which gave the police enormous powers of arrest and resulted in numerous detentions. When the emergency was lifted in March 1986, the UDF undertook to keep a low profile in its operations.[133] With the continuing state of unrest, however, the government restored the emergency on June 12, 1986. Threatened by the planned "appropriate action" advocated by the NF for June 16-26, it took the opportunity also to ban all open air rallies, refusing to grant permission for appeals to hold them.[134] A UDF spokesperson stated that the government had seen fit to declare a state of emergency rather "than heed the demands of the residents of almost every township in South Africa." By the end of August more than 12,000 people were believed to be in detention under the emergency regulations, while others returned into hiding.[135] The Detainee Parents Support Committee (DPSC) gave the number of those detained under the emergency by the end of the year as about 22,000. Of those, about 8,000 were said to be children under the age of eighteen, with half of them still in detention. The Black Sash reported that between 1,300 and 1,800 children under the age of seventeen were being held, while the government claimed that only 256 young people between the ages of eleven and fifteen were being held.[136]

In October 1986, the UDF became the third organization in

South Africa to be declared an affected organization.[137] The first two to be declared as such more than ten years previously were the Christian Institute of Southern Africa (CI) and NUSAS. The CI was subsequently banned with nineteen other organizations in 1977. NUSAS is presently an affiliate of the UDF. As an affected organization, the UDF can no longer receive funds from abroad. It is inferred from this that by receiving foreign funds, an organization becomes a foreign agent and becomes duty bound to please its foreign sponsors. Hence it plays to a foreign audience. By implication, curtailing such funds restricts foreign influence and so limits the activities of the organization. The UDF reacted, however, by saying that the government was only wasting its time. Limiting its funds from abroad would not affect the Front's activities.[138] An official was later forced to admit, however, that as a result of the government's general harassment, the UDF had become less effective, particularly as its members adopted a low profile.[139]

On several occasions the UDF has successfully challenged the government's actions against it and its members. In 1985 a UDF supporter, who had been tortured under police detention as a student after the 1976 uprising, was awarded government compensation of R 6,750 after court action had been brought against it by a UDF law firm.[140] During 1986 the Front successfully challenged several stipulations of the emergency regulations, thus winning the release of some detainees. In some cases the government quickly closed the loopholes in the affected legislation to prevent further challenges. In its actions, the UDF has often presented itself as the last hope for peaceful change in South Africa, warning that if the government were to ban it, this would be the sign that the govenment was only paying lip service to peace, not to mention its desire to change. For this reason the Front has approached its cause with the confidence of an invincible opponent. The government has been confronted with similar challenges in the past and often given the impression of being on the brink of capitulation. Only time will produce the "cup" from which the current resistance will drink, or tell when the mighty Goliath will come to its unexpected downfall.

CRITICAL EVALUATION

Some have speculated about why the government has not yet implemented any drastic action—that is, banning—on the present political organizations after several years of unrest and agitation in the country. More relevant for this discussion is the suggestion that never before has the resistance been so widespread and so intense. Further, it is thought that because the struggle has gained international attention, with the threat of sanctions and with anti-apartheid movements in almost every large center of the world, the government is forced to be more cautious than it has been in the past and must consider seriously the consequences of taking such a damnable step. Besides, in spite of other repressive action it has taken so far on its opponents, the government has wanted to give the impression that it was living up to its promise to bring about evolutionary change, albeit within the existing system.

Such speculation on the whole underestimates the ruthlessness of the South African government. When it feels threatened, this government has no regard for the international community nor for promises it might have made, which are for the most part hollow, anyway. This is what is meant by "withdrawing into the Laager." If the struggle is in fact more intense now than it was on previous occasions, one would have expected the government to have acted even more swiftly with the present organizations than it did with those in 1960 and 1976. Certainly one of the main reasons for the government's calculated approach so far is its intention to capitalize on so-called black-on-black violence, a problem that has plagued the resistance movement in the last few years. This dimension of the struggle may have added to its intensity. Not only have there been witch-hunts for suspected police informers and other marked "servants of the system" but also an apparent lack of tolerance between some movements has led to regrettable interorganizational strife rather than a united focus on the real target, the government itself. Hence the government could afford to relax and take it easy, thus giving the impression of false tolerance.

To suggest that the current struggle is, in other respects, more intense than "Sharpeville" and "Soweto" and their aftermath can thus only reflect what short memories people have and how gullible they are inclined to be. This is not to deny the great mobilization that has taken place and the struggle's internationalization through personalities like Archbishop Desmond Tutu and Dr. Allan Boesak. If anything has been gained from the struggle of the 1980s it is precisely this international aspect: the testimonies and subsequent awarding of the Nobel Peace Prize to Archbishop Tutu; the declaration of apartheid as a heresy by the World Alliance of Reformed Churches (WARC) through the influence of Dr. Boesak; the new campus awakening to the evil of apartheid mainly as the result of the anti-apartheid demonstrations that began at the South African Embassy by Congressman Fauntroy and representatives of TransAfrica; the adoption of and continuing threat of sanctions against South Africa by some members of the international community; and so forth. As far as internal action and mass mobilization go, humility dictates that we should recognize the historical circle it continues to perpetuate, for better or for worse. Hence my opening this chapter with the quotation from Lelyveld, insofar as it affirms this historical aspect.

To a large extent, the practices of these organizations have continued to trail behind their theories. In this respect little effort has been made to learn from the past and improve upon it. AZAPO and the NF have, indeed, reflected a strong awareness of the need for a "principled program of action" to direct their actions. Such a program has, however, been considered on a "touch-and-go" basis and has not quite fully emerged. Whatever has come out of it so far has not significantly improved upon past BCM strategy, except for its more rhetorical emphasis on socialism and the working class. Further, in spite of AZAPO's intention to move beyond past BCM strategy, it still focuses more on the conscientization approach than its actual implementation through some form of challenge to the existing system. Insofar as this "program" has been acted out at all, such action has not transcended the short-term focus of the "politics of protest." In short, the organization's theory addresses both short-term and long-term goals, with an emphasis on the latter; but any action that has been taken toward the realization of these goals has invariably been action aimed at short-term achievements, leaving the long-term requirements unattended. As we saw in the previous chapter, this is mostly what the PAC accused the ANC of doing, though the PAC itself was finally caught in the same trap.

The UDF has not done any better in this respect, despite its acknowledged harassment of the government. The key to its program of action was the "politics of refusal," which was a short-term negation rather than a long-term affirmation. Originally aimed at the government's constitutional proposals in 1983, this program continued to be retained even after the "coloured" and Indian elections it had been aimed at had taken place, and even though the alliance had referred to long-term demands at the same time it was proposing the "politics of refusal." Apart from the challenge to the government's constitutional proposals, the UDF's program differed very little from that of AZAPO/NF, focusing on motivating and organizing the people and their organizations rather than "going out to get it" from the government. It may be said that all these bodies reflected or engaged in the "politics of protest" rather than the "politics of aggression"—or "challenge." From this it was understandable that the UDF's theme for its 1985 annual conference was: "From Protest to Challenge . . !"[141] Yet the steps proposed for achieving this were oriented more toward the organization itself and the community than toward the government.

These organizations, as well as any other future organizations, would do well to review some of the more positive proposals and achievements of the past, such as the 1949 Program of Action and the 1952 Defiance Campaign it inspired. They can both learn from and build on them. This would enable their future action to move forward in a more informed manner, repeating the best of past history instead of its worst. They deserve much credit, however, for keeping the spirit of resistance alive for the present generation. They would do even better if this spirit were informed by an approach to action that is more meaningful than has been the case hitherto. Some of them have begun to review the 1956 Freedom Charter to help put their theory in perspective. It will certainly help more to reorient their practice if they can retrace their steps a few years back to 1949 and 1952, see what those years have to offer and what improvements—not mere repetition—can be made on their approaches for the continuing struggle against apartheid.

Chapter 4

Toward a Conception of Continuity between Philosophical and Theological Ethics

This chapter is the point of transition between, on the one hand, the examination of the goals and policies of the movements discussed in the preceding chapters and, on the other, the socioethical evaluation of these goals and policies. It also paves the way toward a critical examination of alternative strategies for the solution of the problem with which these movements were concerned. My aim in this chapter is to provide a normative frame of reference for the first of these tasks in particular. This frame of reference will consist of an adaptation of the moral laws as conceived by Walter G. Muelder in his book, *Moral Law in Christian Social Ethics.* My chief concern here is to highlight the point of contact between these laws and Christian social ethics with its own principles.

Muelder's book is seen as the culmination of a historical concern of Christian theologians to find a "common ground" between secular (philosophical) and religious (theological) ethics. This concern was first expressed in the natural law teaching of the early church, which St. Thomas Aquinas systematized and later Catholic social doctrine made normative. In recent Protestantism the concern was manifested quite dramatically in the American "Social Gospel" of the late nineteenth and early twentieth centuries. It continues to this day in ecumenical social thought. Although an examination of each of these three traditions would be useful in showing how each attempted to solve the common problem as well as in determining in what sense Muelder's approach could be regarded as a step forward, such detailed examination would be of interest only to a few with an academic background of and inclination to ethics. Besides, it would only serve to delay our progress to an ethical evaluation of the activities discussed in the foregoing chapters.[1] The following sections will, therefore, proceed directly to the consideration of Muelder's moral laws, subject to a few preliminary remarks.

By lifting up the linkage between secular and religious (Christian) moral conceptions as seen in these approaches, it is hoped that we might find a suitable standard by which the movements discussed above—as predominantly secular in orientation—can be judged sympathetically and with understanding not only from the secular perspective but from the Christian perspective as well. Such a standard should be employable by these movements in their quest, and have equal moral significance for Christians and non-Christians involved in them and in their wider communities. In my opinion, we may derive a standard of this kind in a more meaningful way from Muelder's approach than from the others mentioned here.

These approaches share with the moral laws the common concern of integrating the Christian and secular moral orders, while at the same time professing their primary allegiance to Christian principles. Notwithstanding justifiable objections that may be made against some aspects of each, each succeeds in its own way—in theory. In all cases, however, the theory does not go far enough in providing practical guidelines for action in concrete situations. The principles and precepts of natural law, the love commandment and the standard of the kingdom of God in the social gospel, and the middle axioms and the idea of the responsible society in ecumenical social thought would all still require more elaborate guidelines for their fulfillment or practicalization in concrete situations. This is where Muelder's moral laws seem to fit in. They provide guidance on how to will, what kind (in a rational sense) of values to will, and for whom to will them. A description of these laws will follow a general consideration of coherence in social ethics.

COHERENCE IN SOCIAL AND GENERAL ETHICS

The moral laws proposed by Muelder are of philosophical origin, but he assumes certain theological and biblical parallels to all of them.[2] His concern for philosophical, theological, and scientific coherence in Christian social ethics leads Muelder to bring together into one system the philosophical-theological integration of Catholic natural law theory and the theological-social scientific integration of both the social gospel and the ecumenical movement. This makes Christian social ethics an interdisciplinary field of study. None of the disciplines involved in it is entitled to dictate the terms of the coherence; all are equally important.

Thus Muelder is critical of those theologians—such as Barth, Ramsey, and Lehmann—who demand that Christian ethics be coherent (only) with Jesus Christ. He writes:

> The appeal that ethical reflection must cohere with divine revelation does not recognize sufficiently the changing traditions about that self-disclosure, the historical and cultural factors in these changing interpretations, and the part that science and philosophy inevitably play in Christian faith and understanding. There is no completed given event with which ethical reflection can cohere against all other evidence.

His insistence on interdisciplinary coherence means that ethical reflection must be coherent with all the relevant evidence made available through these disciplines. Paul K. Deats, Jr., Muelder's former student and colleague, has described the contribution made in social ethics by each of the disciplines or related fields involved. He sees the contribution of philosophy and theology as being that of "illumination through historically derived loyalties, traditions, insights, and categories of interpretation."

> They should also contribute categories and procedures of logical consistency and rational coherence. . . . Finally, philosophy and theology deal with sources of motivation and concern and with the grounds of hope.

The main contribution of the social sciences is to help in understanding the facts of the case or the situation. They are also a useful aid in the "previsioning of alternative consequences of choices." Coherence, then, concludes Muelder, is not somehow given to man. It must be found continually "as an emergent."[3] From this it is also obvious that there is no necessary or final conflict between faith and reason. "They interpenetrate man's spiritual unity."[4]

Speaking of the specific relationship between theological and philosophical ethics, Muelder states that the first is introduced by faith and is "disciplined and clarified by reason." The second discovers its moral law through reason and "commands openness to faith." The metaphysical law, which commands that all persons seek to know the source and significance of all the moral laws (discussed in Muelder's book), thus urging the coherence of the moral order, necessarily leads to theological considerations. Muelder states that ethics is "logically more ultimate than religion, though not logically or metaphysically more ultimate than God." This is because it is not possible to regard a thing or a being as good, as God is considered to be, unless one has some conception of the meaning of *good*. Since God is regarded as the very embodiment of the good, ethics recognizes that if his existence be a reality, then he is the creator of persons as moral beings. Consequently, moral autonomy depends on theonomy. In this sense ethics not only acquires some of its content from religion,[5] but it can actually be said to extend to religion, which in turn provides ethics with some feedback. "When religion is defined as cooperation between man and God expressed through worship and conduct of life, God is viewed as the embodiment of the moral ideal and as the source or creator of a moral order in the universe."[6] Thus a circular or a reflexive kind of relationship seems to exist between ethics (philosophical) and theology, where the former leads to a religious and theological conception and the latter leads to an intensification and expansion of ethical reflection and understanding. Muelder is consistent and probably correct, therefore, in saying that morality is not entirely independent of religion but depends on it for some of its content.

This leads him to advocate the cause of the Christian faith as one special aspect of the religious life and, therefore, a transcendent source of morality. The moralist, then, must seriously consider Christianity, taking from it "its profoundest ethical values and organiz[ing] them coherently into personal and community existence when these values are criticized and interpreted."[7] There should be no difficulty in doing this, it seems, once one has recognized the continuity between ethics and religion. The universality and impact of the Christian religion in particular should or is bound to arouse some curiosity in the ethicist and compel him to scrutinize the significance and value of its ethical teaching. This is almost a *sine qua non,* if Muelder's argument makes sense, as it certainly seems to.

By the same token, a Christian ethic supposedly based on revelation alone would be a baseless ethic that does not take into account the human contribution and experience, as well as Muelder's point that we conceive of God as Good (and, therefore, as author of the moral order) because we first have an experience or idea of what *good* is. Thus even the Christian ethic is basically an interpretation of human experience, though in the context of its ultimate significance. As such it has its origin in this experience and must continually stoop low to share anew in it and to reinterpret it, as well as to improve itself through the new insights of this experience. In the final analysis, theological ethics needs philosophical ethics to complement it as much as philosophical ethics needs theological ethics for the same purpose. At the same time, both need the human sciences for their better understanding, interpretation, and rehabilitation of the human (moral) experience. This, it seems, is the whole object of Muelder's work.

THE MORAL LAWS

This extremely systematic integration of philosophical and theological ethics, in particular, would not take us very far beyond the other approaches mentioned here—especially natural law theory—were there no provisions of elaborate practical guidelines for moral decision. It is here especially that Muelder's approach seems to excel these others. The two Protestant approaches treated, in spite of their concern for relevance—reflected in their scientific approach—and their attempt (especially that of the ecumenical movement) to work out principles for practical decision making, still seem to have left much to what Duff called an "ethic of inspiration." While there were suitable tools for laying situational facts bare, it does not seem quite clear how one was to proceed in making a decision for action no matter how armed one might be with middle axioms or the idea of responsibility. One simply knew that one had to be responsible, or just, or to love one's neighbor, and so on. Without more elaborate (though not necessarily prescriptive) guidelines on how best to carry out these duties, such concepts remained static in spite of their openness and potential. The conclusion seems to be that only "instant guidance" from the Holy Spirit could have been expected to provide assistance in completing the process.

In Catholic natural law theory one had to make one's decision in accordance with one's nature or with what one regarded as the best means of retaining the harmony of the order of things as planned by God. This meant that the good had to be done and evil avoided. Could there be one universal way of determining the demands of nature in general in a particular situation? The "see-judge-act" formula often proposed by some moral theologians parrots the obvious. It says little on how to judge. Hence Catholic laypeople had to look up to their "superiors," the clergy, who in turn ultimately had to look up to the Magisterium, for perpetual moral guidance on the demands of natural law and for the interpretation of its "precepts." There is little wonder, therefore, that natural law ultimately tended to become a law in the legal rather than in the moral sense.

The "new" moral laws seem to overcome most of the above obstacles. In fact, they appear more deserving of being called natural laws themselves because most of them seem so obvious and "natural" to human beings. The link between these laws and some of the Christian principles is not immediately visible except for the Christian principles that can be compared with them. These Christian parallels, in view of the preceding discussion connecting philosophical and theological ethics, appear to be distinguished from the moral laws only by the language and tradition from which they originate. The basic idea between the two seems to remain the same. Christians are insistent, however, that theirs is a more adequate type of morality. Muelder in his system is one of those few theologians who substantiate this position convincingly. If ethics leads ultimately to God and religion, and religion in turn expands and gives more meaning and direction to ethics, then surely that type of ethics which does not transcend its "earthly" status is an incomplete ethic. The significance of the Christian parallels and other Christian principles to the moral laws, therefore, will depend upon the significance of what Christianity (as a religion) adds to ethics. With the same breath, however, we must admit that a Christian ethic not grounded in experience, and, therefore, in philosophical and scientific exploration, is also deficient. Christian ethical principles, in their basic sense, can be interpretations and recastings of this human moral experience only with added significance in the light of revelation and the mission of Jesus. On the basis of this argument, it is possible that the Christian parallels to the moral laws are not necessarily equivalent to the latter but wider in scope, depending on their religious significance and reconstruction.

Muelder lists a total of fifteen moral laws, divided into four aspects that hang closely together. These aspects are: the formal, the axiological, the personalistic, and the communitarian. The moral laws are normative laws of choice or "principles of responsible decision." Muelder distinguishes them from three other types of moral laws (which do not necessarily comprise the whole list): the prescriptive, the natural law, and what may simply be called normative ideals. He also distinguishes them from Kant's categorical imperative, which, despite some of its high pretensions, finds room particularly under his formal aspects (in the law of autonomy). Muelder also shows that some of those Christian theologians who do not find any type of moral law acceptable, such as Barth and Lehmann, actually presuppose such laws or their equivalents in their ethical thinking.[8]

The moral laws are universal by virtue of their purely formal character. They prescribe no code of conduct, nor do they constitute cultural moral content. They are methodical and regulative, and "comprise the rational structure of all truly ethical choice." Ethics, according to Muelder, deals with responsible action willed by the self. "Moral deliberation leading to decision and action involves choosing among alternatives."[9] This choice is made through the aid of the moral laws, now considered very briefly below.

The Formal Aspects

The first group of laws, the formal aspects, consists of two laws, namely, the logical law and the law of autonomy.

The Logical Law

The logical law exhorts consistency in the intentions of the self, and commands the will to be free from self-contradiction. "A moral person does not both will and not will the same ends." He or she must have a desire for "formal rightness." Refusal to acknowledge the requirements of this law is likely to lead to anomie or normlessness. DeWolf mentions as examples of biblical parallels that support this law the saying of Jesus, "Let what you say be simply 'Yes' or 'No,'" as well as the Old Testament principle not to have or worship other gods besides Yahweh.[10]

The Law of Autonomy

This law may be briefly stated: "Self-imposed ideals are imperative." We are obligated to act in accordance with those ideals or standards we set for ourselves. This law was stated in its extreme form by Kant in his categorical imperative. He urged action according to the maxim that the self would "at the same time will that it be a universal law." Muelder checks Kant by his claim that Christian principles urging obedience to God (theonomy) are not in violation of the law of autonomy if they are acknowledged by the self and self-imposed or adopted as one's own. "God's will is morally binding on man when it is responded to and accepted to be right." Contrariwise, true morality cannot be based on any will other than one's own.[11]

These two laws have to do with the will alone. They are standards of *how* to will, leaving out of consideration questions of *what* to will, which fall under the axiological laws.

The Axiological Aspects

Laws falling under this category are concerned with values, where value is understood in its elementary sense to mean whatever is liked, esteemed, or desired. Such laws deal with the "rational principles by which values ought to be chosen." Values must be self-consistent, harmonious, or coherent.

The Axiological Law

This law urges self-consistency and coherence of values to be chosen. It aims at the *summum bonum,* insofar as consistent and harmonious values are the best good possible. Values are distinguished into intrinsic and extrinsic values. The first stand on their own, while the second depend on them. Values must be supportive of one another, and are of, by, and for persons. While the whole system of values hangs together, priorities may be considered.[12]

The Law of Consequences

The law of consequences, stated briefly, commands: "Choose with a view to the long run, not merely to the present act." It is concerned not only with "manifest functions" but also with "latent functions." Here is one place where the social sciences can help unravel the facts of the situation and possible effects of action taken in the quest for values. Consequences also involve, according to Muelder, questions of "more-or-less." "The end justifies the means only if the whole situation has coherence and unity."[13]

The Law of the Best Possible

"All persons ought to will the best possible values in every situation, hence, if possible, to improve every situation." This law has four emphases, involving the concrete situation, its possibilities, its improvement, and the role of the best. Best values are inclusive, coherent, and consistent with the moral laws. They represent the highest good, as seen under the axiological law. The law commands not only the best, but also the possible. Therefore compromise is always provisional in the light of the ideal.

The Law of Specification

This law is the basis of most present-day situation ethics. According to it, "All persons ought, in any given situation, to develop the value or values specifically relevant to that situation." It is a corrective against abstract laws, against mere idealism. Being situational, it is also a pluralistic law; but taken in itself, it might distort the whole purpose of morality. The law of specification, therefore, like the rest of the moral laws, must be seen in the light of the whole system of moral laws.

The Law of the Most Inclusive End

The law of the most inclusive end is closely related to that of the best possible and the axiological law. All three emphasize the greatest good. It commands that all persons should choose a coherent life in which the widest possible range of value is realized. By urging the "most inclusive," it cautions against complete situational atomism.[14] It goes beyond the axiological law in demanding "a life plan for the person and an overall strategy for social action."

The Law of Ideal Control

All the axiological laws are summarized by the law of ideal control. It also explicitly relates the experience of values to ideals or critical standards. The law states that all persons "ought to control their empirical values by ideal values." Moral judgment cannot occur without ideal control. "Control by ideals, therefore, requires self-criticism of both thought and emotion."[15]

The Personalistic Aspects

The third aspect of the moral laws, the personalistic aspects, focuses on the human person. It affirms that values are of, by, and for persons. Personality is considered an intrinsic value and without respect for it, all other values become almost void. Muelder quotes Edgar S. Brightman, who said that "The person is what he experiences himself to be," and concludes, "A definition of personality in terms of experience is essential to an understanding of the moral laws of personality."[16]

The Law of Individualism

The law of individualism commands, "each person ought to realize in his own experience the maximum value of which he is capable in harmony with moral law." This law must be grouped in particular with the law of altruism and the communitarian laws, which keep it in check. It opposes "tight collectivism" and the extreme altruistic emphasis of some Christian ethicists. Muelder points out the impossibility of loving others when we do not love ourselves. Persons who have never learned to love themselves are incapable of showing love to others.[17]

The Law of Altruism

Individualism finds its counterpart in altruism. These two laws are aptly expressed jointly by the second greatest Christian commandment, "And thou shalt love thy neighbor as thyself"; or the exhortation, "Do unto others as you would have them do to you." Kant also well articulated it: "Act so that in your own person as well as in the person of every other you are treating mankind also as an end, never merely as a means." Muelder puts it: "Each person ought to respect all other persons as ends in themselves, and, as far as possible, to cooperate with others in the production and enjoyment of shared values." This law finds greater expression in the communitarian laws. While urging identification with the wider claims of other persons, it does not counsel neglect of oneself. That is why it is so well expressed by Kant and by the Christian commands to which we referred.[18]

According to Muelder, the law does not settle the question concerning what values in others are to be promoted. It does seem, however, that the Christian exhortation to "Do unto others . . ." does provide some clue, especially where others' particular needs are manifest and where they are in difficulty. The starting point of the law of altruism is simple justice, ascending toward more loving and sympathetic concern: "Love at once fulfills and transcends justice" "because the whole person responding to other persons must include their true good in the pursuit of his own good." This statement is justifiable in terms of the argument already entered into at the beginning of this section.

The Law of the Ideal of Personality

"All persons," according to this law, "ought to judge and guide all of their acts by their ideal conception (in harmony with the other laws) of what the whole personality ought to become both individually and socially." The fulfillment of personality, since it is both product and determinant of culture, calls for both personal life-plans and purposive social change. "What a person ought to do depends [ultimately] on what the community ought to be." In fulfillment of this law, a person may receive guidance from an ideal personality type, such as Jesus or Confucius, though pure imitation of such a type would defeat the aims of morality.[19]

The Communitarian Aspects

The communitarian laws appeal to the experience of the person in community. Personality has both a social and a private aspect. It is interpersonal. A person is a person within a community. Muelder adopts Tonnies's definition of a community as distinguished from an association, that is, where the former is understood as an intimate type of relationship among persons, while the latter is more businesslike and interest-oriented.

The Law of Cooperation

The first communitarian law commands cooperation among persons in the production and enjoyment of shared values. Participation in group life must be productive and oriented toward common values. This law "lifts the interdependence of men to the level of morally responsible participation."

The Law of Social Devotion

According to this law, "all persons ought to devote themselves to serving the best interests of the group and to subordinate personal gain to social gain." The law of social devotion emphasizes the law of the best possible and that of ideal control. Each person must, by subordinating personal to social gain, seek to serve the best interests of the group. This law is not in contradiction with the law of individualism, since self-interest is directly served by service to the community. Rousseau put this in a more crude and self-centered way in *The Social Contract,* where he writes,

> Finally, since each man gives himself to all, he gives himself to no one; and since there is no associate over whom he does not gain the same rights as others gain over him, each man recovers the equivalent of everything he loses, and in the bargain he acquires more power to preserve what he has.[20]

While the motive of the social contract as seen by Rousseau is purely personal gain, the communitarian laws in general, though not completely surrendering personal interest, are truly altruistic.

The Law of the Ideal of Community

All persons ought to form and choose all of their ideals and values in loyalty to their ideals (in harmony with the other laws) of what the whole community ought to become; and to participate responsibly in groups to help them similarly choose and form all their ideals and choices.

The law of the ideal of community confirms the preceding two laws by emphasizing the truth that "personal realization is a partnership in the good life." It raises the question of what constitutes a true community, and recognizes cultural pluralism: "no one 'historical totality' is normative for all others." A world community can be made possible by mutual recognition of symbols, ideals, and goals among the various world communities, leading to some form of world culture.

The Metaphysical Law

The last of the moral laws in Muelder's system is the metaphysical law. We have already described it through several references early in this section.

Muelder stresses the point that none of these moral laws can be fully grasped in isolation from the rest of the others. He affirms Peter Bertocci's statement, "Reason must allow every part to speak, but must go on to assess the relation of the parts to each other with a view to discovering what the testimony of the whole reveals."[21] Coherence among these laws is, therefore, absolutely necessary.

PRACTICAL IMPLICATIONS OF MORAL LAW IN CHRISTIAN SOCIAL ETHICS

While in general Muelder well integrates philosophical ethics and theological ethics, he does not seem to show, in theory, what this integration means in moral practice—that is, how in particular the philosophical moral laws relate or cohere with Christian principles in moral decision making. This, if Muelder is well understood, is his Achilles' heel. Others have also criticized Muelder's work, notably Ralph Potter, Jr., and Oliva Blanchette, S.J.,[22] who point to his interdisciplinary approach in social ethics in general and to his success in integrating ethics and social science. Such criticisms have been justifiably refuted by Muelder himself and by Deats.[23] Our present concern has nothing in common with these critiques. Blanchette has a further objection that Muelder's system does not have room for prudence, which he deems an essential aspect of ethics. Yet, certainly, this aspect does find a place, particularly in the laws of specification and the best possible, and may be assumed in the law of the most inclusive end and the law of consequences.

Several answers may be provided for the functioning of moral law (philosophically considered) in Christian ethics. First, following upon our earlier exposition of Muelder, we may say that moral law has been religiously vindicated and raised to a higher status in Christian ethics. Therefore it is no longer necessary to refer to it in action; one need merely to carry out the Christian command. Such an approach would require a systematic exposition of the Christian principles parallel to Muelder's system, in order to ensure the same broad scope of analysis, coherence, and consistency. It would still be necessary, however, to review the human experience and its moral development occasionally in order for Christian ethics (and its principles) to improve itself and to retain relevance. A completely "Christianized ethic," though relevant for the "Koinonia," would lose the "common ground" aspect necessary for relating to secular social institutions and groups. Hence Christian social ethics would remain somewhat defective.

A second answer could be to focus on certain key Christian principles such as the love commandment, the primacy of the kingdom, the Beatitudes, the idea of the responsible society, and so forth, and to interpet these in terms of the moral laws given in Muelder's book. In other words, one could, for instance, determine the most suitable way of implementing the love commandment by applying the moral laws to the moral situation in an effort to acquire consistency, harmony, and coherence in both purpose and action. It seems to me that most authors of Christian social ethics and ecumenical social thought—except those that reject any form of moral law or "coalition ethics"—would concur with this answer. Many actually do, despite certain limitations (in the light of Muelder's development), conform to this approach. Muelder's construction seems to be this approach at its best and most elaborate form. While this kind of relationship between the moral laws and Christian principles appears to follow implicitly from his work, he does not seem to express it explicitly—at least in theory. His exposition is limited to the integration of philosophical and theological ethics in general, without extending it to their principles in particular.

We should continually bear in mind that these laws presuppose scientific aid and illumination, so that carrying them out faithfully implies the use of the social sciences. Thus Muelder's interdisciplinary emphasis is implied even if it may not be directly mentioned. This is Muelder's main rebuff to Potter. Our present concern is how the philosophical and the theological aspects of the moral laws relate to each other in practice.

The final answer concerning this relationship may be one identical to that offered by natural law theory in Catholic teaching, overlooking its defects. Here one may emphasize human conscience as the law implanted by God in every human being; or take Muelder's point that God, if we acknowledge his existence, is the creator of persons as moral beings. The human moral laws such as those examined here would then be regarded as products of both reason and a morally conscious and concerned conscience, and so, consequently, as willed by God himself. One who acted in accordance with them would by that very fact be considered to fulfill God's will and—directly in the case of Christians and indirectly in that of non-Christians—the Christian teaching. In the case of non-Christians it would not be indispensable to use the Christian language and concepts in order to fulfill the moral teaching endorsed by Christianity; there would be no substantial difference between Christian ethics and philosophical ethics so conceived. Nor would Christians have to insist on such language and concepts in addressing social issues, though their approach might presuppose them and their faith in general.

Such an approach, however, would be unacceptable to most Christian theologians who regard their moral teaching as "superior" and as requiring open proclamation, that is, not to be "hidden under a bushel." Muelder has shown, however, how the Christian teaching is affected by the various traditions, cultures, philosophies, and interpretations of the communities it affects. He has also offered clues, both implicitly and explicitly, on the sense in which the Christian teaching can be regarded as more adequate than one that does not have its transcendence and significance. If such Christian transcendence and significance are accepted implicitly in the moral laws (e.g., through the metaphysical law), then philosophical ethics can be Christian in spirit though not in language. Hence the moral laws could be appealed to and fulfilled "in a Christian way," but not necessarily through explicit Christian concepts, in reference to social issues. Explicit proclamation of the gospel does not necessarily encourage imprudence in delicate situations that, nevertheless, could be influenced in other ways to fulfill God's will. This is the whole point of the Catholic emphasis on natural law.

The thesis of this argument is that while such an approach may be unacceptable in a "Koinonia ethic," it would be most suitable in a social ethic directed particularly toward the "children of darkness." This kind of approach would be more meaningful to the organizations considered in this book as they plan their strategies and engage in political and social action. Such organizations and other secularized aspects of their communities often find no practical "this-worldly" significance in the Christian teaching—at least in its "primitive," colonial form. For them a Christian ethic remains a "pie-in-the-sky-when-you-die" ethic. We cannot solve this kind of situation by boasting about the "superiority" of the Christian religion and its ethic. We must affirm the good in these groups' moral orientation and values. Upon this can the Christian teaching build up; its harmony, advantage, as well as contribution to these values unfolded and explicated. We may then introduce this contribution by way of comparison, emphasis, and similar approaches until the relationship between the two approaches toward morality is grasped and acknowledged. Thus the explicit use of the Christian language and teaching need not be abandoned altogether. Even when this relationship has been grasped, however, this method must be retained; for it is a foregone conclusion that the social order will never be completely Christianized.

It is with this background and concern that we set out in the next chapter to evaluate the movements studied in the previous chapters in terms of the moral laws. The final chapter will then go on to investigate alternative strategies to the problem addressed.

Chapter 5

The Moral Significance of the South African Struggle

In chapters 2 and 3 above we were concerned primarily with outlining the policies and practices of the organizations examined in this study. The time has now come to look critically at these organizations, using the moral laws considered in the last chapter as our norms of judgment. Taking the last of these laws seriously, and recognizing the inherent religious and Christian feedback on the rest of the moral laws as a result, the present approach to them will largely presuppose a Christian influence in their implementation. It will not always be necessary to explain what a particular interpretation means in terms of Christian principles. In this way it is hoped that their "common ground" element will be taken seriously and that they will have the double effect intended in the previous chapter: appealing to both Christian and non-Christian participants and observers.

In the present chapter I will extract what appears to be the salient, ethically significant points in the preceding chapters and present them for evaluation. These will include the organizations' positions on majority rule, minority rights, their approach to political action, violence, and the exclusion of whites in the struggle, among others. The goal will be to determine whether, in terms of the standpoints examined, these organizations have been consistent or inconsistent—both theoretically and practically—with respect to the moral laws. This evaluation does not intend to measure these standpoints against each individual moral law. In theory, it seems quite possible to analyze and evaluate a moral situation in terms of all the moral laws. In practice, however, it would appear to be unrealistic and impractical to appeal explicitly to each one of them for every moral decision. Some have more relevance than others in specific situations, though the rest should be kept in the background since all the moral laws comprise a system.

Generally, ethical or moral practice proceeds on the basis of certain internalized values and principles that are presupposed in such practice. Catholic moral theology, for instance, puts a lot of stake on the moral value of an informed conscience and of virtues or good habits.[1] Since Plato, it is commonplace to say that good people produce good deeds rather than the other way around. Paul Deats has spoken of the importance of building "an ethos of world community and [building] *Moral restraints into the character of Christians,* which restraints will function in the lives of citizens, soldiers, policy makers, or resisters."[2] Muelder also emphasizes the importance of an informed conscience in his *Foundations of the Responsible Society.* In the rest of this book Muelder implements the moral laws dealt with in his earlier book, but on the whole without referring to them explicitly.[3] Perhaps the most recent expression of the in-built moral conscience is Wogaman's methodological presumption.[4] Christians, in particular, are said to have strong presumptions for certain practices and against others. Any challenge to these presumptions leaves the burden of proof against them with the challenger.

I have referred to these other studies to show that not too much, indeed, is to be expected as far as an *explicit,* systematic analysis of a moral situation in terms of the moral laws is concerned. The most that can be done is to determine which laws are specifically relevant (positively or negatively) in a particular case, while presupposing the rest of the others in one's judgment. This is the approach we will follow in this chapter.

REVIEW OF GOALS

It has now become clear that all the organizations treated here were generally agreed on the ultimate goals they envisaged for South Africa. They differed mainly in their means toward achieving these goals.

The ANC, however, did not have the same ultimate goal in view from the very beginning but gradually evolved toward the goal of complete equality and majority rule that was the outlook of the PAC and the BCM from their very beginning,[5] as well as of the current three movements. The main goal of the early ANC was merely representation for Africans in Parliament, while the present structure of the political system was not questioned. The ANC was also concerned largely with sociopolitical reforms such as the removal of discrimination, the abolition of the pass system, the improvement of black wages in labor, and so on. These might have been the best *possible* demands it could make under the circumstances and thus in accordance with the law of specification. However, it is also obvious that they were not the *best* ideal values contemplated or that could be realized by the people in their country. Nor were they the most inclusive values insofar as they did not advocate the greatest good possible for the country's total population. Advocating minor reforms in spite of the country's wealth and the suffering of most of its population was almost tantamount to capitulating to the imposed status of fourth-class citizenship for Africans. This implicitly violated the personalistic aspects of the moral laws. Without bold demands for maximum individual fulfillment it is highly improbable that there could be true altruism—far less toward the oppressor—and thus it would also be impossible to fulfill the law of ideal personality. In short, while more ambitious demands might have been thought to be "unrealistic" under the circumstances, the early ANC appeared generally to have no principles to guide it as to the best values to cling tightly to for both blacks and whites in the country.

It was the Youth League of the organization that revised the ANC's conception of its goals and thus revitalized the organization. In so doing, the Youth League became the predecessor of both the PAC and the BCM, and has affected the positions of current organizations. All stood or continue to stand for the policy of majority rule[6] in an egalitarian society. The Youth League stated its demands very strongly, but even after it had made its impact, the ANC still retained its mild approach and often gave an impression of ambivalence with regard to its true goals. Thus even when it endorsed the idea of majority rule, it did not seem to be willing to recognize the full implications of this position.[7] Only after it had been outlawed in the country did the ANC assume a militant position.

The Youth League, the PAC, and the BCM recognized that majority rule in a country that was predominantly black would necessarily imply a predominantly black government. This did not mean that whites would thereby be excluded from the government. Since "race" would be immaterial in such a state, parliamentary representation would focus on persons rather than on groups. For the PAC and BCM this implied an emphasis on individual rather than group rights. Hence minority rights would not be guaranteed but would be implicit in individual rights. Similar views are held by AZAPO, the NF, and the UDF, with varying emphases. The Youth League, on the other hand, did have an explicit provision for the protection of minority rights.[8]

Majority Rule

From the ethical perspective, majority rule, implying political representation by the majority, would appear to be an ideal form of government. The ideal of rule by all, though it would be ethically the best, is practically inconceivable since there are always bound to be dissenting voices. As the most inclusive form of government, majority rule is more likely to have regard for the rights and best interests of most people than a minority form of government. There is also a better chance of the inculcation and encouragement of cooperation among as many persons as possible for common goals and values in this than in any other form of government.

J. Philip Wogaman has cited the concept of majority rule as one of four "interlocking principles of democratic ideology." The other three are popular sovereignty, equality before the law, and secure civil rights and liberties. Three of these principles, including majority rule, were seen as corollaries of popular sovereignty. Majority rule, according to Wogaman, presupposes equality of all before the law and equal civil rights and liberties. Since unanimity on policy questions cannot always be reached, the majority of persons must carry the presumption (of rightness) over the minority: "there is a greater probability of rightness attached to the views of the majority than to those of any given minority."[9] This, of course, does not imply that minority rights to dissent can be easily violated.

There seems to be little doubt, if any, that all the movements examined, following the ANCYL, had in view similar ideals expressed here for the rest of the people in the country, regardless of their ethnic background or cultural outlook—in spite of their different approaches to the question of minority rights. Both the Youth League and the PAC spoke, implictly or explicitly, of an "inclusive nationalism" of black and white *after* the African had attained his liberation. Even in the BCM, the idea of such a "nationalism" was implicit, while it continues to be explicit in the current movements. In the first two organizations this ideal was contained in the statement that anyone who paid his full allegiance to Africa and to the principles of democracy would be regarded as an African.[10] Such an ideal, adhered to in full compliance with the concept of majority rule and its implications, would be well in accordance with most of the moral laws—except perhaps the final, metaphysical law, which would not be directly relevant. The state would aim at the best possible and most inclusive values for all in accordance with the country's material, spiritual, and cultural resources. Everyone would be able to enjoy, with the cooperation of others, the greatest values of which he or she is capable and there would be mutual assistance toward the achievement of common values.

Some of the conditions laid down for the envisaged "nationalism," however, seem to militate against the spirit of the moral laws. For instance, it was generally recognized and emphasized that Africa was a "black man's country." Hence the Youth League and the PAC took it as logical that the leader of Africans had to "come from their loins."

Such a conclusion would apparently, though not necessarily, be inevitable upon the advent of majority rule. However, intentionally aiming at black leadership would appear to foreclose any possibility of having white leaders even if they might be elected by the majority. This would be discriminatory, undemocratic, and consequently retrogressive. Most of the laws that would otherwise support the ideal of majority rule would then be contradicted, especially the law of the best possible, the law of the most inclusive end, the logical law, and the law of consequences, as well as the personalistic aspects. It should be noted, of course, that taken by itself, the statement that the leader of Africans should "come from their loins" is not necessarily inconsistent with the moral laws—especially if it presupposes the idea of an "inclusive nationalism." Only if the statement is made the conclusion of "Africa is a black man's country" do serious questions arise.

The PAC did state explicitly that majority rule did not imply that a white person might not be elected to Parliament: "for colour will count for nothing in a free Africa."[11] It is not clear if this meant that he might also become a prime minister. The answer to this would depend on whether the statement follows the expression of common "nationalism" or that of the country and continent belonging to black people. On the whole, however, it seems that the PAC had moved to a more open outlook on this issue than had the Youth League. The ANC (Old Guard), insofar as it was for majority rule, also rejected color criteria in any area of the future South Africa, and the BMC's position was almost similar to that of the PAC, as are those of all current movements, *mutatis mutandis*.

The PAC and the BCM expressed the future goal of "inclusive nationalism" in the concept of a nonracial society, which implied equality and common brotherhood compatible with the spirit of all the moral laws and the Christian principle of love. AZAPO, the NF, and the UDF also envisage the same goal along similar lines. The ANC, on the other hand, stood for a policy of "multiracialism," which the other two earlier groups rejected, and both AZAPO and the NF still do, as "racialism multiplied." While it is true that people's external and cultural differences have to be accepted rather than wished away, the idea of "multiracialism," insofar as it lays emphasis on "racial groups" rather than on persons as such, appears to be less ideal and inclusive in terms of the moral laws. It may be incompatible with the personalistic aspects: persons are not valued for their own sakes but as part of an exclusive "racial" group. Because of the expressed desire to work together for the common good, the communitarian laws may not be completely violated. They cannot be completely fulfilled, however, because "racial" considerations always place certain limitations on human action. Primary allegiance is to the group rather than to the whole community. Thus it becomes questionable to what extent even the axiological aspects of the moral laws can be fulfilled, especially with regard to consequences and the axiological trinity: the best possible, the axiological law, and the most inclusive end.

While all these groups aimed or still aim at majority rule, therefore, their total commitment to it seems to have varied—and still does for the new movements. Would color still be the criterion for leadership? Would it still play any part at all in the ideal society? All desired the minimization, if not the complete eradication, of color influence. Even those who spoke in terms of "multiracialism" instead of "nonracialism" believed, in the final analysis, that this was merely a semantic rather than a factual debate. The common goal was—and still is—that of a common society where black and white would cooperate on the basis of human brotherhood and patriotism rather than the color of the skin.

The Status of Minority Rights

As already indicated, among the groups discussed only the ANC, by virtue of its Youth League, had provisions for the protection of the rights of minorities. The PAC and the BCM rejected this idea, as do AZAPO, the NF, and the UDF. They understood it to mean the continuation of the present, ethnically stratified system, with special privileges for a few. In this sense, "minority" was understood to stand for "ethnic minority." Such special privileges for a few were rejected out of hand in favor of undifferentiated individual rights. The question arises: If personality reigns in the form of majority rule, without any regard to color, ethnic, or cultural background, is there still any necessity to guarantee (explicitly) minority rights, particularly ethnic ones?

In a country such as the United States this has seemed necessary in order to attain parity and equalization of sociopolitical benefits for all. Thus, through the Affirmative Action Program, the law favors minorities on certain rights of which they have been deprived in the past. Supposing parity were to be achieved and the rights of individuals fully implemented socially, would the Affirmative Action Program still have relevance? It seems not, though human nature would seem to render such an achievement utopian. But then, human dreams have a utopian element in them; otherwise some human aspirations—especially those that appear difficult to achieve—would not be pursued at all. If, therefore, the Affirmative Action Program were to be no longer relevant, would its scrapping necessarily lead to the state of affairs similar to that before its implementation? One cannot answer this question categorically.

Were the Affirmative Action Program to be completely successful, it seems that we would have a situation where individual rights are fully acknowledged and respected. This, by implication, would mean also the recognition of individual rights to association and, therefore, to forming and participating in whatever groups individuals pleased. Some of these groups might well turn out to be ethnic in constitution or even hold views opposed to those of the majority, but would not thereby be outlawed. Thus we may have religious groups, cultural groups, the Broederbond, and the like. Such groups, however, may not be recognized as groups but merely by virtue of the individuals participating in them. This seems to have been the kind of indirect approach to minority rights envisaged by both the PAC and the BCM, while at the same time avoiding the danger of seeming to sanction the present system of ethnic inequality.

Such an approach to minority rights would, indeed, be ideal if it were practicable. It would be both "color blind" and "blind" to all the differences that cause conflict among groups, while at the same time ensuring the unity-in-diversity type of equilibrium in society. It would also be in accordance with the "blindness" to personal and group statuses expressed in the New Testament, as well as be in fulfillment of the moral laws, especially their personalistic and communitarian aspects. Individuals would be respected as persons rather than as members of a particular group, and the entire community would function cooperatively for the general good rather than for sectarian interests, even within specific interest groups.

Many ethicists doubt, however, if such an ideal is possible and would insist on the explicit protection and guaranteeing of minority rights. "Nothing is to prevent a majority from running rough-shod over a minority," some stress.[12] Without special guarantees for minority rights, even in preference of higher aims and ideals as envisaged by the PAC, the BCM, AZAPO, and the current alliances, it is felt that such rights cannot be ensured at all. Speaking of minority associations, Pope John XXIII stressed that their establishment is "by all means necessary" because they are "capable of achieving a goal which an individual cannot effectively gain by himself." These associations are, according to him, "indispensable means to safeguard the dignity of the human person and freedom while leaving intact a sense of responsibility."[13] Deats quotes a three-man dialogue written by Walter Lippman and related to this issue. It runs as follows:

Socrates: Is the right of the majority to rule a fundamental principle?
  Bryan: It is.
Socrates: Is freedom of thought a fundamental principle, Mr. Jefferson?
Jefferson: It is.
Socrates: Well, how would you gentlemen compose fundamental prin-
          ciples, if a majority ordained that only Buddhism should be
          taught in the public school?
  Bryan: I'd move to a Christian country.
Jefferson: I'd exercise the sacred right of revolution. What would you
          do, Socrates?
Socrates: I'd reexamine my fundamental principles.[14]

The message of this dialogue is quite clear: namely, that minority rights
are not necessarily implied or guaranteed by virtue of majority rule. The
conclusion for the organizations discussed seems to be that, while it
would certainly be more preferable and more compatible with the
moral laws to guarantee full individual rights and thus minority rights
only indirectly by implication, human imperfection (or sinfulness)
makes it imperative for us to go against our better judgment and ensure
that minorities do not suffer because of our utopian ideals. Indeed, this
is a reminder of St. Paul's frustration: "I don't do the good I want to
do; instead, I do the evil that I do not want to do" (Rom. 7:19). The
moral law mainly pertinent to these considerations is that of consequences. Adverse consequences to our ideals here might lead also to
the violation of most of the laws in the system.

As for the reexamination of fundamental principles proposed by
"Socrates," however, it is hard to see what other direction it can go than
attempting to perfect the majority rule system and making it more
"fool-proof" or less liable to discrimination. Is this not what the United
States is attempting to do with its desegregation laws and the Affirmative Action Program? This is in agreement with traditional political
philosophy or what Michael Walzer endorses as a "piece of conven-
tional wisdom": "that governments derive their just powers from the
consent of the governed."[15] A minority government without the consent of the majority of the governed is, hence, almost illegal—especially
if it is unjustly imposed on them. It would be difficult to justify through
the moral laws. It follows that majority rule, as long as it has genuine
regard for the good of all and special provisions for the protection of
the rights of minorities, will necessarily be found to be the ideal form
of government.

REVIEW OF STRATEGIES

None of the six organizations completely followed a strategy similar to that of another. Like its goals, the ANC's strategy was affected by the emergence of the Youth League within it. At this time, the ANC jettisoned the long outdated method of petitions and negotiations, which had perhaps been consistent with the initial, limited goal. In its place it adopted a Program of Action and the policy of noncooperation with oppressive structures. The PAC and the BCM later followed this policy, as do the latest movements. It meant that each organization would stop trying to negotiate with the government and stop participating in the channels of representation set aside for blacks by the government but that had no influence or authority. For the later ANC such noncooperation meant engaging in acts of civil disobedience if certain demands were not met. The Defiance Campaign of 1952 was a climax of this policy. The PAC started differently, but ended with its Positive Action Campaign, which was almost a repetition of the ANC's Defiance Campaign. The BCM took a different approach altogether and remained faithful to it until the end. It coupled its tactics of noncooperation with relative withdrawal from direct action vis-à-vis the government, addressing itself to the immediate political and social needs of black people primarily through consciousness raising. Current organizations have variously implemented what the UDF refers to as the politics of refusal.

Noncooperation

The decision no longer to cooperate or negotiate with the government was born out of forty years[16] of frustration and fruitless attempts to work for change in a peaceful, reconciliatory, and "civilized" manner. Not only had the government not responded to these endeavors, it had also dealt with them brutally on many occasions. This step of the struggle, therefore, appeared to have been long overdue.

The ANC did not reject negotiation altogether. Its political activity normally began with attempts at negotiation, threatening noncooperation if not heeded. This was a sign of refusal to believe that all its years of negotiation could have come to nothing and still continue to remain worthless. It may also be interpreted as a strong indication of faith in fellow human beings and in their capacity for conversion and for sympathy. Since this approach continued to have no effect, the PAC, followed by the BCM, had a change of attitude. These two bodies put aside negotiation attempts altogether and adopted an almost complete noncooperative stance—a trend that is continuing in present-day black politics. The PAC did negotiate on a technical issue once, however, before it embarked upon its Positive Action Campaign. This was when it cautioned the commissioner of police in Johannesburg against police brutality on participants of the planned campaign.

Though refusal to negotiate (communicate) with a fellow human being is a denial of his moral and spiritual dignity and, therefore, a negative judgment upon his personality, it is difficult to guess how meaningful continued negotiation might have been considering past precedents. Merton and Muelder have suggested that one of the reasons for the failure of nonviolent resistance is that little attention is given to its methods and techniques.[17] At the same time, Sharp affirms that there is "no cut and dried answer concerning how this technique might be applied in a multitude of situations in which there is now widespread ultimate reliance on violence. There are no carefully worked out plans."[18] Could it be that the refusal to continue cooperating and attempting to negotiate with the government on the part of the South African resistance movements was untimely or ignorantly carried out in terms of the situation? What could have been the best way(s) of carrying it out to be successful in this particular situation? The failure of noncooperation in early resistance implied a possible violation of the law of consequences during planning, which should have counseled the weighing of the pros and cons of several nonviolent methods before a final choice was made. If this was done, on the other hand, noncooperation might have been found to be the best possible strategy and thus in accordance with this law. Thus, the law of consequences would also not have been broken. But if noncooperation had been found to be the best possible method and yet failed, this would mean—unless the criticisms of Merton and Muelder are applicable here—that all nonviolent methods had their limitations in the South African situation.[19] If the movements concerned were intent on remaining nonviolent, they would then be faced with the dilemma of continuing to employ this inefficient method—since it was, notwithstanding, the best possible—or returning to the old method of petitions and negotiations. As there can be only one best possible strategy, however, the latter method would itself be canceled by the choice of noncooperation. The conclusion would then appear to be that a stalemate had been reached, and unless new vigor and creativeness could be injected into this choice, the struggle would have turned into a pastime and thus be unworthy of the name. This would mean that the moral goal of the struggle had been nipped in the bud through the breaking of the logical law, and so it would not even be necessary to consider how the other moral laws might apply.

Sociopolitical Action

On the whole, the political activities of these bodies held unequal ethical and political significance. The ANC's Defiance Campaign was a political precedent. As almost a repetition of it, with little improvement (if any), the PAC's Positive Action Campaign was ethically idle. Its leaders did not weigh the cost seriously on the basis of past experience. The fact that the ANC's campaign did not succeed in bringing about change suggests that either it was not the right strategy at the time or had certain defects. Gene Sharp believes that the greatest blunder the ANC leadership committed in the Defiance Campaign was to yield to the government's repressive measures when the campaign was at its peak.[20] According to him, the organization's success and credibility depended largely on its response at this very point. "Withdrawal at such a point allows the government to regain the upper hand and for an atmosphere of fear and conformity again to become predominant." Sharp sees the "primary requirement of change" as willingness to undergo imprisonment and other forms of suffering rather than succumbing voluntarily to (apparently minor) penalties such as bannings and house arrests. He directs the same criticism at the PAC and its Positive Action Campaign.

What Sharp seems to overlook, particularly in the case of the PAC, but also in general, is that almost all leaders of both the PAC and the ANC were detained or convicted after Sharpeville. By the time some of them were released, their organizations were banned. Rather than intensify the struggle, the people were leaderless and demoralized. How far, indeed, can any struggle or campaign go without leaders? It might be more symbolic for the leaders to go to prison than to languish quietly under house arrest; but of what good is this if there are no replacements—or is leadership dispensable? During the 1970s and especially after Soweto, the government showed that it could detain and deal with a succession of leaders *ad infinitum,* leaving only those who are prepared to collaborate with it. Does Sharp see any value in leadership—especially good leadership—at all? While Sharp, at the end of his series of articles, offers general suggestions for change in South Africa, he does not answer this particular question.[21]

While the Positive Action Campaign suffered from moral shortsightedness, it excelled the Defiance Campaign in political portent. The question it raises is whether the immediate results (increased political awareness and interest among blacks) warranted the cost in lives. The law of consequences does not seem to have been weighed sufficiently, particularly in view of the experience during the Defiance Campaign. Since the Positive Action Campaign was meant to excel the Defiance

Campaign, it was certainly seen by its leaders as the best possible to date. But this conclusion was contradicted by the lack of near accurate calculation in accordance with the other laws, particularly that of consequences. Theoretically, this campaign was more related to the ultimate goals intended than was that of the ANC. It was seen as the first of a chain of activities that would persist until liberation was won. The emphasis of the Defiance Campaign, on the other hand, was on immediate, alleviatory goals. While quite radical at its time, it lacked the dynamism of a future oriented movement. It aimed at the apparently possible, but not the best. Hence its end was not most inclusive, and it sacrificed all the ideals in the moral laws: ideal personality, ideal community, and ideal control. There was also the danger that these secondary goals might be turned into the main goal of the struggle and thus the ultimate end never addressed. Those who criticized the ANC of reformism already believed this to be the case. The 1984 "politics of protest" of the newer groups may be viewed in the same light.

As forms of civil disobedience,[22] both the Defiance Campaign and the Positive Action Campaign might be morally justified by the fact that they were aimed against an unjust political system that was not prepared to negotiate with the organizations involved—or with the people they represented—toward a better and just society. Such disobedience is now generally recognized as long as it remains nonviolent and those who engage in it are prepared to accept punishment for their actions, since it is a challenge to the law of the state even though it may be unjust.[23] The tradition of civil disobedience is now commonly associated with Thoreau, Gandhi, and Martin Luther King, Jr., though they are not its originators.

Both campaigns were marred and brought prematurely to their end by riots. The ANC managed to survive a few years after its campaign but was finally crushed by the government with the PAC, after its leaders had been subjected to various forms of persecution. On the whole, the oversight of three closely related moral laws—the logical law, the law of consequences, and the law of specification—was specifically responsible for their failure, though we must not minimize, for its part, the intransigence of the government.

The BCM engaged in no direct political activity against the government, coming closest with the 1972/73 student strikes, but particularly during the "Viva Frelimo" rallies in 1974. The former activity was undertaken in support of a fellow student and leader who had been expelled from college for pointing out the government's double standards affecting blacks and whites in the educational field. Its initial aim was to have the student reinstated. The strike soon lost its focus, though, and other demands, crucial for students but of secondary importance under the circumstances, were added. Primarily the law of specification was not carried out by these demands, and the logical law and the law of consequences also suffered, since the main object of the strike was clouded by side issues. The problem was not one of the validity of other moral claims to fair treatment of students and to equal educational opportunities but rather one of priorities at the time.

The "Viva Frelimo" rallies also turned into a challenge of the government only when they were banned at the last moment. A momentous decision involving the safety of the people (who, unaware of the ban on the rallies, might have had to face the wrath of the police alone) had to be made, which did not retract from the position and consistency of the movement. This decision was especially compatible with the law of altruism—concern for the neighbor's safety—as well as those of consequences and specification. Given sufficient time, the movement might have complied with the government's ban.

The 1984 "politics of protest," reflected in resistance to the government's constitutional proposals by the UDF, the NF, and AZAPO, may to some extent, in theory, be related to the ANC's and PAC's campaigns. They differed from these, however, in that the latter were aggressive acts whereas the former were defiant in the sense of negating the government's overtures. In the UDF's own words, it was engaging in the "politics of refusal." Insofar as they were aimed at the short-term goal of discouraging support of the government's constitutional proposals, they were consistent with their aim. To the extent that they were later applied toward the long-term objective of a future South Africa, they were inconsistent as well as unequal to the task. The moral laws mainly affected here are the logical law, the law of consequences, and the law of specification, as in the case of the earlier movements.

Riot Situations

The riots resulting from both the earlier campaigns of civil disobedience had been anticipated and cautioned against by each group. In both cases the organizations had strongly counseled nonviolence, and it was generally believed that the police were actively involved in inciting violence later. Whatever the origin of the riots, it is clear that the people were not prepared to suffer passively but rather reacted in kind. Thus they differed from both Gandhi's followers in India earlier and those of Martin Luther King, Jr., in the United States about the same time.[24] The reasons for the difference might not be as simple as they appear at first sight. The natural question to ask is whether the ANC and the PAC had taken sufficient time to prepare their followers for the nonviolence they advocated. If so, was this preparation adequate? Did they measure the foreseeable consequences—both manifest and latent? As far as the ANC is concerned, there is no doubt that it did spend some days preparing its following for nonviolent action. Whether a few days of preparation was adequate or not—or whether this question is relevant or not—is a different matter. It has been suggested that noncooperation, among other forms of nonviolent resistance, while requiring large numbers, does not necessarily require a large degree of special training for all participants.[25] Certainly, however, training here cannot be referring to discipline, which seems to be the most important aspect of nonviolent resistance. In the case of the PAC, there was apparently less training even in the sense of discipline. The Positive Action Campaign was the result of a sudden decision and there was no time at all for the organization to prepare its following for nonviolent action, except for last-minute exhortations.

We must remember, nevertheless, that during the campaign anyone could participate even if he or she did not actively support the organization or know of its nonviolence stance. Hence there was no way in which nonviolence could be completely guaranteed or rioting forestalled, even if allegations of police incitement were not true. Would considerations of such possible consequences have discouraged the leaders of these organizations from undertaking their campaigns? This seems to depend on what they thought were their chances of overall success (the law of the best possible) and of curbing such possible violence (the law of consequences). If the campaigns were canceled in view of the latter law, the time might never be ripe for undertaking them, especially because the absence of *agents provocateurs*—if they were taken into consideration in the decision—can never be guaranteed. There is always a risk of faith in all ethical decisions and in anything undertaken in search of change. It follows that every political activity, more so if it is of a revolutionary nature, must allow for a certain amount of risk. Consequently, that civil disobedience in South Africa always seemed to end in violence whereas *on certain occasions* in India and the USA it did not, is not an indication that South African nonviolence advocates were less ethical or less disciplined than Gandhi or King, though this might well have been the case. It must be granted, though, that for them nonviolence was mostly only a strategy, while for Gandhi and King it was also a way of life as well as a theological and moral principle.[26]

Once more, the BCM features very little where questions of riots are involved. During the student strikes and the "Viva Frelimo" rallies there does not appear to have been much rioting, in spite of police brutality. As I have already suggested, the Soweto uprising affected the

BCM only indirectly as its manifestation. The violence that issued from it could not be attributed to any particular black consciousness organization, and therefore cannot be blamed directly upon the movement.

As a manifestation of black consciousness, though, the uprising must be accounted for in part—though only indirectly—by the movement, in the same way as the movement takes credit for its positive aspects. The manifestation itself represents part of the latent consequences of the BCM, which the movement should have anticipated to some extent in its inaugural plans. It is not always clear, however, to what extent latent consequences are to be anticipated by an individual or a group. According to Walzer,

> It may be necessary for a man contemplating civil disobedience to worry about the possibilities of revolutionary violence, but only if such possibilities actually exist. It is by no means necessary for him to reflect upon the purely theoretical possibility that this action might be universalized, that all men [or some like him] might break the laws or claim exemptions from them.[27]

What Walzer says here is equally applicable to an organization. He further observes, "It is never possible to know in advance the course of the mass movement or the historic shape of the long revolution."[28] For this reason, he suggests, possible improvements in such movements must always be considered—in fact, there is always room for improvement in a mass movement.

In the case of the BCM, even if the movement had weighed and foreseen the imminent consequences, it might still have thought that the goals to be achieved were greater than and worthy of the immediate negative consequences of its approach—if these were deemed unavoidable—particularly because of their unintended nature. This would be well in accordance with the law of the best possible. Nevertheless, this raises the question whether ethical action, particularly in terms of the moral laws employed here, is an all-or-none process: How much can some of the moral laws be sacrificed without rendering the whole ethical venture abortive, that is, without violating the internal coherence on which they depend for moral consistency?

The internal coherence of the moral laws seems to imply that these laws, taken seriously together, constitute some kind of comprehensive ethical system. We must hasten to repeat that they do not prescribe specific moral action, namely, whether this particular act or that is *always* right or wrong and thus whether it must always be done or not. They are regulative principles to guide ethical reflection and action. Each one of them, taken seriously, compels the moral agent to rethink carefully, revise and readjust if necessary, his prospective act to its best conceivable and moral form rather than that the law should be adjusted to suit a morally questionable act. This does not mean that this use of the moral laws cannot err: there is always the problem of mistaken intentions. The moral laws do, therefore, constitute an all-or-none ethical system, though their faithful fulfillment is often restricted by the limits of human perception. None of them can be fully grasped in isolation from the others, "for each is logically abstracted from the whole."[29]

In their application, the moral laws must stick together and, as such, cohere with the moral situation. Muelder illustrates this point with a quotation from Bertocci. In the moral situation, "reason must allow every part [of experience] to speak, but it must go on to assess the relation of the parts to each other with a view to discovering what the testimony of the whole reveals."[30] A final moral decision may thus be understood as some kind of common denominator issuing from all the moral laws. We can expect that some of the laws often will be more relevant than others in certain situations, thus requiring special emphasis. This puts the moral laws generally in a state of tension with one another, often resulting in some conflict among them. Within the moral laws themselves, however, are built-in moderators or, to put it crudely, laws with some kind of veto power. These laws do not necessarily disqualify the others in case of a conflict. They merely have the last word in determining the best possible way of resolving the conflict and reaching a satisfactory moral decision under the circumstances. These laws are those of specification, the best possible, the most inclusive end, and the general appeal to personality (including the communitarian laws). The law of specification provides legitimation for focusing upon the needs of the immediate situation. It also "protects from the errors of abstract idealism under historical circumstances."[31] It is supplemented by the law of the best possible, which determines the best possible form of action to take under given circumstances. The two laws interpenetrate each other: The law of the most inclusive end is a corollary of the law of the best possible. It seeks to assure the most inclusive and equitable distribution of values within the limits of the situation. Finally, and perhaps even most important, the appeal to personality in general seeks to ascertain that whatever the difficulties of the situation, all persons shall continue to be treated as ends in themselves and not merely as means. When the final weight of appeal is laid on these laws or any one of them, a risk is taken, acknowledging the precarious nature of moral decision-making in general. This risk reflects the active nature of moral coherence, which is applied in an emergent decision.

Moral law ethicists who are also Christian theologians often find appeal to Christian values and convictions reassuring in such cases of moral predicament. This appeal is seen not as an abandonment of the moral laws, but rather as their reinforcement, for even Christian ethics presupposes the moral laws.[32] Christian principles and the moral laws are mutually supplementary, as I argued previously.[33] Muelder himself makes this kind of appeal particularly in dealing with matters of war or violence and nonviolence, probably impelled by what Wogaman has called Christian methodological presumptions. In doing this, Muelder—in accordance with his personalism—certainly lays strong emphasis on the personalistic value of human dignity and the Christian value of respect for human life. Since the focal point of the moral laws, as of ethics in general, is the human person and the ideal of community, this bias seems quite understandable and logical. However, it often seems also rather farfetched and abstract, especially when numbers are involved. The moral laws studied here certainly have their bias in responding to such questions, but cannot offer a definitive answer apart from the moral situation. While they are definitely oriented toward value attainment, they cannot be casuistic about possible exceptional or difficult cases: they do not "prescribe antecedently" any special moral content.[34] They respond to the actual situation in accordance with its demands as perceived by the moral agent. On the other hand, it seems possible to go beyond their dictates (without reducing their commands) and make a permanent commitment on the basis of one's religious conviction, thus supplementing them. This is what moral law ethicists such as Muelder and Deats do in their pacifist convictions and as Christian theologians who place special significance on the death of Jesus on the cross. Such a permanent commitment would not be possible on the basis of the moral laws alone.

From this general discussion of coherence in the moral laws it follows that the BCM—as indeed the ANC and the PAC—was not exempted from weighing seriously the consequences of its actions as a resistance movement, not only upon its members but also upon the community at large and possible negative reaction by it. However, Walzer's point must be taken, and human finitude must—however zealous we may be—be granted particularly in calculating remote consequences. Hence the risk of faith in moral decision-making. Such risk has often been called the basis of an "ethic of distress," of which Goulet has written that

> every ethic except supreme non-violent heroism places men in a distress situation in the face of revolutionary conditions, for it is impossible to follow one course of action to its ultimate consequences without betraying certain ethical values. The reason is that once human conditions reach a certain point, there exists no

fully moral manner of eliminating evil, of attenuating it. In quite literal terms, an ethical dilemma is posed.[35]

The South African situation was worsened by the fact that even after violence had broken out, it was not possible for the leaders of the movements to provide crisis leadership because of instant disciplinary and retaliatory measures taken against them by the government. Such leadership might conceivably have minimized the overall damages particularly in persons' lives by providing guidance that would have shortened the duration of the riots.

Insofar as there have been riot situations in the activities and campaigns of AZAPO, the NF, and the UDF, the preceding argument applies to them as well. A further concern arising from these movements, however, was their animosity toward one another and the fighting that resulted from it. Such fighting was, of course, completely against the aims of the struggle and violated all the moral laws, particularly those of personalism, autonomy, and consequences. The apparent lack of tolerance for the different opinions of others, resulting in their physical abuse, violated their personality and their autonomy of decision. On the other hand, this violent confrontation made it possible for the government to act on the organizations, as it has been alleged, and to capitalize on their lack of tolerance in order to demonstrate the chaos that would allegedly follow black rule in South Africa. Appeal to the laws of cooperation and the ideal of community would be necessary to bring about reconciliation and to restore moral integrity to the objectives of these movements.

Final Violent Confrontation

The problem of police interference and obstruction in the quest for change has led many in South Africa to conclude that change in the country will never be achieved through nonviolent means. The days of nonviolence, it is felt, are over. This conclusion was first reached after the outlawing of the ANC and the PAC in 1960. Although the BCM continued the nonviolent approach in the late sixties until it was banned, it left open the possibility that nonviolence might not be the only way. As an exiled movement, now, it has certainly despaired of nonviolent change. The important question of whether there are any nonviolent options for movements operating in exile is beyond the limits of this study.

Immediately after their banning, the ANC and the PAC evolved violent, underground strategies. To them it was clear that their way of nonviolence had failed to move the hearts of those who rule black people without their consent. There was now nothing left, it was felt, but to resort to force. Surely continuing nonviolent action within the country presupposes the ability to continue organizing and operating freely and openly. If the outlawing of these organizations did not constitute at least some justification for resort to violence—provided such action met certain conditions and fulfilled the moral laws—what does? Yet while such resort might be sanctioned by laws such as the logical, best possible, and specification, it might still be checked by others, especially that of consequences.

It might well be that the ANC and the PAC had no sufficient knowledge on how to employ nonviolent means. What they were certain about at the final stage of their internal struggle, however, was that nearly fifty years[36] of nonviolent confrontation had been almost fruitless. It became clear to them that the problem was not a rational but a psychological one. It was not their inability to convince the government and its electorate that blacks meant well but rather years and years of domination and exploitation that made it difficult for whites to let go of their unjust system. The question was, How does one deal with "racial" hostility and discrimination—with psychological antagonism?

In most cases this has led to the use of brute force as the "only" remedy. Protagonists of nonviolent resistance deny, however, that this can be the *only* remedy in any "special" case. Gandhi and King believed that self-suffering is the most potent remedy against this kind of "enemy." Suffering, wrote Gandhi, "is infinitely more than the law of the jungle for converting the opponent and opening his ears, which are otherwise shut, to the voice of reason." King believed that unearned suffering is redemptive.[37] In South Africa, though, self-suffering, rather than move the heart of the oppressor as both King and Gandhi thought was finally possible, seems to be an indication of weakness to him and thus something to be exploited to the full to drive home the point that it is a waste of time. In a statement quoted earlier, Prime Minister Vorster made it clear that if some of the South African black clergy thought they could do in South Africa what King did in America, "forget it!"

It seems, for many ethicists, that people must first be exterminated before the oppressor's heart can be moved, if at all. Hitler did not willingly surrender his goal of wiping the Jews from the face of the earth. Robert Brown's encounter as a student and his sympathy with Jewish students whose parents lived through the terror of Hitler's Germany led him to the conclusion—though his general view on violence/nonviolence changed twice again later—that "pacifism was at least not a technique that could be expected to 'work' against a diabolical force like Nazism."[38] The South African "homeland" system has been compared to—if only more subtle—Hitler's concentration camps, where black people and their childern are allowed to "suffer peacefully." Because the press (as, indeed, most white South Africans themselves) is barred from its brutal manifestations and because the rest of the world is only remotely and incidentally aware of it, no one, except those who are directly involved, knows the exact damage produced by the system. This is not only a matter of statistics but of human life and dignity. How, therefore, can outsiders really be convinced of the urgency of the situation and how can they help—if at all—before the people are irrevo-cably driven into despair and retaliatory as well as self-sacrificial vi-olence as is continually threatened of late?

The South African problem, as is the case in most exploitative governments, is the problem of the sharing of values—material, spir-itual, and cultural. A group of selfish people seeks to have and retain all, leaving the majority with crumbs and thus subjugating them. This ten-dency has no regard for the moral laws, particularly the personalistic and communitarian aspects, as well as the law of the most inclusive end. Those seeking to change the system must necessarily seek to realize these laws for the benefit of all, but are first confronted with the ques-tion of how to get rid of the present state of affairs. If nonviolence is—rightly or wrongly—thought to have failed, and rather serves to perpet-uate the system, yet continues to be used, a number of moral laws are directly violated. These are, in particular, the logical law and the law of consequences, the law of the best possible, and the law of specification. This in itself precludes the realization of sought values, and con-sequently the fulfillment of all the other laws. If violent action is seen as the answer, the status of the law of consequences is precarious under the present circumstances in the country, though the other three laws may recommend this form of action. Further, this violates a different set of laws, namely, the personalistic and communitarian aspects. This may be regarded as their "temporary" suspension until the situation has been restored to normality. Can this be permissible? We are confronted with the situation of conflict described earlier, with various laws seem-ing to recommend different actions. There can be no simple "yes or no" answer either for violence or for nonviolence—except that the bias for nonviolence always remains in the background—nor can the moral laws "casuistically" prescribe their own violation. The final decision, it would seem, will hang on the four laws referred to earlier as "built-in moderators" within the moral laws and can be made only in actual en-gagement in the moral situation—not in speculation outside it.

It is interesting to note that those who take a strong position on the means of nonviolence as against violence do so mostly on religious grounds rather than on purely ethical ones. Those who reject such a position, however, are quick to remind them that Jesus said the Sabbath (principle) was made for man; not man for the Sabbath. While the moral laws, notably their personalistic aspects, would see nonviolence toward the human person as a normal way of life and would, therefore, be opposed to violence, it is not in their nature as formal laws to prescribe the moral content or to prejudge the situation—as we have been emphasizing all along. Room must be left for analysis of the situation as a whole. The best possible course of action must be determined in terms of the moral laws themselves.

We have already mentioned how Muelder and Deats are able to remain strong advocates of pacifism and still be faithful to their moral law professions. Both believe that any resort to violence, if at all justifiable, can be only through appeal to the just war theory. For a moral law theorist this would not necessarily mean an abandonment of the moral laws, since the determinants of the just war can be calculated through reference to these laws. Though Muelder (and Deats as well) reluctantly concedes the possibility of violence as the last resort, he nevertheless acknowleges that the

> double criterion of egalitarian power and development tends to shift the argument from absolutising either violence or nonviolence by appealing to the conviction that Christianity is not a set of fixed rules, but an existential commitment to justice and redemption in widely differing circumstances.[39]

Nor are the moral laws themselves fixed rules of action but are methodological principles of decision making. Muelder's Christian convictions, which both inform his pacifism and reinforce his moral law beliefs, are quite strong, however. Thus, having reluctantly come to recognize that "at most, to be just, a violent revolution can only be a last resort," he hastens to add: "A people so disciplined as to meet the criteria of such a revolution might well do better by the strategies of non-violence."[40] Nevertheless, if, after weighing all the cost, violence is still found to be the "best" way out, one must resort to it with some fear and trembling and leave it to the mercy of God.[41] However reluctantly conceded, this qualifier offers some relief to those who would see some conflict between nonviolence and the ultimate demands of the situation.

Wogaman's own method of methodological presumption is less strict than Muelder's approach, if only because Wogaman is not a pacifist. According to his method, Christians, by virtue of their faith and its ethic, have a strong presumption against violence to a fellow human being. Because of this presumption, anyone who wishes to challenge the Christian position on violence must bear the burden of proof and show why the contrary is justified on a particular instance. In fact,

Muelder's rejection of violence as a means of settling disputes is based on this method. In the final analysis, Muelder's position is more absolute. Wogaman makes this concession:

> The reader will note that I am very seriously opposed to killing. But the point is that those perfectionists who are willing to sacrifice all concern for the conditions of human existence when necessary to guard what they consider to be perfect obedience to the loving command of God may have undermined the basis of their own case by casting doubt upon the whole realm of worldly conditions and bodily wellbeing.[42]

We may compare the two with Brown's just war approach. As he puts it:

> We are left, then, with a position that must in principle allow for the possibility of violence as a last resort, when all else fails, but that will have numerous safeguards built into it to ensure *that no one easily or prematurely decides that the last resort has been reached*. If properly understood, this need not be a moral cop-out, either in the direction of allowing easy rationalizations for the use of violence, or in the direction of misinterpreting non-violence as disengagement from conflict.[43]

The violent phase of the struggle undertaken by the ANC and the PAC after 1960 might have been a last resort—at least in the eyes of the parties concerned—if only because they were no longer allowed to function openly. However, because of its desperate and hopeless nature, it can certainly not be justified in terms of the moral laws—or even prudence, for that matter. The ANC, at least, gave a little consideration to the problem of violence and its consequences. The PAC does not *seem* to have done so. The ANC rejected killing human beings as yet unwarranted by the current stage of its struggle and wanted to avoid its postrevolutionary effects. This led it to choose sabotage in preference to guerrilla warfare and terrorism as the "best" form of violence to employ at the time.

The term *violence* here requires a little interpretation. Violence is often associated with causing harm or injury to human beings. Citing the WCC's Cardiff Consultation's definition of power, violence, and coercion as adopted from Gene Sharp, Deats defines violence as "the infliction of physical harm or injury, or death to persons, or the threat to do so." Deats also sees force as an inclusive category, while violence goes beyond authorized force.[44] Some of the dictionary descriptions of the adjective *violent* are more general in terms of its object, but confirm the meaning of violence as excessive force. The term is described as "characterized by physical force, esp. by extreme and sudden or by unjust or improper force; furious; severe; vehement."[45] It would be difficult to make this distinction in writing, however, since *violence* is already used generally to refer to both kinds of force. The first definition of the word rules out sabotage as a form of violence. The second would, however, apparently include property as one of the objects of violence, so we may speak of violence to persons as well as violence to property (sabotage). This seems to be quite a reasonable understanding of *violence,* and will be followed here. When the term is used without a qualification, however, it will be taken as inclusive of both types of violence, but with an emphasis on violence to persons.

Sabotage or violence to property is, naturally, less serious morally in comparison to violence to persons. This does not mean that it is necessarily always justified. Our examination here would require us to show in what way it could have been successful in the situation in question to be justifiable in terms of the moral laws. It becomes obvious immediately that, under the circumstances, sabotage was not likely to succeed. To begin with, there was little manpower to do the job and there were no sufficient and sophisticated weapons to carry it out. The enemy, on the other hand, was well equipped with spies, weapons, and other means of thwarting this move and bringing its perpetrators to justice. Several important factors to be considered in selecting opposition methods to be used in a given situation have been suggested. They include

> the type of issue involved, the nature of the opponent, his aims and strength, the type of counteraction he is likely to use, the depth of feeling both among the general population and among the likely actionists, the degree of repression the actionists are likely to be able to take, the general strategy of the overall campaign, and the amount of past experience and specific training the population and the actionists have had . . . [In] military battle weapons are carefully selected, taking into account such factors as their range and effect.[46]

The failure to count the "total" cost was a moral handicap without which the ANC, in particular, might have planned a little more before embarking upon a violent course of action, and that finally led to its downfall underground. Three closely related moral laws would specifically appear to have counseled against violence at this stage: the logical law—since the goal would already be contradicted by the insufficient means adopted; the law of consequences—emphasizing this same fact; and the law of specification—taking all the factors of the situation into account.

This phase of the PAC's struggle, on the other hand—according to available evidence, which is hardly conclusive—was a complete moral failure in the sense that the organization does not appear to have considered the moral significance of its actions at all. Like the ANC, the organization itself might have been justified in abandoning nonviolence, since it was no longer permitted to function openly. It might be wrong, however, to conclude that the PAC made no planning or ethical deliberation before entering this stage, since it operated more secretively than the ANC. Any judgment on it can be made only on the basis of its activities and the conclusions drawn from them.

The question would still remain whether these activities, in view of their aim, consequences, and counterconsequences, can be justified in terms of the moral laws. Since the circumstances were the same, we cannot but return to the conclusion reached in the case of the ANC. It was only a matter of time before the enemy could catch up with his opponents. The same three laws cited above were involved. The PAC, however, went further in its actions. Its targets were human beings, and do not seem to have been selectively sorted out. Thus the personalistic aspects of the moral laws also seem to have been contravened in the persons of the immediate victims. Though the PAC's goal was, in theory, compatible with most of the moral laws and their ideal aspects, the uncalculated violent course adopted by the organization in effect contradicted all these laws. In the end, even this underground movement was completely crushed and driven into exile without achieving its goals.

Without a commitment to nonviolence as an absolute, therefore, I think that in these particular instances violence—both to persons and to property—was not justified by the moral and material resources of the organizations. Nevertheless, their outlaw status seems to have provided at least some justification in considering violence as the means, if they could meet these needs and other criteria sounded through this section. The only movement that has not resorted to violent underground tactics since it was banned is the BCM. The current movements are still determined to continue their nonviolent approach as long as they are not deprived of their legal status.

Exclusion of Whites

One aspect in the internal strategies of both the PAC and the BCM was the exclusion of whites in their struggle. AZAPO currently follows this approach. The ANC also did not have whites in its ranks during its internal struggle, but it provided for them and other "racial" groups in the Congress Alliance. Both the PAC and the BCM based their position against white involvement in their activities (as AZAPO still does) on the historical role whites played in black politics. As already noted in the previous chapters, they were seen as neutralizers of black opinion and aspiration, indirectly serving to maintain the *status quo*. The objections of these groups against working with white liberals, in particular, were almost similar to the view expressed by Richard Shaull:

> Concerning liberalism, the situation today is quite different. If it once represented a dynamic struggle for freedom, equality, and justice . . . today these ideals have become slogans with little power to transform the world. And as it has lost its power to change society, it has placed increasing emphasis upon the defense of the only means it can accept for bringing about social change: gradual progress and reform within the framework and according to the rules of the given social, economic, and political structures. To the degree that we are confronted by a situation demanding the creation of qualitatively new institutions and structures, this liberal dogma becomes the major obstacle to understanding and action.[47]

A moral question in the South African situation is whether there was any justification in generalizing that all whites' motives were similar and negative. If, according to the communitarian aspects of the moral laws, all persons ought to cooperate toward the production and enjoyment of shared values, and to seek the best interests of the whole community, how can the exclusion of other persons in this quest be justified? The late Steve Biko once observed that if the South African government suspected, say, eight missionaries of causing political problems, it had rather deport a thousand missionaries and hope that the eight culprits were among them than exert its effort to search for the unknown eight. Were the PAC, the BCM, and AZAPO guilty of the same crime?

There are, it is often said, two sides to every story or problem. By pointing to historical precedents among liberals, these bodies were saying that the liberals in particular, and all white South Africans in general, had been given the benefit of the doubt for close to a century in all—since blacks changed from armed to political resistance—as co-workers with blacks for change. In all these years, it was felt, the liberals had not outgrown their ambivalence and their tendency toward the establishment. There might have been "radicals" among them—though the PAC thought they were all "quacks"—but how were these to be recognized, since all acted alike in the presence of blacks but always *seemed* to betray their trust in the presence of other whites? For instance, most liberals would never want to be seen talking to a black person in the street. For such reasons the BCM and the PAC thought it was about time to test the other side of the story: namely, to question their motives in general and to see how this might make progress toward change possible.

This approach, of course, offends against the personality of well-meaning whites. It may even be uncharitable and unreconciliatory. As a temporary test of faith, however, it might be moral and even the best way toward love and reconciliation. In other words, it might be in accordance with the law of the best possible. Well-meaning whites might feel disappointed but prepared to sacrifice a little pride for the sake of more meaningful future relations with their injured black brethren. No one has the right to dictate to another. If the other has been continuously offensive, however, it does appear that one has the moral right to shut one's doors to him temporarily until one feels able to trust him again. This seems to be in accordance with what Roberts means when he says that there can be no shortcut to reconciliation.[48] Thus, while the approach may appear to be inconsistent with the personalistic aspects in particular, as well as the communitarian aspects of the moral laws, it might in fact make their fulfillment—and consequently that of the axiological aspects, especially the axiological law, the law of the best possible, and that of the most inclusive end—more meaningful and fruitful after reconciliation. The strategy might have to be revised, and another one tried, however, if reconciliation did not appear within sight. Jesus' exhortation: "not seven times, but seventy-seven times" (Matt. 18:22), must always be kept in mind.

The PAC, once more, went a little further and confessed to hatred of whites. They rejected as hypocritical the popular idea that one could hate the deed but ought not to hate the doer.[49] Is this kind of hating, indeed, possible? Of what significance—as Sobukwe questioned—is the whip or the whipping without the hands of the wielder; and of what significance are these hands without the *inner drive* that directs them to inflict injury? On the other hand, is it really possible to hate a person *as a person,* or is hatred directed rather toward *what a person does in response to an inner drive that is unkind?* Sobukwe seems to have been quite in order, then, when he said that the whites in South Africa are hated as *oppressors,* that is, because of their inner tendency to inflict injury upon blacks. They were not hated as persons. Nor, as he observed, is it possible to hate an abstraction—oppression—or an indifferent instrument that accompanies it. Remove the evil tendency, he stressed, and the hatred disappears—the person remains intact and retains his full human dignity and respect.

The question whether to direct one's hatred to a person or to *the* doing (note the use of the article rather than the personal pronoun) has been belabored beyond proportion and lost all meaning, and must be reviewed. Hatred of persons as persons, if this were possible, would indeed be in violation of the whole system of the moral laws as well as of the Christian principles of love and human brotherhood. However, hatred of a particular evil tendency in a person, only personified in him, cannot be morally reprehensible unless there was danger of this personification turning into hatred of the person himself. This seems difficult to conceive. It is also true, nevertheless, that once the cause of this personification is removed, there would be no basis for such hatred to continue.

Withdrawal of Foreign Investments

Since the emergence of the BCM blacks have spoken increasingly of the discontinuation of foreign investment as the immediate last resort for achieving peaceful change in South Africa. Foreign investment is seen as enriching the white sector of the South African society, thus strengthening it economically and politically at the expense of blacks. This appeal to external intervention is necessary as most of the internal channels for working for peaceful change, except on the government's terms, have been choked by the government, and are continually being made more difficult, as this study has tried to show.

Thus, working for change in any way within the country is becoming increasingly impossible. In the meantime the government is continually depriving blacks of their rights, even the basic right of belonging to the country itself! The appeal for economic sanctions as the last peaceful resort toward change has now become the prerogative of those exiled from the country, except those who have reached the conclusion that nothing short of armed uprising can bring about the desired result.

In recent years economic sanctions have been thought of increasingly in terms of divestment and the withdrawal of foreign companies from South Africa.[50] A common argument used by those who advocate withdrawal of foreign firms is that such a move will have only a transitory effect on the lives of the blacks. Most of them are already suffering more than they can bear, anyway. They would be willing, the argument runs, to sacrifice a little more if this would mean reaping the fruits of change later.[51] This type of argument is often directed at those who advocate improvement of conditions for blacks employed by foreign firms as a first step toward gradual peaceful change in the economic and political fields. One of the champions of this approach was an American minister, the Reverend Leon Sullivan, who was on the board of directors of General Motors. He found support among some black leaders in the country, particularly those who have yielded to the government's "homeland" policy. Rev. Sullivan proposed six principles to be met specifically by all American firms doing business in South

Africa—now commonly called the Sullivan principles.[52] These principles recommended

> (1) Nonsegregation in all eating, comfort and work facilities. (2) Equal and fair employment practices for all employees. (3) Equal pay for all employees doing equal or comparable work for the same period of time. (4) Initiation of and development of training programs that will prepare, in substantial numbers, blacks and other non-whites for supervisory, administrative, clerical and technical jobs. (5) Increasing the number of blacks and other non-whites in management and supervisory positions. (6) Improving the quality of employees' lives outside the work environment in such areas as housing, transportation, schooling, recreation and health facilities.

A black South African trade unionist, Lucy Mvubelo, once echoed this position strongly in the *Voice of America News*. She went so far as to imply that those fellow South African blacks who stood for disinvestment were communists or "emissaries of the East."[53]

Most black South Africans objected to the Sullivan principles because they thought that they were aimed merely at reform. What blacks are interested in, they say, is complete sociopolitical and economic change; not mere "cosmetic changes" here and there. Consenting to such changes, they fear, might lead to complacency and thus inhibit or prolong the urge for meaningful change. This would merely increase the lot of the majority, for there is no question about the fact that only a minute proportion of blacks are employed by foreign firms and only they would benefit from such improvements, while the majority remains unaffected. Nor is it clear how such improvements might lead to eventual change in the system. Economic sanctions, on the other hand (it is believed), are likely to lead South Africa to the bargaining table once it realizes that it cannot completely "go it alone," especially on economies requiring advanced skills and technology.

The Sullivan principles were based on a premise that has been disproved by both a number of observers and the experience of increased foreign investment itself in South Africa, especially over the last two decades.[54] Massachusetts senator Paul Tsongas, who had just returned from a tour of Southern Africa in 1980, directly referred to these principles as a half measure.[55] Speaking in general terms, Heribert Adam points out that "the analytical perspective which focuses on the essential compatibility between economic interests and white political power comes much closer to reality than the *naive* belief in economic growth as the magic defeat of racial discrimination."[56]

It is clear that while the Sullivan principles would greatly aid in improving the standard of living for a certain category of employees, it is certainly correct that they would not benefit the great majority. Besides, they are far from meeting the requirements of the law of the best possible for change in the country, let alone satisfying the most inclusive end for all. The latter law's aspect of the greatest good for the greatest number—as far as the demand for overall change is concerned—would be lost. Further, the consequences of these principles insofar as their reformist tendency seems to dominate their potential for meaningful, radical change might be counterrevolutionary and so against the law of consequences as well. Even now there are already talks of exploiting them by creating a black bourgeoisie that will have a stake in the South African system and thus be reluctant to fight it for the benefit of all. If these are some of the possible effects of the principles, what hope would there be in them for gradually influencing change in the system? Rather, would their application not merely divide the black people and strengthen the camp of the oppressor? Even if such consequences were not likely, it is still hard to see how the changes contemplated in the economic field would finally influence change in the political field. They seem more likely to become an end in themselves, thus confirming the fears that they are merely reformative.

Those who suggest a little more suffering coupled with the hope for a better lot later would seem a little cruel in expecting this, particularly of the most deprived people (who live mostly from hand to mouth). When we remember, however, that the most deprived are rather the millions who have been sentenced for the rest of their lives to their so-called homelands, and who do not even know the name General Motors, the situation assumes a different picture. Surely those who have been blessed with jobs for the rest of their lives would be willing to sacrifice a little comfort for a little while in order to identify with those who do not know where their next meal, if any, is coming from, and so speed up the cause for change? Such self-sacrifice would be true altruism and humanitarian, as well as Christian, concern for the neighbor. It would also be an expression of desire for the sharing of the best possible values realizable from one's country by all, while keeping in view and working for the realizaton of the ideal community. It is refreshing to recall in this particular respect the words of Gandhi, that "things of fundamental importance to people are not secured by reason alone but have to be purchased with their suffering."[57]

Were the question of withdrawal of foreign investment merely an altruistic, moral issue, it would indeed be very difficult to understand why the United Nations and its member countries—particularly the leading Western nations—have been so hesitant in acting upon it. Those familiar with the world economic situation and South Africa's place in it seem to think that not only would such withdrawal be a weak instrument for inducing change within that country but it would also involve "greater potential losses to those imposing [such economic measures] than to the Republic" (South Africa).[58] For this reason, few countries have been willing to urge their withdrawal. Rather, some have been more accommodating on the question of restrictions on new investment than on these more drastic measures. Among the problems anticipated from the total withdrawal of foreign investments from South Africa, Hance has named the following: (1) investor and investing nations would incur heavy losses; (2) it is impossible to repatriate much of the investment, such as in mines and manufacturing establishments; (3) the impact on South Africa would be minimized because of the relatively low present (1965) dependence on new foreign capital (at this time it was estimated that South Africa could provide 80-90 percent of its capital needs from domestic resources);[59] (4) South Africa could counteract through the imposition of higher taxes, additional restrictions on the outflow of funds, or nationalization of foreign holdings.[60] While the countries involved would be strongly unwilling to forego their national interests threatened by such consequences, some believe that if they consented to restrictions of new investments, this might have enormous psychological impact on white South Africans. This would be so especially because the latter have interpreted continuing investment in this country as evidence of support of its policies or of unwillingness by Western nations to take any positive actions against South Africa.[61] Indeed, the limited sanctions imposed by several Western countries in 1986, including the U.S., have somewhat shaken South Africa off its psychological complacency though the actual economic consequences were still too minimal to persuade the government to change its policies in any significant way.

It is not our task here to consider the merits of these arguments. Suffice it to say that those strong advocates of foreign withdrawal have to be aware of some of these problems and try to offer positive solutions or compromises to them. In the final analysis, the underlying problem in the search for a solution may not be a moral versus an economic one, as most protagonists on either side are inclined to argue. Nor is it the problem of South Africa versus the world, if we recall Muelder's point that "mankind is the unit of cooperation." The problem is a joint moral and economic one, and it is a world problem—a family problem of humanity. Hence to try to evade concern for the victims of apartheid for the sake of "national," "sectarian" interests might be a betrayal of the law of altruism and all the communitarian aspects of the moral laws on the part of those who refuse to take action for a better South Africa. On the other hand, it is ultimately the responsibility of each country involved to determine the most suitable action to take to help bring about the desperately needed change in South Africa. As every action has its own limitations, so the various participants in the debate are morally obligated to decide what is the best possible moral course to follow in the light of all the relevant facts. At the same time, the generally accepted warning must be noted that no single country acting on its own to try to influence peaceable change in this troubled land has a chance of succeeding.

CONCLUSION

The use of the moral laws in the past South African struggle in general could have led to a more serious scrutiny and refinement of the goals and activities of the mass organizations involved. Among the goals examined, the question of rights would have required a little more study. Considerations would have had to be given to the problem of human weakness, thus demanding the introduction of some checks for the rights of minorities in particular, especially by the PAC and the BCM, as well as by AZAPO, the NF, and the UDF in the continuing struggle. This would have been necessary even though minorities were not meant to have special privileges nor considered as "separate" groups from the rest of the community. In the activities engaged in, a little more study on the methods of nonviolent revolution in general might have helped "perfect" their strategies. We must bear in mind, however, that most literature having to do with change is taboo in South Africa and likely to have been banned—whether it is concerned with violent or nonviolent methods of change. The leaders of mass organizations thus depend mostly on their own personal resources and thus have their limitations.

It is difficult to imagine how these organizations, notably the ANC and the PAC, could have carried on their activities nonviolently after they had been banned. At the same time, both organizations should have calculated more seriously the pros and cons of a violent struggle. Naturally, this calculation would have followed the pattern of the just war or just revolution theory, determined on the basis of the moral laws themselves if they were used. Judging from the resources available to the two organizations at that time, more time and preparation would have been required before this resort to violence could have been justified.

This discussion has made it obvious that the use of the moral laws depends mostly on their previous assimilation and character-formation, since they cannot practically be called forth individually in each moral situation. Deats has written:

We act on the basis of certain assumptions, often implicit, both of fact and of the nature of reality. Unexamined values, those which we take for granted, may confirm our choices without adequate criticism.[62]

Further, while the moral laws call for coherence, some are more relevant than others in particular moral situations, requiring special emphasis. This places them in a state of tension with the rest of the system. Often a conflict among various laws may arise as a result. In this case, however, certain laws seem to have the prerogative of restoring coherence by determining the best way out of the moral predicament and suggesting the final decision. These laws have been found to be those of specification, the best possible, the most inclusive end, and the general appeal to personality as the point of reference of all the moral laws. These are the built-in moderators of the system as a whole. Most decisions in the situation examined would have finally depended on these moderators, which include an element of risk in their invocation.

Chapter 6

Future Action: How Viable?

It has not been my intention in this work to do an extensive study of either violent or nonviolent methods of resistance in the quest for change in South Africa. Nor have I intended to justify either method. Rather, my concern with these issues here is mainly contextual and peremptory. I will retain this approach in the present chapter, in which our main focus will be on strategy. In considering the various possible strategies for bringing about change in this country, the emphasis will be more on their practical effectiveness or viability, while moral judgment will be mainly implicit, except for occasional raising of explicit questions. One must bear in mind, however, that in the actual formulation and execution of strategy, moral questions and principles must be made explicit, as the adopted guidelines will show. It is not my goal in this chapter to formulate a strategy or strategies as such but merely to examine the practicability of the ones indicated in the South African situation.

There are very few options in selecting strategies for working for change from within South Africa. Each one seems to have its own limitations and problems, primarily because South Africa is basically a police state that will brook no challenge to its government. The five options we will consider are guerrilla warfare (urban), appeals for both international economic sanctions and United Nations intervention, direct Christian action, and intensified noncooperation with the government within the country. Working within the system (through bantustans) is rejected as a nonoption or as a pseudo-strategy. Before proceeding to examine these options, we need to look at two questions. First, is there still any suitable structure left within which the search for change can be effectively pursued in South Africa? Second, what guidelines may be used to inform and guide those involved in working out more effective and morally defensible strategies?

SEARCH FOR ALTERNATIVE STRUCTURES

Any search for a new structure that may serve as an agency for change in South Africa must take into account the advantages and disadvantages of past and current structures of national organization. It may be necessary to ask whether, in view of past experiences in the struggle, we still need mass organizations. If so, how are such organizations to forestall or to overcome the government's intolerance such as that demonstrated by its treatment of past organizations, particularly when they appeared to be gaining ground in their struggle? How are the new organizations to improve upon past strategies? If a mass organization is not needed, what alternative structure or structures can be employed in its place to achieve similar goals?

Precedents: Present Difficulties

From the foregoing chapters it has become clear that the history of the "liberation movements" inside South Africa has been characterized by failure. This has been so primarily because of the intransigence of the government, and because, as Schlemmer and others have pointed out, whites will not easily vote away their privilege and class status.[1] Schlemmer states that both English- and Afrikaans-speaking South Africans have strong class interests, but that among the Afrikaners "these same interests are reinforced by greater racialism and by the general orientation in regard to cultural diversity." Similar obstacles to change have been echoed by Marais, who asks, "Where on earth will you find a racial or other group of three million highly educated and developed people who, having for three centuries ruled the country and built up a great material civilization, will voluntarily vote themselves into another group or just hand over under conditions such as prevail in South Africa today?"[2]

For such reasons both the English and Afrikaans groups have increasingly entered into an alliance and supported the ruling National Party for its firmness in handling black protest. A survey conducted in the country over ten years ago suggested that some 54 percent of English speakers and roughly 77 percent of Afrikaners agreed with the government on "all or most points of policy." In Schlemmer's own study, about 65 percent of the largely English-speaking area of Durban were found to agree with the government on "all or most points of policy."[3] For most white South Africans in general, therefore, blacks dare not hope ever to participate in the government of the country. General political campaign slogans have become, "[Black participation] over our dead bodies!" By 1971 more than 60 percent of whites believed that apartheid and the bantustan system are the only way to solve the so-called bantu problem.

When weighed against this resoluteness, past black protests and organizations appear to have been knocking against steel doors. We have observed certain deficiencies in their internal, nonviolent campaigns. However, one wonders how their strategies, made more perfect, might have been or might still be effective against a group determined to die rather than share power with its disenfranchised. Significantly, the three older groups studied first were crushed just when change appeared imminent and when it appeared that the government and its electorate would not resist it any further. At the same time, government action against these groups was followed by intensification of the system and by acceleration of its bantustan program. The longevity of a resistance movement in South Africa is measured by its ineffectiveness or by its apparent ineffectiveness in the eyes of the authorities. As soon as it shows signs of influence both socially and politically, it is outlawed and its leaders silenced. During the period between this outlawing and the gathering of momentum of a new organization to replace it, the government strengthens itself and takes further precautions against future challenges. Thus each new organization works within a new set of restrictions and may easily be charged with "furthering the aims" of its predecessors. This makes organization and the movement of black leaders very difficult. It was on this organizational problem that objections were raised earlier to Sharp's suggestion that nonviolent methods can be as effective in tyrannical states as in democratic ones. The very amount of freedom of protest and organization allowed by democratic governments makes quite a difference when one is confronted with a police state like South Africa.

Any present and future attempt in South Africa to organize along the lines of past resistance movements, therefore, must seemingly have some underground element, especially in the leadership, to evade government interference. This in itself is already a restraint in organization and cannot be expected to overcome the limitations of the past very much. For a few months between late 1960 and early 1961, Nelson Mandela managed, after the expiration of a banning order that had been imposed upon him, to evade the police successfully while continuing his organization work before another order was served on him. How far this can be carried out is difficult to tell, but may be worth considering. Other alternative ways of organizing will have to be sought while new methods of mass organization are being investigated. The answer to South Africa's future might well depend upon these alternatives.

Bantustans

Diametrically opposed to this approach are the structures of "homeland" or bantustan politics. These structures are at a serious disadvantage among Africans for three main reasons: (1) they are not alternative structures for change at all but part of the apartheid system and its implementation; (2) they have not been chosen freely by Africans, but are imposed upon them on a take-it-or-leave-it basis; (3) they represent the collaboration of those African leaders who accept them in the "final" disinheritance of their own people. Most of the African leaders who participate in these structures—most of them government-appointed chiefs—claim to do so for practical reasons and as a lesser evil for their people rather than in submission to white domination. Some seem to think that they can be used as vehicles for change, though there are often contradictions since it is also believed that these structures themselves can no longer be undone.

In his preface to the book *African Perspectives on South Africa,*[4] which is mostly a book on bantustan politics, Professor H. Ntsanwisi summarizes the views presented in the book as a clear expression that "the sooner the ruling class ceases deluding itself in thinking that they have gradually won African backing for the question of "andersoortigheid" [otherness] the sooner will black and white in South Africa come to real grips with the issues that divide them."[5] According to him, "homelands" are supported as an "interim measure," representing "the first crumbs falling from the rich man's table." It is not clear how this view relates to those bantustan leaders who have accepted "independence" for their ethnic groups in the last ten years in spite of the government's refusal to concede to certain demands the leaders had made conditional for accepting this "independence."

The claims and practices of two of these leaders have seemed quite contradictory, often causing much confusion. One of these men, Chief K. D. Matanzima, now retired, openly declared his support for "separate development" "provided that it is carried out to its logical conclusion." However, he goes on, "if it fails, as it seems to be failing, the alternative is an integrated South Africa with full equality amongst all races."[6] In fact, though, Matanzima is known to have been an unconditional supporter of apartheid, as shown by his ruthlessness in enforcing the bantustan system in the Transkei. In his election manifesto of 1973, Matanzima stated in the same breath that:

1. South Africa belongs to black and white equally and all its wealth should be shared by all inhabitants without discrimination.
2. The homelands should be developed to full independence and

that the division of land in terms of population numbers is basic for the fulfillment of such independence.

3. There should be "freedom to seek work anywhere in the Republic of South Africa and freedom from pass laws."

Whatever their objections to certain details of implementation, all bantustan leaders seem to have come to agree with Lucas Mangope, chief and leader of "Bophuthatswana," that the bantustans are "a reality with which we have to learn to live." Mangope claimed that he would never abandon the "permanent ideal" of one man, one vote in a united South Africa. However, he said, "historical realities and their practical implications" that are responsible for the white fears of being overwhelmed by a black majority had to be taken into consideration.[7] What seems ironical about this apparent concern for the white countryman is that it seems tacitly to sanction white domination and exploitation of black people as an understandable means of alleviating or eliminating white fears. When Mangope and Matanzima accepted "independence" for their bantustans in 1977 and 1976, their land and economic as well as citizenship claims had not been satisfied. Their ethnic groups' South African citizenship was legally ended and, despite the disagreement between the white and bantustan government leaders concerning the position of the so-called urban blacks, the latter were also stripped of this last right of citizenship and made the responsibility of bantustan governments.

An idea that seems to be prevalent among some bantustan and white leaders concerning the instrumentality of bantustans toward change is that of federation, expressed variously as pluralism, partition, or the like. Alan Paton, for one, declared himself in 1971 to be opposed to the then United Party policy of race federation, and also rejected the policy of "perpetual white control." However, he believed that his own goal of the common society "must now be striven for in the framework of separate development" because "it has the monopoly of the instruments of power."[8] Like most supporters of change through the medium of bantustans, Paton seemed to believe that the changes that were "bound to come about," even through these structures, would "not be in accordance with the designs of the architects of separate development, but [would] in fact hasten the inevitable progress towards a common society." At the same time, Dr. Paton could not help seeing "integration" with Africans as some kind of impossible dream, and rather recommended the immediate integration of whites with "coloureds," Indians, and Chinese as the first step toward a common society.[9]

Many blacks have expressed dismay at Paton's misunderstanding of the real issue and this display of insensitivity to the black plight, after he had acted as a leading South African liberal for so long. His new position merely strengthened black suspicion of their supposed liberal friends and sympathizers. Now that his dream of the common society within the context of "homeland" politics seems to be becoming more and more remote, they are waiting to hear how he continues to justify it.

Those bantustan leaders who have come out in support of a "race" federation also see it with different eyes from those of the former United Party. In talking of a "race" federation, however, these leaders do not seem to see an anomaly in considering all South African whites as constituting a single group, while, with regard to Africans, they have fallen into the government's divide-and-rule trap of stressing separate ethnic units. In his proposal of 1974 of a future South African federation, Gatsha Buthelezi originally suggested a single "homeland" for all the whites, with certain unified areas of the country for their territory. On the other hand, Africans would have their "Kwa-Zulus" and "Kwa-Xhosas," for example, in accordance with the present government policy. Buthelezi insisted though, that the whites must not continue to determine the future of the country alone.[10] His tentative "blueprint" for a "South African Federal Republic" would be (1) states in which the interests of an African ethnic group are paramount; (2) states in which the interests of white people are paramount; (3) special federal areas that are multi-ethnic in character, in which no particular group interests are designated.[11] These would be especially those areas where the economic resources of the rest of the country are concentrated.

According to Buthelezi this system—apart from being based on "race"—would be similar to that of the United States and other corresponding governments, particularly with regard to citizenship. He failed to realize, however, that some of the aspects he proposed—for instance, an internal passport system in the place of pass books—would be as restrictive as color or ethnic considerations themselves, which is not the case (at least legally) in the countries cited for comparison. Buthelezi also expressed the common belief of most bantustan leaders that "Africans are . . . realists enough to understand that since homelands are now set up, they cannot be undone at this stage."[12] This seems to be a contradiction, of course, since they also continue to claim to recognize these political structures as vehicles for change toward common citizenship rights. It seems to follow, therefore, that the relevance of bantustans as alternative structures toward social change in South Africa is questionable.

In 1986 Kwa-Zulu and Natal province jointly sponsored and produced a model blueprint for cooperation between these territories and

their black and white populations. It was largely believed that the
model would be adopted by the whole country and serve as the basis
for change in South Africa's racial policies. The report on this model,
issuing from a so-called Kwa-Natal–Kwa-Zulu Indaba, was very controversial in government circles and was rejected even before it was fully
discussed.

Among the whites the idea of a plural or federal government similar to that proposed by Buthelezi was represented by Denis Worrall as
anticipated by Walshe. Worrall rejected the ultimate aim of a common
society. He saw this as recommending "a reversal of white attitudes
since Union toward non-white participation in the political system."
Worrall was firm in his rejection of a common society, and his view is
reminiscent of those expressed by Schlemmer and Marais:

> Quite apart from its workability in theoretical terms, the common
> society course does not recommend itself to either the short-term
> or the long-term interests of the dominant white minority, and it
> appears unlikely to gain acceptance within the foreseeable future
> when one considers that after ten years the Progressive Party,
> surely a conservative party in terms of the common society, gained
> no more than 3.5% of the total poll in the April, 1970, general
> election.[13]

These considerations seem to lead to the conclusion that while, not
long ago, there used to be polarization in South African society between white conservatives and liberals as between black "radicals" and
"collaborators," today this polarization among whites appears to be
fading away in common resignation to apartheid and the endorsement
of bantustans as the "only" solution to the "black problem." In the years
since Worrall wrote in 1971, however, the problem has become more
complex and the attitudes of many whites confused and less predictable.
Among blacks the gap seems to be widening. At the same time, while
whites refuse to compromise their privileges, especially with regard to
the proportional sharing of land and economic benefits, they, like some
of the bantustan leaders, seem to be thinking more and more in terms
of a pluralistic or federal government for South Africa. This leaves the
"radical" group, with its remaining white supporters, as the only one
that rejects categorically all politics of separation and inequality presented to blacks in the form of an ultimatum. By the same token, all
black "collaborators" are seen as part and parcel of the system of white
domination.

Other Agencies or Nonconstitutional Groups

Because of the setbacks suffered by past organizations and the precarious conditions under which their successors find themselves, there appears to be dire need for the establishment of alternative structures that will transcend these disadvantages and shed off the stigma imposed upon these organizations.

During the Soweto uprising in 1976 and in the next two years, a number of "emergency" groups arose and took it upon themselves to mediate between the students and the authorities. Prominent among these groups were the Black Parents' Association and the Soweto Action Committee, followed later by the still existing Soweto Committee of Ten (SCT). These groups were concerned not only with crisis intervention but also with bringing home to the authorities that the students' grievances were not to be dismissed lightly. Rather, they expressed political and social hardships blacks in general are forced to endure under the apartheid system. Thus, the government would be wrong merely to search for scapegoats, "agitators," believing that after dealing with them the situation would continue as before.

The SCT continues to function today as some form of pressure group. After the banning of the BCM in 1977, in spite of the government's victimization of its members with the rest of the BCM, it took up leadership and maintained the pace of the struggle, posing a challenge to bantustan and apartheid institutions and leaders. Later the SCT worked side by side with a new mass organization that filled the vacuum left by the BPC. This seems to be commendable. Other similar committees were also set up later, namely, in Port Elizabeth and other places. Thus, future political and social action would seem to depend on a multitude of such groups all over the country and in many districts and locations. They need not be a duplication of existing mass organizations, since they are not concerned with membership but more with increasing awareness of unwarranted oppression and keeping up the spirit of resistance. In fact, their "conscientization" efforts should be able to increase the membership of mass organizations and to prepare these members for action within them. A recent development of such local organization has taken the form of "street committees," believed to have been inspired by the UDF.

While blacks are rightly concerned with continuing their fight in their own way, any efforts still undertaken by concerned whites to change their own part of the community—with ultimate cooperation between the two groups—should be welcome. Similar structures for change by white "radicals" were contemplated at one time under the label of "white consciousness." Kleinschmidt described the concern of white consciousness as making the white people in South Africa aware that "each time we inflict a racist practice we are putting not only our victim into prison but we are putting ourselves into prison too."[14] White consciousness aimed at making whites aware that they, not Vorster, the government, or the Nationalists, are the oppressors. They were to realize that Vorster did not vote himself into power but was put there by white acquiescence. Through white consciousness they would learn to act rather than to react. They would come to a better understanding of their whiteness and its role in the South African situation. This understanding would make possible their eventual meeting with blacks, as they recognized that the only solution to the present conflict in the country lay in "a changed consciousness on the part of both blacks and whites."[15] In short, the role of white consciousness groups would be to rouse whites to the fact that

> white prejudice against blacks is based on ignorance, whereas black hostility to whites is based on the hard facts of exploitation. Secondly, it is probable that, in South Africa at least, race prejudice plays an important role in justifying to the whites their right to treat blacks in the way they do. That is, it is in some way a rationalization of exploitation: . . . Conflict will not end until [black] grievances and [white] privileges end. But once these have ended, there is no basis in race difference for further conflict. That is, there is no reason why whites should expect to be discriminated against in a democratic South Africa because of their whiteness.[16]

Black and white pressure groups such as the ones implied here would appear to be among the very few alternatives left for relatively "safe" pursuance of meaningful change within the context of South Africa. While the government may easily ban a named organization including its branches everywhere in the country with a single act, it would have to go to more pains to find and outlaw various groups scattered all over the country under the labels of Black Consciousness and White Consciousness—that is, unless it bans "consciousness" itself! Of course, we cannot be too sure of this, since the South African government has in the past been capable of banning any kinds of gathering of specified numbers. It might bring this down until even as few as five people might be deemed to constitute a "crowd." No proposal of an alternative structure for change can, therefore, be completely "waterproof" in South Africa. Hence organizers are always preoccupied with searching for loopholes in the existing laws to determine if some improvement is possible on the very outlawed structures. This is why an outside observer may often think that there is an undue repetition of past mistakes.

Churches and Religious Bodies

Like these pressure groups, the church in South Africa seems to be one of the few remaining options for influencing change in the country, if it will begin to take its mission seriously. While the church is not "of" the world, it is "in" the world and ministers to people "in" the world. This means that it must not try to extract the soul from the body and try to save it alone for the life to come. It must make the body livable by the soul, so that the body can serve as a worthy temple from which the soul can communicate with God and perfect itself for him. When the church concentrates its mission merely on the human soul, it relegates the body to the very bonds that "preoccupy [man's] mind to the extent that he can no longer even meditate on his God or find opportunity to offer sacrifice unhindered."[17] It is thus self-defeating for the church to claim to seek salvation for people's souls, while their other human aspects are left unattended. This view seems to find clear expression in Deats and Stotts in the following words:

> The central social goal of the Christian ethic is a redeemed society: the release of persons from all those aspects of group relationships which corrupt life, obstruct personal growth, and hinder the divine purpose; the establishment among groups of relationships which provide the maximum concern of persons for each other's welfare, further the realization of their highest potentialities, and facilitate their communion with and service of God.

This statement in turn finds elaboration in this description of the task of the church:

> The task of the church is not primarily in the church, except to see that its own life expresses its message, but in the world of which the church is part. It is within the framework of this larger goal that the subordinate goals find their proper place and their relationship to each other . . .
>   Certain alternatives are thus excluded from the choice of the Christian. He may not withdraw from the world to seek his own salvation. He may not conform to the secular world. He may not separate his life in the church and his life in the world into distinct spheres of activity. His life will be lived out in the continuing tension of reconciling the world to the love of God and man as known in the life of the church. Social action becomes not just an important task of the church but a necessary dimension of life in the redemptive fellowship of the church.[18]

Larry Coppard and Barbara Steinwachs have accurately observed that the church has spent many years developing various forms of crisis ministry to people in need. All these activities, however, rarely addressed the basic issue of institutional racism, "for it is in its institutionalized forms that racism continues to oppress people and create untold suffering."[19] This observation is no less true of the history of the church in South Africa. The first chapter of this book has shown that, although racial oppression is endemic in South African history, the church did not begin to address this issue—except for a few individual clergymen here and there—until after 1948. The reason for this sudden change was more English mistrust of the Afrikaners, who were now taking over the government, than concern for black human rights. Words were seldom accompanied by action, and to this day the church still discriminates on the basis of color.

During the 1970s, as throughout certain periods in history, the church's attitude was severely challenged by black theologians and ministerial students in South Africa. Black theology itself guided black ministers in their pastoral and social duties, but no particular strategy of social action was devised as a result of it and it remained more of an intellectual rather than adequately practical tool for effecting change. Nevertheless, it inspired many black religious organizations and seminarians, as well as influenced more openness in white-administered religious bodies such as the Christian Institute and the South African Council of Churches. Until quite recently these organizations remained more what might be called relief organizations than vehicles for complete change in the country.

Today, more than ever, both black and white aspects of the church in South Africa need to develop channels that will inspire and work for change not only in the church, where it is still very much needed, but also in society as a whole. What is needed is aptly expressed by Dom Helder Camara in reference to Latin America:

> Instead of letting people repeat in their terrible resignation that "some are born rich and others poor: it's God's will" (. . .), let us openly declare that the social and economic structures of Latin America are unjust and must be replaced by others which are more just, more humane . . . [B]rotherly counsel and pathetic appeals are [not] enough to make socio-economic structures tumble like the walls of Jericho.[20]

Even the church's participation in social change has often been conceived in terms of the creation of religious pressure groups that might cooperate with other social groups. It seems that such groups might be tried in the context of South Africa within that country's restrictions. According to Richard Shaull, such groups would "try to break the situation; confront the present forms of domination; insist on freedom to build the political power of peasants, workers, and students; and support students, labor leaders, intellectuals, and priests who are now working to build a new order."[21] In other words, they will enable the oppressed, "in all the precariousness of their existence," to "discover how to move from a dead end to a new beginning." For Camara these pressure groups would operate within the law but, "within the limits of the law, to risk everything."[22]

Another supporter of the idea of pressure groups within the church, Arthur Gish, has suggested that they should not attack social problems from the center of power, but operate on the periphery, "on the cutting edge of society." These "creative minorities," he believes, will direct themselves more to individual conversion within the group, extending to the whole community through these groups. Although Gish states that decisions and strategies begin in these groups, he suggests that a revolution is not planned for. "People just start living differently": that is, "groups of people who have a common commitment and who meet regularly to share their hopes and fears, joys and frustrations."[23] This view seems to be more monastic or "pentecostal," and therefore more a matter of individual change than of social action. It is likely to find little, if any, favor with black South Africans. This is not to deny the importance of individual reform as a primary step toward meaningful participation in social action. Personal change, as Coppard and Steinwachs stress, "plays a much needed supportive role in structural change. The effort to change a structure or practice also fosters attitude re-examination."[24] The problem with Gish's emphasis seems to be that of concentrating on personal change and letting social change follow on its own. But without planned and purposive action there can be no guarantee that personal change will automatically lead to such results. Rather, the two kinds of change should be pursued concurrently, even though the first type may initially be focused on for a limited period of time as preparatory for full-scale social action. Once the process has begun, each side might even reflect upon the other, thus making influence and growth mutual. What are required, therefore, are structures of both personal and sociostructural change working jointly.

"GUIDELINES FOR STRATEGY"

Alongside organizational structure, another crucial question in South Africa's liberation struggle is that of "the how" of effecting change. It is crucial because past failures in the struggle naturally imply that hitherto adopted strategies and methods employed for change have either been insufficient or inappropriate responses to the ruthlessness of the regime. Before examining some of the few possible, alternative strategies that remain open for blacks struggling within the country, it seems appropriate to pause briefly and consider some of the elements required in formulating an effective strategy. As our model we shall adopt in very condensed form those general aspects of strategy worked out by Paul Deats and Herbert Stotts in their book, *Methodism and Society: Guidelines for Strategy*.[25] Our interest in this book lies more on what is expressed by the subtitle than the main topic itself. The concern is with guidelines as a general method toward action rather than as related merely to Christian action.

The alternative strategies that follow this section will not be directly based on these guidelines since the intention there will not be to formulate strategies as such but to examine options. It is incumbent upon those inclined toward any particular strategy to see that it meets the requirements of the proposed guidelines or any others corresponding to them. This section is thus relevant as some kind of testing ground for qualifying or disqualifying any adopted strategy, as well as for working out its details.

The Meaning of Strategy

Deats and Stotts define strategy as "the clarification of ethical norms, the appraisal of social needs, the assessment of costs and resources, and the deployment of energies to establish and accomplish institutional goals."[26] Put differently, five considerations seem to go into the formulation of strategy. They are (1) the definition and clarification of goals, (2) the statement of principles, (3) education and planning or preparation, including the assessment of costs and resources, (4) social action, and (5) evaluation and review of previous successes and failures. Strategy involves further the "continuing process of revising goals, confronting changed situations, weighing alternatives, and reconsidering institutional forms and procedures."

Concern for social change leads to study and planning as the basis for policy making. Policy in turn must result in action.[27] The initial education and planning should take into account both long-range and short-range goals of the institution and of those involved in it. Accordingly, the program of action will also involve steps ranging from action for the realization of immediate needs to concentration on long-range achievements. Present achievements become an inspiration and a source of hope for future goals and also provide a lesson for the ensuing steps of the process. Strategy will, of course, differ in each situation and period, "depending upon the estimate of the balance of forces regarding a given problem."[28]

The authors warn against considering the mere possessing of a strategy as the solution to the problem. Having a strategy does not, therefore, rule out contributions and resources of other independent individuals and groups. There is room in social action for both charismatic and crisis leaders as well as for conservatives and nonconformists. "The limits of strategy are best dealt with when they are recognized and when there is continuing assessment of crises, drift, and other groups seeking change."[29] A strategy is always open to improvement and there might well be much to learn from the approaches of other groups.

Goals

Organizational strategy is formulated on the basis of goals to be achieved. This means that goals must be well defined and clarified for an appropriate strategy to be forged in relation to them. "A fragmented approach to strategy [resulting from unclear goals] precludes consistent and purposeful action and opens the way for ad hoc solutions."[30] Clarification of goals is an integral part of social education in strategy. Members of an organization are likely to identify more readily with goals they understand, especially if they have helped to formulate them. Goals must be formulated with a view to priorities among them, the distinction between goals and preconditions necessary for reaching them, the people for whom they are formulated, and their costs.[31]

The main question involved in establishing priorities is, "will energy and other resources be concentrated first upon those uncertain of their motives and commitments, or upon those antagonistic to proposed action?" The educational approach chosen will depend upon the target singled out. The question of priorities seems to enter also in distinguishing goals from their preconditions. Preconditions may be regarded as instrumental goals or intermediate steps toward goals. One must not confuse them with the ultimate goals, if the latter are to be reached and worked for at all. This ultimate achievement depends also upon clarity concerning the people for whom the goals are formulated and those to whom they are addressed. Nor is it sufficient merely to be aware of needs. Goals must be weighed in terms of costs (e.g., perceived difficulty of proposed actions, challenges to existing satisfactions, and choice among competing claims) and resources. Fulfilling these goal requirements demands rational and faithful choice. This must be tested by the coherence of goals, the acceptance of obligation to act upon goals established, the inclusiveness of concern, and the awareness of consequences.[32] In making these calculations we need the guidance of ethical and, especially in the case of religious bodies, theological principles.

Ethical Norms

Deats and Stotts recognize both philosophical and theological ethics as providing normative guidelines in the formulation of a social strategy. They see the need for continuing interaction between the two: philosophical ethics as "the critical, rational interpretation of experience," and theological ethics as "the guidance of life in existential situations in accordance with Christian norms."[33] These disciplines are important in providing "principles of discriminate criticism, ethical illumination for situations presently faced and to be faced, some of them different from any we have faced before." It is inevitable to have foresight as well as hindsight, to learn from history, and to be able to anticipate decisions reflectively.[34] While individuals must internalize normative principles, for purposes of social action they must also make them explicit in policy statements.

The authors enumerate five principles in terms of which the Christian, in particular, is to define his ethical goals. Although these principles are addressed to the church, they appear to be quite relevant to secular bodies engaging in social action as well. They are:

1. The dignity and worth of the human person; "All institutions . . . are judged in terms of their effect on persons."

2. Human freedom: "Persons cannot be fulfilled in love apart from their freedom to choose (and so to err) and from the responsibility that inheres in moral choice."

3. The inclusiveness of the human community in which Christian concern for neighbor is expressed.

4. Social salvation: the transformation of institutional life.

5. The community of the forgiven and the forgiving: "A barrier-less community transcending all man-made divisions," "a human and divine institution always judged and renewed by God."[35]

The concern of these principles is in accord with the aims of the moral laws studied in the last two chapters. It even appears that one might use these laws as elaborate guidelines to fulfill these same principles. All five principles, for instance, can be fulfilled through reference to the personalistic and communitarian aspects of the moral laws. Since the effectiveness of these laws themselves depends on their harmony with the other moral laws, it follows that the whole system is involved in providing principled guidelines for realizing these Christian goals. It is also obvious that these Christian principles and values are not—except for their higher appeal—only Christian but also humanitarian. They represent some of the common concerns of both Christians and humanists alike, and may be the basis for a "common ground" ethic emphasized especially in Chapter 4.

Education and Planning

It is in planning that activists carefully study their goals, evolve principles, assess costs and resources, devise methods of action or action programs, as well as continually revise previous undertakings. Education and planning might well be the central part of strategy, for without planning there can be no direction in action; without education, no understanding of the issues and goals. Planning concentrates on the duties of the various individuals and sections of the organization as well as on what is to be achieved socially and in what manner. An education program must necessarily issue in action. Without this, it is sterile,[36] in the same way as action without education is blind.

The authors understand planned change as "purposeful intervention to accelerate, retard, or direct processes that are already in motion." This conception of change is based on the understanding of society as an organism rather than as a "machine": "change and growth are seen as normal rather than as exceptional processes." Human responsibility is sometimes to initiate change, but more often to guide it.[37] The authors are critical of equilibrium models of science, which they see as preoccupied with stability rather than a continual state of change in society. In accordance with their view of society, they see strategy as a dynamic process: "the situation to be met is normally not static but involves a complex of moving forces" and policy attempts to "shape the future by exerting influences upon trends that flow from the past into the present."[38]

In planning, the initiating agents measure the readiness for action of other persons and groups. They try to determine which people share the concern, which are motivated and to what extent, and how many are ready to share in preliminary decisions. The following steps are involved, and may be phased according to the readiness of the groups for whom they are meant: exposure—attracting and holding attention; understanding—securing and sharing information to correct errors, break down stereotypes, awaken need; concern—appealing to conscience and value commitment; decision—exploring alternatives and adopting positions; training of competence and providing realizable goals.[39] Timing is very important in planning for action. It must take into account the readiness of the organization in general, the disposition of the social situation with regard to change, and the phasing of social action itself. This last aspect involves determining the kinds of action to be taken and in which order. In general, the timing of action has to take into account "the stage of growth of the institution, the involvement of leaders in other tasks, the amount of stress or dissatisfaction, the ability to act in the direction of achieving goals, and the urgency of the task."[40]

In considering the disposition of the social situation for change, the kind of action to be taken must also be based on the degrees of change already in progress. Revolutionary change calls for crisis intervention or response, and generally allows for little or no planning or education except those already incorporated in original general planning. Nevertheless, crises can be anticipated even in general planning.[41]

Social Action

Action to achieve goals is the ultimate goal of strategy. It is the consummation of strategy through the execution of all its elements as contained in social education and planning. Social action represents direct engagement in the actual campaign for change and takes form in various tactics. The following section will be concerned primarily with this aspect of strategy in trying to discover how feasible each of the strategies investigated may be in the South African context.

As Deats and Stotts define it, social action is "the organized participation of [individuals and groups] in processes by which decisions are made and implemented in the church, the community, voluntary associations, the nation, and international bodies."[42] Such participation finds preparation in social education and the continuing study that accompanies action. The goal of action is the achievement of social ends. Such action may involve member participation, exercise of leadership, decision of a group, use of physical resources, or other means of power and influence. All these activities are carried out by individuals.[43]

Two important elements in social action seem to be those of power and cooperation among persons. Power is here defined as the "discretionary [use and] control of resources and influence over the decisions of persons and groups."[44] As an essential ingredient of political life, it cannot be dispensed with in social action. Only by awareness of our own power and of the problem of power in general can we use power effectively to achieve our goals. Cooperation is made much more possible by our recognition that we engage in social action not in opposition to an enemy but in order to solve a problem. The process of cooperation increases from the initiating agent through intermediate change agents in action directed toward a common target or goal.[45] Cooperation is enlisted through appeal to individuals and groups having various degrees of influence in the community; for instance, the commission on Christian Social Concerns, the school committee, the platform committee of the political party, and the like. The general aim is to affect "institutional forms and processes such as jurisdictional structures, housing practices, and foreign policy."[46] When a particular strategy is ineffective in achieving its aims, it becomes necessary to review its tactics, to plan anew, or to evolve an alternative strategy with a more probable chance of success. Organizations often grow rusty and sterile because of failure or inability to devise new strategies, more especially because they make no room in their original planning for continuing evaluation and review of actions adopted.

Evaluation and Review

Evaluation and review are also a crucial part of strategy, if there is to be any meaningful progress at all in social action. This aspect recognizes the limits of strategy, particularly those limits resulting from crises, drift, and other groups engaged in work for change.[47] No strategy, as already stated, is ever so perfect as to preclude room for improvement. There must be continuing review of policy, goals, and activities, particularly under ethical and theological insights. This should be done with a view to testing whether and how well goals are being accomplished; redefining goals, redesigning means, and even abandoning some programs; discovering the reason for successes and failures and so to build up a body of principles for effective strategy. "We evaluate not to justify ourselves but to guide us in obedience, not to rate institutions or programs but to learn how each may be more effective."[48]

Evaluation and review have to play a very central role in strategies adopted for situations such as that of South Africa, where the government has seldom, if ever, responded positively or directly to people's demands for change. They must also lead to new alternatives and better worked out strategies that will transcend the limitations of the past. This should be even more so because the law makes it difficult to retain and improve upon past strategies, thus continually forcing the formulation of new ones from scratch. We must keep this difficulty in mind as we proceed with the next section.

On the whole, these general guidelines can be employed in formulating more effective strategies for the kind of change sought in South Africa. The theological and ecclesiastical orientation of Deats and Stotts has been revised here to make their application more relevant to the secular bodies involved in the quest for change in this country. Another thing that we must keep in mind in applying these guidelines in the South African situation is that change there cannot be achieved through direct participation by blacks in the structures of government, since such participation is not allowed: this, in fact, is the main problem addressed by black resistance to begin with. Therefore social action should be concentrated more on obtaining the participation of more blacks, especially those with influence, in those structures engaged in seeking sociopolitical change, the more to pressure the government and its electorate to yield to the demands.

ALTERNATIVE STRATEGIES FOR THE INTERNAL QUEST FOR CHANGE: LIMITED OPTIONS

Among the first three organizations studied here, each of the latter two represented a review and improvement of its predecessors' strategies. And within the first organization itself, there had been at least two significant reviews and reforms of past approaches, the first of which had been apparently long overdue. Despite these changes in organizations and strategies, there has been little impact on the political system in the direction of the changes desired. Instead, the organizations involved have themselves been disabled. As already seen in Chapter 3, current new organizations have departed little from the approaches of their predecessors and thus very little improvement has occurred in their form of struggle. It is time once more to revise these past or present strategies in order to see what improvements, if any, can still be made on them. We have already examined alternative structures and must now proceed to an examination of possible strategies, paying more attention to their workability.

Critical Rejection of Working within the System

Before going on with this task, it is necessary to criticize briefly and dispense with one pseudo-alternative, or what blacks have often referred to as a "non-option." This is the "homeland" politics approach invented by the government and "reluctantly" welcomed by some black leaders, which is what is meant by "working within the system." It is important to recognize that the bantustan system is part of the design of the apartheid system. It is the way apartheid is implemented, to rid the cities and most of the country of blacks and so to reduce the challenge to white domination. When this system has been fully implemented, blacks who are allowed to work in so-called white South Africa will be reduced to beggars and obligers: knowing that they "do not belong" here, they would—it is hoped—do everything they can to retain their residence, least of all challenge white domination and sovereignty of South Africa. The rest will be dumped in "their" homeland inventions, there to "blush unseen" and to die secretly of starvation, disease, old age, and uselessness.

From this it becomes questionable whether the bantustan system can be an alternative strategy or goal for Africans. To begin with, they have not chosen it. It is imposed upon them as their only means of political expression and "self-government," lest they retain hopes that some day they might be allowed to participate in the government of the entire country with their white countrymen. Because the bantustans represent their political and land disinheritance, therefore, most blacks reject them. Bantustans receive their only support from those African leaders—most of them government-appointed chiefs—who probably see in them a shortcut to power and wealth, notwithstanding the will of their people.[49] A survey conducted by Mayer as early as the 1970s with the urban Africans contradicted the government's propaganda that the bantustans had the support of most Africans. As Mayer reported,

> When people referred to their ideal model of society as they felt it ought to be, they generally did not speak of independent Bantustans, but of a single South Africa, whole and undivided, with equal opportunities, where race and color would not matter. As we know, this ideal was held out by African leadership for nearly a century with the support of large sections of European opinion. . . . Even today, the opposition party in the Transkeian Legislative Assembly adheres to it and continues to belittle the symbols of independence in Umtata [capital of the Transkei].[50]

While the bantustan leaders themselves portray the bantustans as an alternative strategy toward change, they have, as already seen, accepted the premise that "since the bantustans are here, they cannot be undone." Their conceptions of change are, therefore, obviously modeled along the lines of apartheid. They center mainly upon negotiations for land and economic privileges, now conceived more in terms of a "race federation" with more land concessions as opposed to the government's own idea of a "Constellation of Southern African States" based both on race and the present land allocation. The government's goal is that most of the twenty-six million blacks should be allowed to govern themselves in less than 13 percent of the land, leaving the rest of the country to the four million South African whites. Heribert Adam has written concerning this allocation:

> Political independence for separated tribal units, on altogether 13% of the country's land for 70% of the population, would hardly mean anything in the face of continuing dependence on the all-powerful white state. A large part of the African population, still living as a necessary labor force in the so-called white areas, would possess no rights in places where they were born and in fact, had lived and worked for several generations.[51]

Steve Biko (among others) made the same point, noting that not only are Africans restricted to an amount of land gravely disproportionate to their population numbers; even worse, these scattered pieces of land are the least developed in the country, dry, and often very unsuitable for agriculture and pastoral breeding. The logical result is for Africans, though supposedly self-governing, to remain economically tied to so-called white South Africa.[52] It becomes obvious, then, that the design of the so-called border industries is calculated to see to it that the bantustans, notwithstanding the mockery of their land allocations, do not become economically viable, and thus not really independent. Their residents would be compelled to commute to the "white areas" for work during the day, subject to apartheid industrial laws with the present job reservation and wage discrimination, and return to their "concentration camps" after work. By going along with the government, therefore, the bantustan leaders have been co-opted into the system and are thus presenting no alternative strategy for blacks toward change. Nor do blacks in general conceive of change the way these leaders have come to do, as Mayer's survey shows. Change has to be negotiated—not imposed by the guilty party. A national convention of all South African groups, suggested by black leaders for so long and supported by some church and liberal white groups, seems to be the natural vehicle for such negotiation. Such a convention must, understandably, be called by the government. Apparently, however, the South African government "will not do so until it has been brought to the point of recognition that an alternative to *apartheid* must be found."[53]

If the idea of partitioning the country were to be acceptable at all among blacks, which seems very unlikely at the moment, it would have to be by mutual agreement of all the parties concerned and dealt out proportionately according to black and white numbers. The government might continue to represent its electorate, but would have to stop imposing artificial separations among blacks. One of the weaknesses of "homeland" leaders is that they have allowed these divide-and-rule tactics of the government to penetrate their ideas, especially in talking about a federation, while at the same time they regard the various white groups as constituting a single bloc. This is a further reflection that these leaders stand not with their people, but with the ruling party and fulfill its will without the consent of the people they claim to represent. If no solution other than partition were to be found possible—most blacks would reject out of hand even this hypothesis itself—blacks would insist on a single, undivided black state side by side with the white state desired by whites, but would also insist, for their part, on an open society once the partition has been accomplished. The first three chapters of this book lead to this conclusion, except that the idea itself was not even given the dignity of consideration. The organizations studied refused to consider balkanizing their country. A United Nations expert committee on South Africa made the following conclusion in the early 1960s, and the position is unchanged today:

> No line of partition could be established by agreement, and an imposed partition would create a long frontier and continuing conflict. Nor could partition be politically or economically viable, for there is no substantial area of South Africa in which there is a majority of whites, and the economy of South Africa . . . is entirely dependent on non-white labor. Partition would not solve, but would intensify and aggravate racial conflict.[54]

Adam has observed that partition along the lines proposed by the government, obviously imposed by force, would remain as long as "the real opponents of Apartheid were not allowed to raise their voice, were prevented from organizing themselves for effective counterpressure, and therefore, were unable to have at least a share in such a far-reaching decision."[55] Adam's prediction has been proved right especially in the last few years, during which the government clamped down with fearful anger on its opponents. He also agrees with Mayer's study that the supposed African majority support of the bantustan policy cannot be considered to be representative of African opinion. The "basic rules of this game," he affirms, "are laid down by the ruling group and the alternative of a common non-racial society is excluded from African political activity within Apartheid rules."[56]

It follows that at least four requirements would be necessary, in the last resort, for any idea of partition, the chances of which are as yet very remote indeed: it must be by *mutual agreement* between the black and white parties; the states must be proportionate to population numbers (blacks vis-à-vis whites); ethnic separation must not be imposed upon black people among themselves—they must determine the ethnic composition of their own state; a common agreement must be reached concerning the management or allocation of the country's economic resources—there must be no economic subserviency. Many observers have thought of and agree with some or all of these conditions. We must continue to emphasize, however, that any idea of partitioning the country in any way is far from the minds of the majority of black people and is supported only by those leaders who have accepted the bantustan system.

While the present position of bantustan leaders fails to provide an alternative strategy for change, other strategies adopted might lead to negotiation between the affected parties that—purely hypothetically— might reluctantly find proportionate partitioning of the country as the final compromise possible. Such a solution cannot be imposed on them, as we have seen. In general, blacks in South Africa are positive that there can be "no liberation through collaboration." But while perfectly clear in their minds about which areas may be open to compromise and which not, if negotiation were to be finally realized, it would have to be entered into with open minds so that all areas discussed may be judged on their merits for a meaningful solution.

Urban Guerrilla Warfare

One of the far-reaching alternative strategies presently being practiced or considered by some quarters among blacks in the South African struggle is guerrilla warfare, undertaken both internally and from the borders. I do not intend in this subsection to return to the discussion on violence in general as the genus of this type of warfare. The general conclusion reached on issues of violence and nonviolence in the previous chapter should be understood to apply here as well.

There are certain problems involved in both urban and rural guerrilla warfare as it relates to South Africa. Our present concern is with urban warfare. Apart from our focus on the internal struggle, certain difficulties underlying specifically border or frontier guerrilla warfare as it affects South Africa have led many observers to conclude that guerrilla tactics here have a much better chance of success, however remote, if conducted internally than from the borders with bases in a host country. For this success to be possible, it is believed, the fighting would sooner or later have to approach the cities as key industrial areas and economic sources of the country. South Africa's economic strength in comparison to the rest of Africa has been singled out as her Achilles' heel in the event of a well-planned revolution or strike, and the one thing that is likely to lead this country to the bargaining table. So far, economic strikes have not been effective. There are, it seems, three main reasons for this failure. (1) Prolonged strikes are impossible or difficult to accomplish because black wages are calculated precisely for immediate consumption in order to assure the continued supply of labor by blacks for white industry. Thus few blacks earn enough to save anything for future needs. (2) There are no alternative sources of income or livelihood in the case of a prolonged strike. (3) Trade union organization has been hampered by government interference in various ways to keep it ineffective in organizing the workers for any sustained periods. In the face of these obstacles, and in view of past failures in the peaceful struggle for change, many blacks—especially "returning" exiles—have turned to urban guerrilla warfare as the only meaningful option left worthy of further consideration and worth sacrificing their life for.

General Chances of Success

Guerrilla warfare in general has been described as "par excellence the weapon of the materially weak against the materially strong."[57] At the same time, Fidel Castro has cautioned against the city, in particular, as "a graveyard of revolutionaries and resources."[58] Moss observes that the possibility of a successful urban uprising is ruled out by modern techniques of police control, "unless a political crisis cripples the government or the loyalty of the security forces is in doubt." Moreover, ruthless police states such as South Africa and the Soviet Union seem to rule out completely any possibility of a successful urban guerrilla revolution.[59] Referring to South Africa in particular, another observer has pointed out the preparedness of that country's government for internal conflicts since the disturbances of the early 1960s. Strategic considerations played a major role in the planning, design, and location of African townships.[60] It is not clear from Adam, however, how these considerations can affect the operations of small bands of urban guerrillas, which can easily disappear into the crowds and assume an innocent posture after causing some disturbance. These considerations appear to be more suited to large-scale uprisings such as those of Soweto and Sharpeville, though this does not necessarily suggest that urban guerrillas can have a free play. The government's preparedness for frontier incursions as described by Adam seems more convincing, but is not our present task to consider.

The exiled ANC, for one, recognizes both the military strength of the government and the relative weakness of guerrillas in the struggle for liberation.[61] Though the organization has committed itself to the armed struggle, the leadership seems to see the progress of the internal struggle more in terms of the urban proletarian revolution than in terms of armed struggle. "The revolution in our country," it has stated, "cannot succeed unless the working class is mobilized and exercises hegemony over the revolution in practice and in fact."[62] The chances of such a mass proletarian revolution seem precarious, however, in view of the problems described earlier, of past experience, and of the ruthlessness of the South African government.

It has been argued that slum dwellers—such as South African urban blacks and most of the Third World poor—are "basically conservative so long as life is barely livable" but "catapult to revolution the moment that life is no longer seen as livable for whatever reason."[63] If this is so, it is difficult to understand why South Africa has not yet had a real revolution since life for most blacks has been seen as worse than "barely livable." Moss is led to conclude that the "slum fringes of the third world cities contain a volatile mass that may explode during periods of rapid social transition or economic recession."[64] According to him, de Toqueville's celebrated argument that the French Revolution was triggered by the amelioration of the lot of the poor works equally in the reverse. South Africa's present goal of creating a contented black middle class may be aimed at forestalling part of this threat. At the same time, its implementation may backfire as the people's expectations are raised. But since the general aim is not to improve the condition of all blacks but rather to balance the few rich against the poor as a buffer between black and white, the situation is meant to take care of itself with feuding growing among blacks themselves rather than against their white oppressor.

Some observers have questioned the supposition that the material and military strength of the oppressive government is itself a decisive factor in the guerrilla struggle. If it were, it seems, guerrilla warfare would lose its meaning as a "weapon of the materially weak." Even Moss seems to agree with this observation, noting that public reaction has much to do with the success or failure of urban guerrilla warfare. According to him, the weakness of most present-day guerrilla movements is their failure to mobilize popular support. "Where they can find this support, they have a chance of success; where they can't, they fail."[65] He also agrees with Tupamaro that whereas the safety of the rural guerrilla depends much on his hideout in the jungle, discretion plays a very important role for the urban guerrilla.[66] However, Moss finally concludes that terrorism as an aspect of the guerrilla movement rarely makes a revolution. Urban guerrillas are useful as "political catalysts whose actions can radicalize a society and bring about the kind of social and economic confusion that will lead to a decline in popular belief in peaceful solutions. The end results may be indirect."[67]

Also challenged is the suggestion that the environment where guerrilla warfare is conducted must be well equipped with natural cover to provide camouflage for the fighters. Different environments reportedly call for different guerrilla methods and responses. The only universal prerequisite is thought to be the general political situation.[68] To win popular support, urban guerrillas must be able to explain their actions as purposeful rather than let them appear as random criminal assaults.[69] This means that guerrillas must select their targets well and avoid antagonizing their prospective supporters. Carlos Marighella has emphasized the difference between the activities of the guerrilla and those of the outlaw. The guerrilla must know this difference and act accordingly, if he is not to alienate the people whose support he needs. The activities of the outlaw, according to Marighella, issue from selfish motives and he pays no regard to his target. The guerrilla, on the other hand, follows a political goal. He does not attack ordinary people, only the government and its sources of power. His aim is to distract, to wear out, and to demoralize the militarists, the dictatorship, and its repressive forces.[70] He also aims at exposing both the ruthlessness of the government and its weakness when he confronts it, so that the people may lose complete confidence in it and throw their lot with the guerrilla. If the support of the people cannot be won, at least they must be neutralized not to act against the guerrillas in support of the enemy. Only under extreme circumstances will this have to be achieved by use of force, that is, if the people remain antagonistic to the guerrilla and threaten to expose him to the enemy in any way.

The general conclusion to be drawn from this discussion seems to be that urban guerrilla warfare as such does have some chance of success, notwithstanding the strength of the opponent or the environmental conditions under which it is waged. Human relations appear to be the main determinant of success or failure, though other important factors go with them, as we will soon see. Still, given the prohibitive obstacles that have to be overcome on the way to success, we cannot help but feel that the final results of urban guerrilla warfare cannot be definitely predicted but depend ultimately on chance or the circumstantial turn of events.

Techniques

Stating that a "hypothetical revolution in a western country would have to be city-based," Moss named three main forms of urban guerrilla warfare: "technological terrorism" in the industrial cities, ghetto revolts and separatist uprisings, and urban violence in preindustrial cities. These forms of warfare are carried out through four main "techniques": armed propaganda, political kidnapping, "stiffening" riots and strikes, and subversion of the security forces.[71] Their aims are: to convey the message to the person in the street; to capture publicity, free political prisoners and induce other concessions, and expose the government's weakness; to establish closer links with popular grievances; to demoralize and subvert the army and police in order to neutralize them. Marighella adds some detail to these "techniques," emphasizing the following aspects: aggression rather than defense, attack and retreat, avoiding unnecessary heroism, surprise, mobility, alertness, good information service, and knowledge of one's terrain.[72]

> Surprise mobility and tactical retreat make it difficult for the enemy to bring into play its superior fire-power in any decisive battle. No individual battle is fought under circumstances unfavorable to the guerrilla. Superior forces can be harassed, weakened and, in the end, destroyed.[73]

Marighella proposes the following "action models": assaults, raids and penetrations, occupations, ambush, street tactics, strikes and work interruptions, desertions, diversions, seizures, expropriations of arms, ammunition, and explosives, liberation of prisoners, executions, kidnappings, sabotage, terrorism, armed propaganda, and the general causing of anxiety on the part of the enemy.[74] Most of the guerrilla's equipment is captured or diverted from his opponent. His arms are mostly light and variegated, and he often experiences a severe shortage of ammunition and other disadvantages. He may also purchase his own arms or make them on the spot himself. Money and other necessities are expropriated from the opponent and his banks. Above all, the urban guerrilla must be able to live among and appear as one of the ordinary city people for his own protection.[75] "When the insurgent abandons guerrilla tactics and seeks to fight on the enemy's terms, he discards the peculiar advantages that the insurgent mode of conflict confers upon him."[76]

Most of the methods suggested here for this kind of warfare are directly opposed to the principles of Christian ethics and will find approval by the moral laws discussed earlier difficult to obtain. This may be the reason why many ethicists had rather dispense with the idea of a violent revolution altogether than try to dig for moral loopholes justifying it or any kind of war, for that matter. We are not concerned, however, with such controversies at this stage. Suffice it to say that the moral difficulty experienced in trying to justify such methods now makes it clear why some ethicists, like Denis Goulet,[77] relegate the violent form of revolution—rightly or wrongly—to the so-called ethics of distress.

Application to the South African Situation

Three main logistic problems would have to be overcome before urban guerrilla warfare as described, particularly in the form of "technological terrorism," can be possible in South Africa. These are the problems of recruitment, arms supplies, and the infiltration of armed exiles back into the country and the cities. Exiled black South Africans are generally *more* motivated for armed struggle than those inside the country. This may be because exiles have no way in which they can return to their country except by either begging for amnesty or fighting their way back. Since amnesty means surrender and the tacit acceptance of apartheid, it seems to follow that the only option left is armed struggle. Another reason is that those inside have no idea where to procure arms, nor do most of them have a military mind, since blacks were traditionally not allowed in the army in South Africa. Except for some businessmen, police, and other civil servants, blacks are also not allowed to buy or carry guns or any other lethal weapons, and few have any idea of manufacturing their own. If they were motivated by the continuing crisis and its climaxes, or even by utter despair in the effectiveness of nonviolent methods of change, they would have to depend more on obtaining their arms from their opponents through the methods described, initially using crude and primitive weapons. The success of such an operation and the rest of the venture cannot be guaranteed, as already stated in general terms. It will be more a matter of chance than of course.

In the absence of motivation on the part of blacks inside the country the uprising would have to depend more on the infiltration of armed exiles into the country and cities, possibly engaging in skirmishes with border patrols and other custodians along the way. Such infiltration would be very difficult to accomplish, with the kinds of neighbors South Africa has, who are almost completely dependent on the country for their existence and dare not antagonize it militarily. An ANC guerrilla has illustrated this difficulty. After being recruited in the country and spending a few years of military training abroad, mainly in Tanzania, the time finally came for him and some of his colleagues to return to South Africa and put into practice what they had learned. Naturally, they expected some trouble in Zimbabwe (still Rhodesia then) on their way through, and encountered many challenges there, losing a few of their men in combat with Rhodesian soldiers. The main obstacle, however, came when they least expected it. On entering Botswana, a "frontline state," and beginning to feel safe, they were arrested and taken into custody for being in the country illegally and for carrying weapons. Their identity and destination made no impact on their captors. They were given seven-year sentences and promised to be returned to the country from which they had entered Botswana on their release. After appealing their sentences and falsely insisting that they were from Zambia, their sentences were reduced and they were returned to Zambia after serving their time.[78]

It thus appears that South Africa does not have to protect itself from guerrilla incursions but has effective buffers, even in those countries which are in principle sympathetic to the cause of black South Africans. In practice, these countries cannot overlook their precarious position in relation to South Africa. The difficulty of penetrating this country from any of these buffer states is now worsened by the change of strategy by the white armies from "hot pursuit" of the guerrillas into the host country to directly attacking and destroying the economies of such countries as a means of deterrence from their sheltering guerrillas or allowing them passage. South African forces employed this strategy in their penetration into Zambia, Mozambique, Lesotho, and Botswana in the past several years. It was also instrumental in leading to the Nkomati Accord between South Africa and Mozambique.

Of the three problems, the first two may not be so insuperable, given good organizational ability and the possibility that the guerrilla may initially get by with very simple equipment. Marighella writes that the urban guerrilla must increase his disturbances *"gradually in an endless ascendancy of unforeseen actions* such that the government troops cannot leave the urban area to pursue the guerrillas in the interior without running the risk of abandoning the cities and permitting rebellion to increase on the coast as well as in the interior of the country."[79] All of these obstacles, however, cannot be minimized and final victory, if at all achieved, might even be Pyrrhic and remorseful.

Economic Sanctions

A less drastic alternative strategy, but one considered to be the penultimate before the final resort to violence (guerrilla warfare), is that of appealing for general economic sanctions. The call for sanctions against South Africa was first introduced by the older South African liberation movements, especially following Sharpeville. It was taken up by the United Nations General Assembly, which adopted its first resolution recommending economic measures against South Africa in 1961.[80] Compared with the issue of foreign disinvestment, economic sanctions would apparently be more challenging both to those who impose them and to the South African government. The possibility of their effectiveness, however, has been questioned in the same way as that of disinvestment itself.

At least three forms of economic sanctions have been considered in the past. They include (1) a total trade embargo of all South African exports and imports, (2) partial sanctions, limited to an embargo on certain key South African commodities, and (3) a special oil embargo against South Africa. Other forms of sanctions have been contemplated as well, affecting South Africa's communication and transportation links with the international community. Economic sanctions can be carried out also through the denial of loans and various financial services to this country, as well as through restrictions to South African personnel movements internationally.[81] All these measures would be recommended to countries through the United Nations, and once accepted each country would enforce them on their own multinational companies and other sectors doing trade with South Africa. Individual countries might even add their own peculiar measures. A study by the British Council of Churches in 1965 recommended a four-point measure for Britain, concluding, "unless there is a preparedness to take such limited steps, any discussion of sanctions must be ruled out of court." The council lamented the fact that "hitherto all the world community concerning South Africa has on all sides been more characterized by hot air and hypocrisy, than by effective action."[82] It was recognized, however, that the reason for this was the immense difficulty of accomplishing anything except by force in trying to appeal to the South African government to bring about change in its system. The view often put forward that strengthening South Africa's economy would open doors to liberalism was rejected out of hand: "This view has been advanced for the last forty years, during which time the rights of Africans have been steadily reduced, not increased."[83]

Partial sanctions would center mainly on prohibiting gold exports and oil imports. This would also affect the extensive imports of capital goods items, textiles, petrolatum, and chemicals; exports of wool, uranium, fruits and vegetables, and diamonds. Maizels believes that sanctions on capital equipment would be likely to bring the greater part of South African industry to a standstill because of the country's lack of materials and components. An embargo on gold is certain to affect South Africa gravely, since it supplies more than 60 percent of the gold needs of the world outside the Soviet bloc. The loss of this market would cut South Africa's exports "by an amount not far short of the value of her entire imports of industrial materials, on the basis of the situation in 1956–57."[84] While the gold-mining industry might be able to continue production in spite of the embargo, since it is virtually self-sufficient in equipment, there would be no returns for such production and the country's income would be reduced while the embargo lasts.

An oil embargo as a partial sanction would also have rather far-reaching results, it seems. In the last few years before 1980, South Africa had started an extensive oil rationing program in anticipation of this threat. The situation was exacerbated when Iran stopped supplying this country with oil after the 1979 Iranian revolution, and the price of oil continues rocketing ridiculously. In 1986 the price of gas had reached about $3.00 per gallon. South Africa's industry is less dependent on oil than are the major Western industrial countries as it makes more use of its coal resources than imported oil. Most of its oil imports go to farming, the defense force, and private and public transportation. Those sectors of South African life would be affected much in the event of a total oil embargo,[85] even as they—especially private motorists—are already suffering under the present high prices. Although South Africa is the world's leading extractor of oil from coal through its Coal, Oil and Gas Corporation (SASOL), this source provides a very small part of the 10 percent that takes care of the country's fuel needs. SASOL will thus not be able to ward off a complete oil embargo.[86]

Whatever impact any amount of sanctions might have on South Africa, it is generally agreed that great sacrifice and endurance would be required of those countries imposing them. It has been observed that "sanctions test the strength and patience of their initiators rather than the survival power of the sanctioned."[87] Several conditions have been laid down for their successful implementation and possible effect:

1. They must receive the full cooperation of the leading industrial countries, especially of the United States and Britain.

2. They must be supervised or monitored by a United Nations army in order to prevent their violation by countries sympathetic to South Africa. On the whole, it is suggested that partial sanctions would be more difficult to monitor than complete ones.

3. Those countries dependent on South Africa for income through labor and for imports might have to be subsidized by the United Nations.

4. In the case of oil, only an embargo with a clear prospect of outlasting South Africa's stocks would be worth attempting.[88]

The policy of sanctions against South Africa has not been a very successful nor popular one in the United Nations, particularly with some Western bloc countries. The crisis in Iran in 1980 involving the taking of American hostages reveals what a thorny subject sanctions can be, especially when the country to be punished is a source of material resources crucial to the international community—more so to the developed countries. Few countries are willing or able to sacrifice their material needs to achieve an international objective or some moral goal. Other factors also seem to be involved in relation to South Africa, such as the readiness by Western countries to believe the South African government's propaganda that political change in that country would result in a "communist takeover." How genuinely they believe this is hard to tell, but most often this threat seems to be used merely as an excuse to keep supporting South Africa's minority government and trading with it.

Arguments against the imposition of sanctions on South Africa cover a wide range. At one extreme is the suggestion that they would not be effective, at the other is that economic links are themselves an effective means for effecting change.[89] The latter point has, of course, been repudiated, as just seen. Other arguments are that world trade should not be used as an economic tool, that the cost would be prohibitive, that the sanctions would hurt most those they are designed to aid:

> . . . the Government would obviously proceed to carry out its
> threat of making the impact of any sanctions fall as far as possible
> on the non-whites. The Black unemployed would be shifted off to

their supposed tribal homelands where of course there would be nothing for them to eat, let alone jobs.[90]

It seems, in general, that the possible damage of sanctions on South Africa is minimized as compared to their cost to those who would carry them out. Marvin points out, for instance, that South Africa's prosperous industry was, to begin with, the result of the partial blockades prompted by the two world wars.[91] It is believed that South Africa's endurance in the face of sanctions can last several years, requiring the unity and determination of her opponents. On the other hand, an embargo of this country's imports would lead to soaring world market prices for some commodities and there would probably be a shortage of certain items.[92]

The response of South African blacks to these arguments and our response to both have already been stated in the previous chapter in connection with the issue of disinvestment. They need not be repeated here. We may only add that the likelihood of the idea of meaningful sanctions ever being implemented against South Africa is grim, considering its history and the general economic interests of the powerful Western countries in particular. Limited sanctions imposed by some of the Western countries in 1986 were not meant to be coercive or punitive but more symbolic. They are indicative of these governments' embarrassment at the worst side of the apartheid policy. It may be worthwhile for black South Africans to begin concentrating on what they can accomplish by themselves, without placing too much reliance on what help they can receive from those who appear to sympathize with them. All countries have their own problems and generally find it difficult to respond positively to issues that do not affect them directly or that require them to forego certain of their interests for the sake of some principle. Typically, practical needs are given more attention than theoretical ends. Yet it is also true that outsiders will be prompted to offer their help only when they see true determination and sure progress in the struggler himself in achieving his goal. Perhaps this is the significance of current limited sanctions, however halfheartedly they were adopted by some.

Appeal for United Nations Action

It is thus also questionable how much reliance should continue to be placed on action by the United Nations as a body of nations to help bring about the solution in any way to the South African problem. Past United Nations mediations have failed, in regard to both apartheid and South Africa's relinquishment of the mandated territory of Namibia. In the last decade South Africa has flouted further negotiations with the United Nations, represented by five Western countries, including the United States and Britain, on behalf of the Namibian people. The main question facing the United Nations in any mediation attempt is: What if negotiations fail?

Amelia Leiss has remarked that the United Nations has had a much higher degree of success in stopping or preventing violence than in imposing a solution or enforcing a settlement. "There is not much evidence in the United Nations record to suggest the conclusion that it is highly successful in itself changing situations."[93] Wann Rawles finds its weakness in that its members are themselves divided. Besides, "people generally tend to react unenthusiastically to a problem that is remote from them."[94] In the case of South Africa, not only has the United Nations been unable to halt the trend of apartheid so far, but the trend is moving at an enormous pace, involving much suffering and approaching the total disinheritance of some sectors of the African people in their own land. It also seems only a matter of time before those United Nations members who are still surreptitiously supporting the South African government's policy of "homelands" will surface openly under the pretext: "It is unrealistic to wish them away; they are already here." In the meantime these "homelands" continue to be moderately condemned, but not threatened. After all, "the devil I know is better than the one I don't."

The world body first became involved in South African issues in 1946. The initial issue concerned the treatment of Indians and Pakistanis in South Africa, and it was raised by Asian states.[95] By this time some African and Indian leaders from South Africa had already made some representations at the League of Nations. Pressure on the United Nations increased in 1960 after the Sharpeville event, however, with the African states taking the lead. Ghana, at their head, urged economic and diplomatic sanctions. A Security Council resolution in April of that year stated that continuation of the state of affairs in South Africa "might endanger international peace and security." A year later another resolution asked for the consideration of separate and collective action against that country in accordance with the provisions of the United Nations Charter.[96] In the same year a resolution recommending economic measures was adopted. The seventeenth Session of the General Assembly in 1962 recommended the closing of ports by member states to South African flag vessels and prohibiting their ships from entering South African ports, a boycott of all South African goods and a ban on exports to that country, the refusal of landing and overflight privileges to aircraft belonging to the South African government or to companies registered under its laws. However, the Security Council rejected the call for a total boycott of South African goods and for an embargo on the exporting of "all strategic goods of direct military value."[97]

In 1963 an arms embargo was imposed on South Africa.[98] By this time the Security Council had twice resolved that the policies of the South African government were a "grave disturbance to international peace." Britain and the United States rejected the word "threat" in this resolution. They feared that it would justify the imposing of measures under chapter VII of the United Nations Charter, "but felt no longer able to oppose recognition and condemnation of the facts of the case."[99] Articles 42-47 of this chapter provide for the use of military force by the United Nations in the event of unsuccessful attempts at peaceful negotiation. Both countries and France had continuously refused to support the view that apartheid, though evil, was a threat to world peace.

In 1964 South Africa rejected a United Nations expert committee recommendation—even before this recommendation was taken up by the Security Council—to hold a national convention of all its citizens for the planning of South Africa's future as a just society.[100] Not a single United Nations resolution has ever been taken seriously by South Africa to this day, but resort to chapter VII of the charter seems completely ruled out of consideraton as an inducement to change. Even during the 1976–77 South African crisis the United Nations failed to do anything beyond what it had already done in the past, notably emphasizing the question of an arms embargo.

The United Nations, therefore, particularly those of its Western members with the power of veto, seems to rely more on South Africa's change of heart for achieving any political change in that country. If change was really thought desirable, coercion would be resorted to only when and if these powerful members make "the political judgement that it is required."[101] The fate of the world body's effectiveness rests, therefore, with these countries and with the solution of the dilemma whether it will sometimes have to be achieved through the use of force or be entirely sacrificed for the sake of peace. Hance states that total economic sanctions have never been applied by any group except during wartime. Their application by any one country or any small number of countries cannot be expected to succeed.[102] This seems to imply that South Africa must be at direct war with a United Nations member state before economic sanctions against it can be seriously considered. Leiss, however, concludes:

[The United Nations has been an] instrument of peaceful change. Those who press upon it a role of forcing the creation of a just society in South Africa call upon it to depart on a new path. The concept of using United Nations collective measures to enforce change, whether among states or within them, would chart a new course for the United Nations.[103]

Until quite recently it seemed probable that a view similar to this, especially in its general form as expressed by the quote above, was held by those member states that have been seriously opposed to collective economic measures against South Africa. Certain international events that led to the calling of collective measures against Iran and the Soviet Union about eight years ago and Libya recently call this to question, though. As already indicated, such measures against Iran, as against South Africa especially because of its gold, were unlikely to be very popular because of the importance of Iranian oil for Western economy. The apparent determination of some powerful countries to protect South Africa from these same measures seems to leave those who would hope for some help from the world body in resolving their country's disputes with no final court of appeal.

Christian Action

Appeals for both economic sanctions and United Nations pressure on South Africa constitute indirect action by black South Africans to achieve their goal. One direct form of action, which stands at the other extreme from urban guerrilla warfare, is Christian action or, as we will understand it here, social action undertaken by the churches and by Christian groups. This form of action has not been fully investigated in South Africa as a strategy for sociopolitical change. In this section I will attempt a few suggestions by reference to some of the works that have already been noted earlier.

We have already seen that the church in the past, in South Africa, has been more concerned with "charity," so to speak, than with "justice." Unhappiness with this restriction of the gospel teaching led to various reactions by black Christians. The first of these reactions found expression in the establishment of the African independent churches. John de Gruchy writes that

> the independent churches symbolize the black revolt against European spiritual and cultural domination. However, while they soon became apolitical, their rise was coterminous with and paralleled by the awakening of black nationalism.[104]

In recent years this revolt has been represented by the rise of black theology, as distinct from African theology.[105] Black theology is not only a challenge to the church to face up to the implications of its mission, it is also the first brick of reconstruction in that direction, beginning with the "reevangelization" of black people that will lead to their spir-

itual freedom and simultaneous striving for their political and social liberation. The primary focus of black theology is thus conscientization in
the grass roots. "What is the gospel but a form of conscientization?"
Davis expresses this fact well when he writes,

> As the poor and exploited learn, on the one hand, to perceive the
> truth of their existing socio-political conditions, and on the other
> hand, hear the gospel call to freedom, they are motivated to act
> against dehumanization.[106]

This is the aim of black theology for black Christians in South Africa.
But if "the church be the church," this must be the goal of the whole
church—not only in South Africa, but wherever it ministers to all the
childen of God, especially the poor and the oppressed.

The rest of the church in South Africa is, therefore, called to this
type of grass roots reevangelization. Awareness of injustice and the effort to eradicate it can no longer be merely an academic affair of theologians and other intellectuals. Part of the mission of the church is to
exhort and help Christians to "make a total break with the unjust established order and make a forthright commitment to a new society."[107]
The Thessalonica Report of the World Council of Churches affirms
that not only is God at work in "rapid social change" but that he also
urges persons, through his church, to challenge social and political stag-
nation. God

> is bringing forth more justice and equality; . . . He is awakening
> multitudes of men to challenge the social stagnation in which they
> find themselves, and opening up new possibilities for the develop-
> ment of personal and social life.[108]

Apart from the church's preaching of prophetic and critical sermons in
South Africa, there are at least two other ways in which this reevangelization can be accomplished. One of these may have been exemplified in
the Boston crusade of religious leaders that led to the "Covenant of Justice, Equity, and Racial Harmony," on November 19, 1979, and the
appeal for commitment to it. This type of crusade will not be meaningful, of course, if it is merely a crisis-within-a-crisis oriented event. It
would have to be well planned and organized, scanning not only the
large cities and townships but the whole country and permanently arranged in local action groups. In other words, it might be some kind of
Billy Graham-type evangelization writ both large and small, but focused on social justice and change rather than merely on spiritual en-
richment. Of course, if the participation is nonracial, the South African
government might try to stop it, but this is precisely where the conflict
arises between church and state and where the challenge to the church

lies. For the church to submit would be for it to obey man rather than God. It would be interesting to find out how the government would react if all the participants were advised to carry their Bibles and, in case of police interference, raise them high in silence or in common prayer. Such portable sanctuaries, if violated, would explode the Christian pretensions of the South African government leaders and, if they approve of its action, those who support it.

A similar kind of crusade to that of Boston, probably an imitation of it, was conducted in South Africa in the city of Durban in 1979.[109] Its theme was described as "*Repentance for the injustices of our society,* and commitment to strive for a *more just society*." As already suggested, unless this event were to cover the whole country and become more than a crisis affair, it can have little effect on South African society or its politics. At most, it would express merely the commitment to justice of those who organized it. In 1980 church ministers and bishops in a significant move marched to John Vorster Square in their apparel to demand for the release of a priest and other detainees. On Easter in 1986 priests, bishops, nuns, and other Christians marched for the same purpose, carrying crucifixes. Crosses in this case were a good substitute for Bibles, suggested above.

Another grass roots approach to evangelization could find a basis in organizations such as the Inter-Denominational African Ministers' Association of South Africa (IDAMASA) and their white counterparts or other ecumenical associations. Following the pressure-group theory that we discussed earlier in this chapter, members of such organizations could serve as a stimulus for the establishment of local ministers' caucuses, who in turn would stimulate the formation of "social awareness and action groups" in their parishes. A proliferation of these groups with a common purpose in both black and white churches all over the country would create not only awareness but also concern about the country's injustice, mutual trust, and the overcoming of past suspicions, as well as the desire to unite together against racial oppression and hatred. Apart from the programs that would be planned on local and national as well as on ministerial levels, there might also be occasion for sharing, cooperation, and interrelation between the black and white sides as progress is made on each side. While South African society is separated, the church need be subject to this un-Christian division only if it is an uncritical reflection of its fallen communities. In fact, the church is called to "keep open channels of communication between 'enemies' even during the conflict, to serve as a reminder and embodiment of reconciliation."[110] But the church must also realize that it is in danger of failing in its mission of love as long as it is surrounded by unjust structures and if it does not do its part in working to dismantle them.

> To actualize neighbour-love is to create a new world in which the neighbour will be freer tomorrow than he or she is today. Neighbour-love is not some romantic I-Thou island; it must include social awareness and an obligation to create healthy cultural, economic, political, and social-structures for all.[111]

Like the other strategies investigated, a program such as this one would not necessarily, as Dom Helder Camara has observed, "make [evil] socio-economic structures tumble like the walls of Jericho." If the church fails, however, let it fail trying as hard as it can to fulfill its social mission to South Africa—not folding its arms in apathy or promising relief only in heaven when all of this life had been meaningless.

These are only a few of the ways in which the church can attempt to carry out its social mission, while at the same time cooperating with other social organizations wherever possible. The church rightly strives for a peaceful solution to all kinds of conflict in the world. If violent revolution should suddenly become inevitable in South Africa, however—as it seems imminent in the absence of any viable solution—then the church must heed the words of Bennett:

> Christians in the revolutionary situation have to do all in their power to exercise the ministry of reconciliation to enable the revolutionary change to take place non-violently or, if this is not possible, with the minimum of violence. But we must realize that some Christians find themselves in situations where they must, in all responsibility, participate fully in revolution with its inevitable violence.[112]

When this situation is reached, the Christian can only place himself in the hands of God and chant in desperation: "*In manus tuas Domine commendo [facta et] spiritum meum.*"

Active Noncooperation: "Black Power"?

As a secular counterpart of this last type of Christian action we may envisage, on the general social level, social groups operating similarly at grass roots. Such groups might find their bases on black consciousness and white consciousness groups such as those described under "structure" above. Whereas Christian action in general tends to emphasize the change of heart, it would be naive for any secular group to depend only on conversion of whites for social change to come about in South Africa. Gail Gerhart has correctly pointed out that because the prosperity and status of whites under the present system rests to such an extent on the exploitation of blacks, only the most sanguine optimist could foresee an evolutionary process of voluntary white capitulation leading to a just redistribution of resources between the races. The present political system precludes such a possibility.[113]

Blacks must, therefore, welcome the assistance of white "radicals" working for change within their own communities, but cannot help but retain a minimum of doubt and suspicion that any meaningful change would result from this exercise, nor need they be in a hurry to cooperate with such groups in any serious way.

At least three mechanisms of effecting change have been noted: conversion, accommodation, and coercion.[114] Whites who sincerely want change in South Africa will naturally depend on converting their own communities. Blacks can no longer rely on this method alone, but must resort to some form of coercion. The probability of receiving any accommodation from the government outside its apartheid system is quite remote. The question facing blacks is, What form of coercion will be used?

Internal, above-board social action will necessarily remain nonviolent in motivation, if only to minimize casualties while blacks are still building up their strength. The question is how to carry it out without government interference and with an assurance of a sustained and effective leadership. Concerning South Africa, Sharp has written that "every means of change has been dammed up. The flood waters are rapidly rising."[115] Is there still room for above-board nonviolent action in this country? Sharp himself has offered a few suggestions that may be useful to examine briefly.

He begins by pointing out the dilemma of the South African situation in the quest for change. There is no way out, he feels, which does not involve severe suffering and bloodshed. "Whether nonviolent or violent means of resistance are used, great suffering will be incurred by the nonwhite people. Anyone who opposes action on the grounds that it will lead to suffering is profoundly ignorant of the situation." The question is how to act effectively, and whether the suffering will finally be rewarded.[116]

In his general exploration of nonviolent action Sharp sees the basic approach of nonviolence as "denying the enemy the human assistance and cooperation which are necessary if he is to exercise control over the population." He sees three main classes for such action: nonviolent protest and persuasion, noncooperation, and nonviolent intervention.[117] The first includes pilgrimages, marches, picketing, vigils, "haunting" officials, public meetings, issuing and distributing protest literature, renouncing honors, protesting emigration, and humorous pranks. The second involves various types of social noncooperation (e.g., social boycotts), economic boycotts (e.g., consumers' boycotts, traders' boycotts, rent refusal, and international trade embargo), strikes and political noncooperation (e.g., boycott of government employment, boycott of elections, administrative noncooperation, civil disobedience and mutiny). The third includes sit-ins, fasts, reverse strikes, nonviolent obstructions, nonviolent invasion, and parallel government. Some aspects of all three classes of action have been attempted in South Africa by one group or another, but for blacks the culmination was in some forms of the second, especially social and economic boycotts and political noncooperation. Sharp insists that the success of nonviolent resistance is highly dependent on the persistence of the activists in abiding by their own methods of opposition and in overcoming all pressures and temptations to succumb to the opponent's violent methods. While nonviolent action is likely to earn some sympathy and support for the resisters, even from the oppressor's own camp, any amount of violence will alienate popular support for the cause.[118]

In reference to the South African situation, Sharp says that the government there is no different from any other government in owing its continued existence to the continued willingness of its subjects to obey it and cooperate with it. Without the submission and cooperation of blacks, therefore, the South African government and its system of apartheid is sooner or later bound to fall. The only problem that remains in effecting this fall is, according to Sharp, that of organization and of strengthening the black masses and their resistance. Above all, once these objects have been achieved, blacks must be willing and determined to persist in defiance despite government repression. Real freedom, he insists, is something that has to be earned and taken, "and which can therefore be defended and extended even in the face of new threats."[119]

Sharp then goes on to list five factors he thinks are especially to be taken into consideration in working out a strategy for change in South Africa. These are:

1. The present conditions in South Africa—pros and cons to the resistance: (a) the government, (b) white opposition, (c) black activists and organizations, (d) potential white resistance, (e) the whole population.

2. The techniques of nonviolent action, its dynamics, requirements for success, and possible experience elsewhere.

3. How to reduce or remove present weaknesses among blacks that would increase their ability to cast off oppression.

4. How best to split the white South African population from support for the government, including liberals, religious groups, etc.

5. How to stimulate maximum international assistance and how to use it most effectively.

Sharp makes several criticisms of past black resistance, the most important of which have already been alluded to in the last chapter.

It has been suggested that much of what Sharp says here and in his other works has to be studied seriously and tried in practice for the growth of any meaningful nonviolent resistance in South Africa. Our only dissatisfaction was with his apparent insensitivity to the difficulties of organizing and mobilizing the people for resistance if their leadership is removed and restricted by the government. Part of the reason for the long lull in activity among blacks after Sharpeville was not so much weakness or apathy on their part as lack of leadership because of the government's imprisonment of most of the leaders. Banning orders might be successfully violated, as Sharp suggests, or evaded, as the case of the late Steve Biko and many others prove. But when a banned leader is then removed, another leader must emerge to take his place. Otherwise, the possibility of meaningful action seems slight, and the government has proved during the BCM era that it has an insatiable capacity for black "leader-consumption." We may agree with Sharp that often little organization or quite spontaneous action (without an established leadership) is "highly effective."[120] However, even well-organized activities have failed in South Africa. It seems that spontaneous, unorganized action depends more on chance for its success than does well-planned organized action. It would be unfair to say that failure in this regard is due mainly to weakness in black people and their determination to change the system. Rather, the problem here is that black leaders, except those who support the government's policy, are never permitted to make their full impact on black organization and action. This means that to preserve leaders, black organizations must concentrate mostly on how to be effective without creating identifiable "superstars" among their leaders. There always must be leaders, it seems, but they must level their stature and encourage more participation by ordinary people in the decision-making processes of their organizations, so that anyone may be able to serve as a leader in case of emergency.

During its time, the BCM managed to produce one leader after another in response to government action, probably because of its democratic process and its leadership-training programs. However, the leveling process suggested here, though originally aimed at, was not quite successful and the key people in the movement remained exposed, making it possible for the government to chop off their heads, so to speak. Only when this leadership crisis has been solved can Sharp's other suggestions have a better chance of being analyzed and tried. The suggestion that blacks attempt to split the white population from the support of the government sounds too optimistic, and few blacks would take it seriously. Most blacks feel that it is no longer for them to approach whites for possible assistance. However, the last few years have witnessed some withdrawals from white political parties by disillusioned whites who felt that the main white political leaders and parties had too narrow a vision of the future of the country and its real needs. Any such reconsideration of stance and help by whites working with their own communities for change is generally appreciated. However, blacks feel that they themselves must continue to "do their own thing" until they see a clear prospect for improvement and meaningful cooperation with whites. While they remain open to the future, they want to continue to strengthen and empower themselves, the more to demonstrate to the government and its electorate that stability in the country cannot be assured for as long as things remain as they are. When their power to change the system has been increased and is no longer threatened, they will then be able to cooperate more freely with those who sympathize with them. At this time there will be no more fear of being used or neutralized. The time of reckoning will be near. This will be the moment of "black power." Whether it will come through this way of nonviolence or through guerrilla warfare—the two extremes very much disputed today in South Africa—will depend on the lateness of the hour in the struggle, on the disposition of the government at that time toward change, and especially on the ethical choice to be made by blacks in the face of the situation confronting them.

CONCLUSION

With some reorganization in structure, strategy, and leadership in the South African struggle, it may still be possible for blacks working internally for change to press for a peaceful solution of their problems. Such a solution excludes their acceptance of the bantustan system, which is not seen as a strategy or a solution but as part of the program of the oppressor. The peaceful solution will depend very much on the success of the organizers to evade the government. It will also depend on the stage in which the exiles are in their organization, who have more or less abandoned hopes for nonviolent change, are committed to guerrilla warfare, and may gradually infiltrate back into the country to carry out their plans.

Internal blacks still seeing some hope in nonviolent action may find the study of Gene Sharp useful, especially because he has not only studied nonviolent resistance in general but has also given suggestions on how it may apply to South Africa. It is probable, however, that his books are banned in the country as "subversive" literature. The guidelines for strategy also studied here can be used in formulating more effective and morally worthy strategies as well. Though they were worked out with a particular denomination in view, they may easily be adapted for Christian action in general and for other social groups working for change within South Africa.

The present study is not, as such, committed to nonviolence exclusively as a method nor as the only ethically justifiable strategy for change. Rather, it accepts the view that there is a strong moral and religious presumption for nonviolent action in effecting social and political change. It also sees nonviolence as an expedient form of action in the South African situation because of the repressive power of that country's government. In the event of complete failure of nonviolent action to attain its objective, the just war or revolution theory remains open for consideration as a possible means of minimizing suffering.

All the forms of strategy discussed here have their own limitations, which vary in their seriousness. Urban guerrilla warfare has both moral and certain strategic difficulties. Ethically, it may belong to the realm of what has been termed the "ethics of distress," though this is not necessarily a valid type of ethics. Strategic problems involve recruitment, logistics, and guerrilla infiltration (into the country and the cities). Like all the other strategies considered, but perhaps more so, the success of urban guerrilla warfare in South Africa would depend more on chance than on necessity. It seems that blacks in South Africa would do better on the whole to rely more on what they can accomplish themselves to achieve change than on what they can achieve through sympathy from other countries either in the form of economic sanctions or through general United Nations intervention. Unfortunately, past appeals for both forms of assistance have been futile and even demeaning.

Positive action by the church in South Africa is also restricted by its greater reliance on personal conversion than on direct and coercive action. Unless there is a purposeful systematic reevangelization and conscientization effort, which will lead Christians themselves to engage in direct action for change, such Christian action is doomed to failure. This is especially so among whites, considering that they have always believed that their policies are compatible with Christian teaching.

It seems probable that change in South Africa will ultimately depend on the maturity of "black power," if this is understood as a direct, lasting challenge to the system by blacks after summoning their strength and uniting in unrelenting action against it for better or for worse. All black South Africans hope that this will come about peacefully. At this stage, however, very few have categorically ruled out of consideration solutions that may be less peaceful.

Afterword

It was made clear from the very beginning of this study that it would be a selective one. Its focus has been limited to examining the challenges posed by black national resistance movements to the South African government's policy of apartheid and its implications on the lives of black people. This limited focus by no means implies that there are no other forms of opposition to apartheid, as Chapter 1 tried to show. Especially since the national school boycotts and subsequent unrest sparked off by Soweto students in 1976, students throughout the country have been at the forefront of resistance to government policy. Often they have preferred to stay out of school completely rather than continue to accept the inferior status of black education. Around 1985 they adopted the slogan "Liberation now; education later." Until the beginning of 1987 it was as if black children might have to forget about continuing their formal education until years more to come.

As the slogan indicates, even for students the issue has gone beyond educational matters. They are talking of total liberation not only from a bad system of education but also from domination by a minority in the land of their birth. Their determination is often expressed in such terms as to imply that they are the ones who will bring the government to its abdication. Whatever the impact of student action on national politics and the struggle for change in the country, it is becoming increasingly clear that no comprehensive study of black opposition and challenge to apartheid can be undertaken without giving any consideration to the role played by the student movement in this challenge. This is particularly so since the Soweto eruption in 1976, as student involvement during the whole black consciousness era cannot be successfully extricated from national politics.

The same can be said of the role of the church and some of its organizations, primarily the South African Council of Churches (SACC) under its leadership since the late 1970s. Much has already been written separately about this role in confronting the country's policies toward blacks. There is, of course, much that has been negative in the church's approach throughout its history in South Africa, as we tried to show in Chapter 1. A greater part of the institutional church in South Africa may still be lukewarm toward apartheid, but within it have been encouraging and prophetic voices that have testified that the church need not be restricted in its mission to so-called religious matters, while letting "Caesar" do as he pleases with the people of God. These voices have aroused international interest in what is happening in the country and have helped put South Africa in the political map of the world. Some of the individuals behind these voices have worked from wider church platforms not restricted to particular congregations or denominations. From these platforms they have helped radicalize the role and image of the church and to wrench it from old stereotypes of the radical separation of the gospel and politics.

Traditionally, the church in general views its social mission more as a prophetic one and thus one of challenging the ills of society than of active participation in the actual "nitty-gritties" of social change. It is the conscience of the world. Hence its work in society is largely restricted to warning society—the government—of its injustice and wrongdoings and trying to restore it, through exhortations, to rule in accordance with divine ordinance. Churches make their official pronouncements on such matters mainly in church councils, synods, episcopal convocations, and so forth, as the case may be. These official bodies can, for the sake of more effectiveness, authorize the establishment of relevant smaller bodies for more actual involvement in social action, while their own involvement as governing bodies remains somehow restricted to proclamations. Traditional bodies similar to these have, however, tended to be too spiritual in a conservative sense that saw no "temporal" role for the church in society.

There is need for a church strategy that considers human beings not only as spiritual animals to be liberated from their material prison, but rather as complete wholes in their entire sociopolitical and economic environments. We need not go into detail here about this possible role and contribution of the church, which is not unknown in other countries. Suffice it to say that in South Africa the church was reluctant for too long even to execute its ordinary prophetic mission toward society.

In addition to the church and the student movement, another indispensable agent to consider in studying black challenge to apartheid is the labor union movement. The involvement of the labor movement is not a new phenomenon in the black struggle for change in South

Africa. Trade unions have always worked hand in hand with national movements not only in agitating for a living wage but also in trying to pressure the government for political change. The stayaway is an old political weapon of black national movements that was always carried out with the cooperation of the trade union movement. Through the years, however, the effectiveness of trade unions was gradually eroded through legislation, but this did not completely affect their activity until perhaps after Sharpeville in 1960 and the subsequent lull in black political organization. With the rise of the Black Consciousness Movement in the late 1960s, union activity was revived mainly through black consciousness–oriented trade unions. Although the links between these unions and the national movement persisted, the link between union activity and the exerting of political pressure on the government was reduced because of the new BCM strategy. As stated in the second chapter, the BCM's strategy before its representative organizations were banned in 1977 was to suspend direct political challenge of the government until it had accumulated sufficient strength and motivated the people enough to do so.

Current cooperation between trade unions and the national movement is thus a tradition of black resistance in the country. The specific cooperation of the two groups in implementing stayaways is a reenactment of the pre-1960 approach in applying political pressure on the government. The last five years, particularly, have experienced more and more such cooperation, even involving the student movement at times. In 1985, for instance, students asked for the support of the Congress of South African Trade Unions (COSATU) in enforcing stayaways to pressure the government to meet certain demands. It also received the support of the United Democratic Front. Since then, the union–national movement–student trio has been involved together often in certain campaigns, more often with the cooperation of church organizations such as the SACC. Early in 1987 some of the unions explictly adopted a political strategy, endorsing the need for their involvement in contributing directly to black national liberation.

A significant number of books already have appeared on each of these forms of resistance to apartheid and it may not be necessary to suggest the need for a comprehensive treatment of the challenge posed by each one of them in a single study. Nevertheless, while such a need might not have arisen a few years ago or when some of the books devoted to a particular focus were written, it now seems more urgent to meet this need in view of the cumulative events and significance of the current decade. This postscript is in itself an acknowledgment of this fact. It is at the same time an admission that it would have been beyond the original goal of this book to have attempted an expansion for the purpose of meeting this need.

Even more serious than the significance of the movements just discussed, it may be considered a defect of the present study that it only mentions in passing the events of Sharpeville, Soweto, and the circumstances surrounding the death of black consciousness leader, Steve Biko, as well as recent school boycotts. If this book was conceived as a historical study, it would have been inevitable to try to discuss in it all apsects of these events in some detail. However, the emphasis of the study is on theory and practice and their ethical significance in the black struggle for change. It has seemed proper, therefore, to pick up from these events only what seemed immediately relevant for this purpose. This in no way diminishes their historical significance both for the struggle itself and for arousing world consciousness to the evil of apartheid as a current embodiment of "man's inhumanity to man." Be that as it may, an additional page or two to this postscript in reference to these events will highlight their importance to the black community of South Africa as well as their historical significance in the black challenge and resistance to apartheid.

The campaign that led to the Sharpeville event[2] was meant by its implementors to be the ultimate "No!" to the pass system. As already seen, this system restricted the movement and employment opportunities of the African people. In form, the campaign somewhat resembled the Defiance Campaign of 1952[3] in the participants' self-assertiveness and challenge to the government. Like the latter, it was nonviolent. Far more than the Defiance Campaign, however, the violence that it unintentionally provoked on the part of the government exceeded proportions. The government had previously responded violently to challenge by the national movements and trade unions, but never perhaps to such an extent with regard to the number of deaths. For the first time in years, because of this brutality, apartheid came to the attention of the world. The United Nations openly condemned it, coming just short of declaring it a threat to world peace. Instead, at the insistence of Britain and the United States, it was declared a "grave disturbance to international peace," thus averting the imposition of measures against South Africa under chapter VII of the United Nations Charter.[4]

Just as there was a lull in political activity in the country following the Sharpeville tragedy and the banning by the government of the ANC and the PAC, so was the evil of apartheid soon forgotten by the world as headlines began to disappear from the media and life resumed its normal course. Less attention was paid to occasional sporadic news sprinkled on the world press afterward. Then Soweto erupted in 1976. It was the children's revolt, ostensibly against the imposition of the

Afrikaans medium of instruction in some school subjects. The language issue, however, is now generally understood to have merely provided an occasion for the expression of underlying grievances. Their root cause was to be found in sociopolitical and economic conditions of blacks in the country.[5] A Soweto student leader is later reported to have said: "Even if the White man's regime would give concessions to our people they are no longer interested in that. All they want is to hit at [uproot] the system and to hit very hard."[6]

The actual uprising came when the police opened fire on students marching across one of the Soweto townships to hold a meeting at one of the schools. A thirteen-year-old pupil named Hector Peterson became the first police victim in this unprovoked shooting incident, with many more to follow. Helplessly, the students responded to this brutality with stones and other forms of angry reaction that left the township up in smoke. Any symbol of government presence was attacked, including government offices and vehicles. Other areas of the country also became involved and called for the removal of the entire system of Bantu education and apartheid itself. For the next year and a quarter there was almost absolute chaos and schooling was greatly interrupted.

The government responded with thousands of detentions without trial, accompanied by torture, under its new Internal Security Act. Hundreds more were convicted for unrest-related offenses. After about fourteen months of unrest the death toll was over seven hundred—far exceeding that of Sharpeville and its accompanying incidents. It was as though the government had completely lost its conscience and ceased to value life if it belonged to a black person. Once more, South Africa was in the headlines of world newspapers and other media. Condemnations of varying import were heard from all corners of the world.

These condemnations became even stronger when Steve Biko died in detention under highly suspicious circumstances that became fully exposed only years after his death. He was reported to have been carried half naked in a police truck, purportedly to a government hospital about five hundred miles away, after undergoing torture and suffering a collapse.[7] Commenting on his death, then minister of justice, Mr. Kruger, caused a stir by remarking that it left him cold. Although the government later implicitly accepted responsibility for the death by paying Biko's family $78,000[8] in compensation, it did not find the doctors who treated him before his death guilty of any misconduct. It was not until the medical council initiated its own investigation that, almost five years later, unethical behavior was discovered on the part of the two doctors. Disciplinary action was taken against them by the council. In the havoc that followed Biko's death the government clamped down on twenty organizations, two newspapers, and a periodical.[9] In this way it ended the dominance of the black consciousness era in the country.

Students have continued to be at the forefront of political activity in South Africa following the Soweto outbreak. This has been so particularly since the new wave of student unrest that began in 1980. Most of this activity appears to have been spontaneous, though some form of organization and adoption of crisis leadership began with the establishment of new student organizations in the late 1970s and early 1980s. The specific roles played by each of these organizations will have to await a detailed study and research, which is not part of the present task. On the surface, most of the recent activity originated with individual local schools, but once it started, it influenced other schools until it spread through the entire country. As the unrest spread, student organizations seem to have become involved with crisis leadership, which took the form mainly of coordinating student demands and action as well as assuming the role of mediator and conveyor of student grievances.

In the first few years of this decade student activity was focused on protesting age restrictions in black schools, corporal punishment, and the elimination of student representative councils by the Department of Education and Training. Students went on to demand the abolition of apartheid education and consequently apartheid itself. Their demands culminated in the slogan "Liberation now; education later," as already explained. By 1984 the students led the move to protest against rent increases in the Vaal area. Thirty-one people were killed in ensuing police action and unrest. The rent protests subsequently spread through the entire country, leading to consumer boycotts in some areas. In March 1985 nineteen people were killed in unrest at the Langa Township of Uitenhage, Cape.[10]

Boycotts of schools continued throughout the year and by year's end it was impossible for examinations to be written. The following year, 1986, was the tenth anniversary of the Soweto outbreak. Long before the beginning of the year there had been rumors that there would be a complete boycott of schools for the whole year. By the middle of the year a second state of emergency was declared following countrywide violence against people responsible for implementing the government system in black townships and suspected government informers. The first state of emergency had been declared in October 1985 and lifted in March 1986 after a world uproar. One of the persisting grievances in 1986 was the army occupation of schools and the ubiquity of armed soldiers in all black townships. They constantly provoked violence and shot people at will. Throughout this entire year there was virtually no schooling and by the end of the year there was concern that protest might spill over to 1987. It was a relief to most parents when the boycott was called off in the latter year and students voluntarily returned to school.

South Africa has remained continuously in the world news as a result of the continuing unrest since it first erupted at Boipatong and the whole Vaal area in 1984. Reports of this unrest represented a new wave of interest in the country by the international community and its media, following upon the examples of Soweto and Sharpeville. Because of the two states of emergency and persistent government interruption of news coverage, however, there have been occasional news blackouts as well as restrictions on the movement of news and television crews for the purpose of obtaining firsthand information. Hence such waves in the provision of news do not necessarily reflect the actual trend of resistance activity in the country. Rather, they reflect what is accessible, more often because of its spectacularity, or rather because it is considered more likely to interest overseas readers because of its extreme nature.

At the same time, it is true that black political activity is not always sustained at the same level for a prolonged period but rather reflects peak periods and times of "normal" operation. "Sharpeville," "Soweto," Biko's death, and the "Vaal" represent such peaks in the black challenge to apartheid and the state repression that accompanies them. Further, the 1980s so far seem to represent the longest sustained agitation against the government in the history of black political resistance since 1960. Such agitation, however, can be understood only in the light of the Soweto event in 1976, as there has never been real calm in the country since then.

Notes

INTRODUCTION

1. Although in the last few years the government has been engaged in reviewing its policy on the permanence of urban Africans in "white South Africa," this fact does not alter the government's aim as whites will still remain dominant politically and Africans will continue to be deprived of voting rights and other privileges of citizenship.

2. On the basis of the 1985 population census the total South African population was 29,443,614. Of this number, 21,197,253 people (72 percent) were Africans.

3. See Chapter 3 below.

CHAPTER 1: GENERAL HISTORICAL OVERVIEW

1. Thomas G. Karis, Gwendolen M. Carter, and Gail M. Gerhart, eds., *From Protest to Challenge: Documents of African Politics in South Africa 1882–1964,* 4 vols. (Stanford: Hoover Institution Press, 1972–1977), 1:5.

2. See the next section below.

3. Alex Hepple, *South Africa: A Political and Economic History* (London: Pall Mall Press, 1966), pp. 83, 86.

4. Karis, Carter, and Gerhart, *From Protest to Challenge,* 1:5.

5. Cf. Albert Luthuli, *Let My People Go: An Autobiography* (New York: Meridian Books, 1962), pp. 140, 239-43.

6. Christopher R. Hill, "The Future of Separate Development," in *Southern Africa in Perspective: Essays in Regional Politics,* ed. Christian P. Potholm and Richard Dale (New York: Free Press, 1972), p. 60.

7. L. Schlemmer, "Factors Underlying Apartheid," in *Anatomy of Apartheid,* ed. Peter Randall (Johannesburg: SPROCAS, 1970), p. 22.

8. See Chapter 2, below.

9. Cf. Muriel Horrell, comp., *A Survey of Race Relations in South Africa: 1977* (Johannesburg: SAIRR, 1978), pp. 36-37.

10. See Mary Benson, *South Africa: The Struggle for a Birthright* (n.p.: Minerva Press, 1966, 1969), p. 119.

11. N. J. Rhoodie, *Apartheid and Racial Partnership in Southern Africa* (Cape Town: Academia, 1969), pp. 50, 53.

12. Schlemmer, "Factors Underlying Apartheid," pp. 19ff.

13. L. E. Neame, *The History of Apartheid* (London: Pall Mall Press, 1962), p. 14.

14. Ibid., p. 16.

15. Ibid., pp. 22-23.

16. Ibid., p. 39.

17. Karis, Carter, and Gerhart, *From Protest to Challenge,* 1:63.

18. From 1910 to 1961 South Africa was known as the Union of South Africa. In 1961 it attained the status of Republic and severed ties with the British Commonwealth.

19. A. N. Pelzer, *Verwoerd Speaks: Speeches 1948–66* (Johannesburg: APB Publishers, 1966), p. XXIX.

20. Cf. Freda Troup, *South Africa: An Historical Introduction* (London: Eyre Methuen, 1972), p. 218.

21. See Pelzer, *Verwoerd Speaks,* pp. XXIX-XXXI.

22. Benson, *South Africa,* p. 35.

23. Andre Brink, "Some Aspects of Culture and Apartheid," in Randall, ed., *Anatomy of Apartheid,* p. 40.

24. This amount was increased to 13 percent in 1936. See Benson, *South Africa,* p. 65.

25. Cf. Neame, *History of Apartheid,* pp. 18-20.

26. Ibid., pp. 16, 23.

27. For instance, color was already a factor in marriage questions by 1685. See Neame, ibid., p. 13.

28. Steve Biko, *I Write What I like: A Selection from His Writings,* ed. Aelred Stubbs (San Francisco: Harper and Row, 1978), p. 88.

29. Neame, *History of Apartheid,* pp. 73-74.

30. Kenneth N. Carstens, "Church and Race in South Africa," *United Nations Unit on Apartheid,* no. 23/71 (May 1971), p. 7.

31. Rhoodie, *Apartheid and Racial Partnership,* p. 81.

32. Ibid., pp. 131-32.

33. Neame, *History of Apartheid,* pp. 132-33.

34. Quoted by Neame in ibid., p. 141.

35. Ibid., p. 153.

36. Troup, *South Africa,* p. 383.

37. Neame, *History of Apartheid,* p. 157.

38. Alex Hepple, *Verwoerd* (Baltimore: Penguin Books, 1967), p. 167.

39. See Rhoodie, *Apartheid and Racial Partnership,* p. 68.

40. Hepple, *Verwoerd,* p. 153.

41. Troup, *South Africa,* p. 379.

42. Neame, *History of Apartheid,* p. 21.

43. Ibid., p. 23.

44. Ibid., p. 27.

45. Karis, Carter, and Gerhart, *From Protest to Challenge,* 2:76.

46. Horrell, *Action, Reaction and Counteraction* (Johannesburg: South African Institute of Race Relations, 1963).

47. Brink, "Aspects of Culture and Apartheid," pp. 34-41.

48. Cosmas Desmond, *The Discarded People* (Middlesex: Penguin, 1971).

49. Ibid. See esp. pp. 147-54.

50. See Neame, *History of Apartheid,* pp. 86, 220. Brink has pointed out the irony of these assertions. Speaking in reference to Dr. Verwoerd, he says that the late prime minister first set out to create separation where it did not exist nor was necessary, then went on to claim that it was a normal state of affairs among all South Africans. He quotes the following statement made by Dr. Verwoerd on December 4, 1963: " . . . it is only by *creating* [italics mine] separate nations that discrimination will disappear in the long run." Brink draws particular attention on the italicized word to show the folly of apartheid rationalizations ("Aspects of Culture and Apartheid," p. 33).

51. Nelson Mandela, *No Easy Walk to Freedom,* ed. Ruth First (New York: Basic Books, 1965), p. 21.

52. Karis, Carter, and Gerhart, *From Protest to Challenge,* 2:6; also p. 63. This act raised property qualifications and introduced educational requirements for blacks to register as voters.

53. Quoted by Bloke Modisane, *Blame Me on History* (London: Thames and Hudson, 1963), p. 163.

54. Schlemmer, "Factors Underlying Apartheid," p. 30.

55. Janet Robertson, *Liberalism in South Africa: 1948–1963* (Oxford: Clarendon Press, 1971), pp. 112, 117, 196-99, 221, 230.

56. Ibid., p. 186.

57. Ibid., p. 224.

58. Cf. Biko, *I Write What I Like,* pp. 13-14.

59. Ibid., p. 14.

60. See Modisane, *Blame Me on History,* p. 158.

61. Biko, *I Write What I Like,* pp. 23-24.

62. Modisane, *Blame Me on History,* p. 163.

63. Basil Moore, "What is Black Theology?" in *Black Theology: The South African Voice* (London: C. Hurst and Co., 1974), p. 2.

64. See John de Gruchy, *The Church Struggle in South Africa* (Grand Rapids: Eerdmans, 1979), p. 47.

65. Neame, *History of Apartheid,* p. 13.

66. Cf. Carstens, "Church and Race in South Africa," pp. 4-5.

67. Statement by the Commission for Current Problems of the Federal Nederduitse Geref. Kerke. Quoted by Fr. Trevor Huddleston, *Naught for Your Comfort* (Johannesburg: Hardingham and Donaldson, 1956), p. 62.

68. Ibid., p. 69.

69. From a meeting of the WCC delegation with eight S. A. member churches, including the DRC's. Cf. *Apartheid: Its Effects on Education, Science, Culture and Information,* 2d ed. (UNESCO, 1972), pp. 179-80.

70. See Karis, Carter, and Gerhart, *From Protest to Challenge,* 1:7.

71. Carstens, "Church and Race in South Africa," p. 16.

72. His white colleague, coming after him, was let into the main hall of the church. See Modisane, *Blame Me on History,* pp. 186ff.

73. UNESCO, *Apartheid,* p. 181.

74. Carstens, "Church and Race in South Africa," p. 19.

75. Ibid, p. 20.

76. UNESCO, *Apartheid,* p. 181.

77. Huddleston, *Naught For Your Comfort,* pp. 79, 77, 70, 75.

78. UNESCO, *Apartheid,* pp. 181, 182.

79. Cf. "Seminary to Close Down," *Post,* 28 December 1977.

80. Carstens, "Church and Race in South Africa," p. 25.

81. However, see below.

82. UNESCO, *Apartheid,* pp. 182-83.

83. See Horrell, *Survey 1977,* pp. 40-41.

84. In 1975 the monthly income gap between white and black average households was R546.00 or an 8.5 difference. See *Survey 1976,* p. 276.

85. See Horrell, *Survey 1968,* pp. 21-24.

86. A Parliamentary Commission of Enquiry appointed to investigate activities of four organizations including NUSAS, UCM, and the Wilgespruit Fellowship Centre.

87. See *Pro Veritate,* June 1975, p. 7.

88. Ibid., pp. 8-9.

89. Carstens, "Church and Race in South Africa," p. 35.

90. Ibid., p. 37.

91. See Horrell, *Survey 1977.*

92. See page 8 above, concluding paragraph.

93. Karis, Carter, and Gerhart, *From Protest to Challenge,* 1:8.

94. Ibid., p. 5.

95. Benson, *South Africa,* p. 19.

96. Neame, *History of South Africa,* p. 27.

97. Karis, Carter, and Gerhart, *From Protest to Challenge,* 1:11.

98. Benson, *South Africa,* p. 20.

99. Ibid., pp. 24-25. See also Chapter 2 ahead.

100. Ibid., p. 29. Also Karis, Carter, and Gerhart, *From Protest to Challenge,* 1:63-64.

101. Benson, *South Africa,* p. 111.

102. Ibid., p. 32.

103. Ibid., pp. 38, 40.

104. Ibid., p. 158.

105. Ibid., p. 42.

106. Ibid., p. 66. Also Karis, Carter, and Gerhart, *From Protest to Challenge,* 2:6, 3.

107. Ibid., p. 89.

108. Benson, *South Africa,* p. 113.

109. Hepple, *South Africa,* p. 155.

110. Neame, *History of Apartheid,* p. 102.

111. Hepple, *South Africa,* p. 165. Cf. also Ambrose Reeves, *Shooting*

at Sharpeville: The Agony of South Africa (Boston: Houghton Mifflin, 1969), esp. p. 40.

112. See D. A. Kotze, *African Politics in South Africa 1964–1974* (Pretoria: Van Schaik, 1975), p. 74.

113. Cf. Steve Biko, *I Write What I Like*; idem, *Black Consciousness in South Africa,* ed. Millard Arnold (New York: Random House, 1978); *Black Review* (published annually by the Black Community Programs, 1972–1976); Basil Moore, ed., *Black Theology: The South African Voice* (London: C. Hurst and Co., 1973).

114. This brief exposition should suffice at this stage. The BCM was engaged in at least three types of activity, two of which may be liable to misinterpretation if merely glossed over here as done with the preceding treatment. There were black relief and education projects (see esp. Biko, *Black Consciousness in South Africa,* pp. 92-98), which apparently did not attract much attention from the authorities. In addition, there were what has been described above as crisis leadership and what may be called "latent functions" or unintended confrontation with the establishment. These latter activities have probably been responsible for the government's unhappiness with the Black Consciousness Movement. Fair and detailed treatment of these activities—and, therefore, the rest, will have to await Chapter 2. However, see the next section on some of the consequences suffered by the BCM members and other members of the black community, especially after the 1976 student unrests.

115. "Political Imprisonment in South Africa," *An Amnesty International Report* (London: Amnesty International, 1978), pp. 23-24.

116. Ibid., p. 19.

117. Ibid.

118. Cf. Horrell, *Survey 1968,* p. 45.

119. *Amnesty International Report,* p. 20.

120. Ibid., p. 21.

121. Ibid.

122. Ibid., p. 22.

123. E.g., in passing a sentence on one of the people who had been convicted of having attempted to leave the country for military training abroad in order to use it against the country, the judge remarked: "I consider five years' imprisonment to be a severe penalty and were it in my power, I would have imposed a lesser sentence or suspended a large portion of the five years. I am obliged to give effect to the law even though I am unhappy that my discretion should be fettered to the extent that it is" (quoted in *Survey 1976,* p. 138). In another case the judge said that he was compelled by law to impose a five-year sentence on each of the two counts of conviction. However, he found ten years disproportionate to the offenses committed. He ordered four years of one sentence to run concurrently with the other, and that the accused should be granted immunity from further prosecution (ibid.).

Such impartiality in South African courts, perhaps acclaimed highest after the treason trial of 1956–1960, is gradually being curbed by the government. One of the ways in which this is done is by substituting local magistrates, who are civil servants, for judges in political trials (cf. *Amnesty International Report,* p. 29). They can impose prison terms of up to ten years, whereas formerly they could not exceed three.

124. Hepple, *South Africa,* p. 172.

125. Karis, Carter, and Gerhart, *From Protest to Challenge,* 3:674, 677.

126. Horrell, *Survey 1967,* p. 50.

127. Horrell, *Survey 1968,* p. 57.

128. Horrell, *Survey 1977,* p. 132.

129. *Amnesty International Report,* p. 38.

130. Cf. Horrell, *Survey 1977,* p. 132.

131. *Black Review* 1973, p. 100.

132. Cf. Horrell, *Action, Reaction and Counteraction,* p. 67.

133. Ibid., p. 72.

134. Ibid., pp. 73-79, 68.

135. Horrell, *Survey 1969,* p. 41.

136. Horrell, *Survey 1977,* p. 167.

137. Ibid., p. 126.

138. Ibid., pp. 33-34.

139. Horrell, *Action, Reaction and Counteraction,* pp. 64-67.

140. *Amnesty International Report,* p. 36.

141. Horrell, *Action, Reaction and Counteraction,* p. 64.

142. See the following surveys compiled by Horrell: *1967,* p. 44; *1971,* p. 68; and *1977,* pp. 127-28.

143. *Amnesty International Report,* p. 27. This statement is supported not only by a look at the periods in which this measure has been applied, but also at the types of people detained—for instance, since 1976, even though this followed the declaration of a state of emergency. Not only were students, BCM leaders, and "potential troublemakers" held; among detainees were "responsible" community leaders: sixteen churchmen, thirty-five teachers and lecturers, sixteen journalists, and twenty-seven people from other black community organizations, social workers, and women's groups (cf. Horrell, *Survey 1976,* p. 113). We may even question what part the CI and its periodical could have played in brewing up any unrest and rebellion.

144. Horrell, *Survey 1977,* pp. 144-45.

145. Ibid., p. 145. See also *Amnesty International Report* on accounts of some cases and pictures, pp. 56-76.

146. See Horrell, *Survey 1977,* pp. 159-64.

147. Horrell, *Survey 1976,* pp. 122, 126.

148. Horrell, *Survey 1970,* pp. 56-57.

CHAPTER 2: THREE MOMENTS OF RESISTANCE

1. See Peter Walshe, *The Rise of African Nationalism in South Africa* (Berkeley: University of California Press, 1971), p. 37.

2. Reverend John Dube, quoted by Walshe in ibid., p. 37.

3. ANC Constitution, Chapter IV, sec. 13 (1919).

4. Walshe, *African Nationalism,* p. 39.

5. See Thomas Karis, Gwendolen M. Carter, and Gail M. Gerhart, eds., *From Protest to Challenge: Documents of African Politics in South Africa 1882–1964,* 4 vols. (Stanford: Hoover Institution Press, 1972–1977), 2:168.

6. ANC, "African Claims in South Africa." Unless otherwise indicated, this document and subsequent primary material cited can be found in the collection by Karis, Carter, and Gerhart, *From Protest to Challenge.* To facilitate the location of the citation in the book, the title of the document will be followed by KCG1, KCG2, etc., and the page number. E.g., KCG2:215.

7. Ibid., pp. 219, 221.

8. Walshe, *African Nationalism,* p. 379.

9. ANC, "African Claims," KCG2:210.

10. ANCYL, "Basic Policy of Congress Youth League," manifesto issued by the National Executive Committee of the ANCYL, 1948, KCG2:327.

11. A. M. Lembede, "Policy of the Congress Youth League," KCG2:317.

12. ANCYL, "Basic Policy," KCG2:328-29.

13. Gail M. Gerhart, *Black Power in South Africa: The Evolution of an Ideology* (Berkeley: University of California Press, 1978), p. 75.

14. Muriel Horrell, ed. and comp., *A Survey of Race Relations in South Africa 1958–1959* (Johannesburg: South African Institute of Race Relations, 1960), p. 10.

15. See KCG3:505-6.

16. Horrell, *Survey 1958–1959,* p. 15; Patrick van Rensburg, *Guilty Land: The History of Apartheid* (New York: Praeger, 1962), p. 165; Report by the National Executive Committee to the Annual Conference, December 19-20, 1959, KCG3:549.

17. See Steve Biko, *I Write What I Like,* ed. Aelred Stubbs (San Francisco: Harper and Row, 1978), p. 10 (Hereafter referred to as *IWWIL*). He gives an account of the historical background of SASO in this book, pp. 9-16; Steve Biko, *Black Consciousness in South Africa,* ed. Millard Arnold (New York: Random House, 1978), pp. 5ff.; Gerhart, *Black Power in South Africa.* pp. 257ff.

18. See Biko, "SASO—Its Role," in *IWWIL,* pp. 5-6.

19. See D. A. Kotze, *African Politics in South Africa 1964–1974: Parties and Issues* (Pretoria: J. L. Van Schaik, 1975), p. 89.

20. See Sipho Buthelezi, ed., *The Black Peoples' Convention—South Africa: Historical Background and Basic Documents* (1978), pp. 2-11.

21. A. J. Luthuli, "The Road to Freedom is Via the Cross," statement issued on November 12, 1952, KCG2:488.

22. A. J. Luthuli to Prime Minister Strijdom, May 29, 1957, KCG3:399, 401.

23. ANC Constitution (rev.), Art. 2, Sec. c (1957), KCG3:413.

24. Nelson Mandela, Treason Trial Testimony, March-October 1960, KCG3:592. See also KCG3:735.

25. Z. K. Matthews, Presidential Address, ANC (Cape), June 18-19, 1955, KCG3:172. Also trial testimony, KCG2:620.

26. Gerhart, *Black Power in South Africa,* p. 83.

27. Mangaliso R. Sobukwe, "Future of the Africanist Movement," *The Africanist,* January 1959, KCG3:507.

28. Ethel Khopung, *Apartheid: The Story of a Dispossessed People* (Dar Es Salaam: Sharpeville Day Association Mbizana, 1972), p. 63.

29. See Sobukwe, "Future," KCG3:507; PAC, "Policy and Programme," in *Time for Azania,* ed. PAC (Toronto: Norman Bethune Institute, 1976), p. 18; PAC Manifesto, in *Speeches of Mangaliso Sobukwe* (np., nd.), p. 43.

30. See Mangaliso Sobukwe, "The PAC Case," in *Time for Azania,* p. 12.

31. Ibid., p. 13.

32. Mangaliso Sobukwe, "Inaugural Address," in *Speeches,* p. 21; idem, "Africa's Future as Seen by Sobukwe," in ibid., pp. 27-29.

33. Sobukwe, "The PAC Case," pp. 12-13.

34. Sobukwe, "Inaugural Address," pp. 20, 15, 17; PAC Manifesto, p. 41.

35. See Buthelezi, *BPC—Basic Documents,* p. 5.

36. Ibid.; Biko, *Black Consciousness,* p. 42.

37. Biko, "Our Strategy for Liberation," in *IWWIL,* pp. 149, 151.

38. Donald Woods, *Biko* (New York: Paddington Press, 1978), p. 102; Strini Moodley, "Black Consciousness, the Black Artist and the Emerging Black Culture," *SASO Newsletter,* May-June, 1972, p. 18.

39. See Biko, "The Definition of Black Consciousness," in *IWWIL,* p. 52; Woods, *Biko,* pp. 55, 52.

40. See PAC, "Policy and Programme," p. 17. See also the subsection on "Response to Specific Legislation," below.

41. See van Rensburg, *Guilty Land,* p. 177; P. K. Leballo, "The Nature of the Struggle Today," KCG3:502.

42. Biko, "Black Souls in White Skins?" in *IWWIL,* p. 24.

43. Ibid., p. 23; Adam Small, "Blackness Versus Nihilism: Black Racism Rejected," in *Black Theology: The South African Voice,* ed. Basil Moore (London: C. Hurst and Co., 1973), p. 15.

44. Biko, "Definition of Black Consciousness," in *IWWIL,* p. 51.

45. See Khopung, *Apartheid,* pp. 92-93.

46. Gerhart, *Black Power in South Africa,* p. 94.

47. See Jordan K. Ngubane, *An African Explains Apartheid* (New York: Praeger, 1963), pp. 99ff.; Khopung, *Apartheid,* p. 92.

48. Albert Luthuli, *Let My People Go* (New York: Meridian Books, 1962), appendix B.

49. See Mary Benson, *South Africa: The Struggle for a Birthright* (n.p.: Minerva Press, 1966, 1969), p. 217.

50. Leballo, "Nature of the Struggle, " KCG3:503.

51. Peter Raboroko, quoted by van Rensburg in *Guilty Land,* p. 162ff.

52. PAC, "Policy and Programme," p. 19; Report of the National Executive Committee to the Annual Conference, 1959.

53. Luthuli, *Let My People Go,* pp. 200-201.

54. Ibid., p. 204.

55. See Biko, "Let's Talk About Bantustans," in *IWWIL,* p. 82; B. A. Khoapa, *Black Review 1972* (Durban: Black Community Programmes, 1973), p. 77.

56. Alex Hepple, *South Africa: A Political and Economic History* (London: Pall Mall Press, 1966), pp. 131ff.

57. See Gerhart, *Black Power in South Africa,* p. 287; Buthelezi, *BPC— Basic Documents,* pp. 29-31.

58. Brian Bunting, *The Rise of the South African Reich* (Harmondsworth, Middlesex: Penguin Books, 1964), p. 147.

59. See Brian Bunting, *Moses Kotane: South African Revolutionary* (London: Inkululeko Publications, 1975), pp. 245-46; KCG2:564.

60. Bunting, *South African Reich,* pp. 149ff.

61. Africanists to the ANC, KCG3:505; also Leballo, "Nature of the Struggle," p. 500.

62. See Khoapa, *Black Review 1972,* p. 40.

63. James North, "The Hopelessness of 'Working Through the System' in South Africa: Capitalism and Apartheid," *New Republic,* May 5, 1979.

64. See Walshe, *African Nationalism,* p. 312.

65. See ANC "Bill of Rights," KCG2:219; Freedom Charter, KCG3:206; and Nelson Mandela, "In Our Life-Time," *Liberation,* June 1956. Also KCG3:245ff., 268.

66. Sobukwe, "Inaugural Address," p. 15; idem, "PAC Case," p. 13.

67. PAC, National Executive Report, p. 552.

68. See Woods, *Biko,* p. 100.

69. See Buthelezi, *BPC—Basic Documents,* p. 22; Biko, *Black Consciousness,* p. 51.

70. Biko, "Our Strategy for Liberation," in *IWWIL,* p. 149; idem, *Black Consciousness,* p. 53.

71. See Khoapa, *Black Review 1972,* pp. 21-22.

72. Ibid., p. 28.

73. See Biko, *Black Consciousness,* pp. 30, 211-17.

74. See Bunting, *South African Reich,* p. 206.

75. ANC, Resolutions of the Annual Conference, December 16-19, 1954, KCG3:1648.

76. Mangaliso Sobukwe, "Address on Behalf of the Graduating Class at Fort Hare College Delivered at the 'Completers Social,'" October 21, 1949, in *Speeches,* pp. 6-12.

77. See Silumko Sokupa to the Editor, *SASO Newsletter,* November-December 1975; Buthelezi, *BPC—Basic Documents,* p. 13.

78. ANC Constitution, Chap. III, Sec. 4, KCG1:77.

79. Leo Kuper, *Passive Resistance in South Africa* (New Haven: Yale University Press, 1957), p. 238.

80. ANC to Prime Minister of South Africa, n.d., quoted in Kuper, *Passive Resistance,* pp. 233ff.

81. Kuper, *Passive Resistance,* p. 125.

82. Sobukwe to Major General Rademeyer, March 16, 1960, KCG3:565.

83. See Biko, *Black Consciousness,* p. 83.

84. ANCYL, "Basic Policy," KCG3:330.

85. Benson, *Struggle for a Birthright,* p. 199.

86. Luthuli, *Let My People Go,* p. 154.

87. Bunting, *Kotane,* p. 245.

88. See Sobukwe, "The PAC Case," pp. 10-11.

89. See BPC, *Quest for a True Humanity,* p. 7; Buthelezi, *BPC—Basic Documents,* p. 28.

90. Buthelezi, *BPC—Basic Documents,* pp. 6, 28.

91. See Fatima Meer, "African Nationalism: Some Inhibiting Facts," in *South Africa: Sociological Perspectives,* ed. Heribert Adam (London: Oxford University Press, 1971), p. 31.

92. These were the repeal of the pass laws, the Group Areas Act affecting mainly the Indian community, the Suppression of Communism Act, the Bantu Authorities Act, and stock limitations in the reserves.

93. Kuper, *Passive Resistance,* p. 111.

94. Ibid., p. 112.

95. Ibid., p. 122.

96. In a statement read in court, one of the volunteers, Mr. S. Mokoena, included these remarks: "You will be the first to agree, Your Worship, that we have exhausted all attempts to air our genuine sufferings through the so-called proper channels. . . . It is common knowledge that, because of our color, we are a voteless and voiceless majority."

97. Luthuli, *Let My People Go,* p. 127.

98. Ibid.

99. Walshe, *African Nationalism,* p. 420.

100. Sobukwe, "The State of the Nation," in *Speeches,* p. 33.

101. Sobukwe, "Calling the Nation," flyer announcing the launching of the anti-pass campaign on March 21, 1960, KCG3:564.

102. See Horrell, *Survey 1959–1960,* pp. 56ff.

103. Ibid.; Gerhart, *Black Power in South Africa,* p. 238; Ambrose Reeves, *Shooting at Sharpeville: The Agony of South Africa* (Boston: Houghton Mifflin, 1961), p. 40.

104. Gerhart, *Black Power in South Africa,* p. 244.

105. See Khoapa, *Black Review 1972,* pp. 21, 25-26.

106. See Pascal Gwala, ed., *Black Review 1973* (Durban: Black Community Programmes, 1974), pp. 164-68.

107. See Khoapa, *Black Review 1972,* p. 22.

108. Ibid., p. 180.

109. See Biko, *Black Consciousness,* p. xxi.

110. Ibid.; *Pro Veritate,* December 1974, pp. 7-9.

111. Biko, *Black Consciousness,* p. xxi.

112. See Kuper, *Passive Resistance,* pp. 190ff.

113. Ibid., pp. 190, 192.

114. Ibid., p. 135.

115. Benson, *Struggle for a Birthright,* pp. 155-56.
116. Ibid., p. 166.
117. Ibid., p. 232.
118. Horrell, *Survey 1959–1960,* p. 73; Gerhart, *Black Power in South Africa,* p. 245.
119. Benson, *Struggle for a Birthright,* p. 225.
120. House of Assembly Debates, 29 March 1960, col. 4302-3.
121. Horrell, *Survey 1959–1960,* p. 84.
122. Ibid.; Ngubane, *Apartheid,* p. 106.
123. See Benson, *Struggle for a Birthright,* pp. 248-49.
124. See next section, below.
125. See Khoapa, *Black Review 1972,* pp. 22-24.
126. See Gwala, *Black Review 1973,* pp. 92-93.
127. See Hilda Bernstein, *No. 46—Steve Biko* (London: International Defence and Aid Fund, 1978), p. 16.
128. Cf. Biko, *Black Consciousness,* pp. xiii, xxii.
129. See Chapter 1, above; also *Focus* 18 (Sept. 1978): 6.
130. *NBC News,* July 17, 1979.
131. Nelson Mandela, *No Easy Walk to Freedom,* ed. Ruth First (New York: Basic Books, 1965), p. 109.
132. *Umkhonto We Sizwe,* flyer, December 16, 1961, KCG3:716ff.
133. See KCG3:648, 667; Benson, *Struggle for a Birthright,* p. 239.
134. KCG3:674, 741.
135. Ibid., p. 778.
136. Benson, *Struggle for a Birthright,* p. 253.
137. Ibid., p. 257.
138. KCG3:743, 745.
139. See Ngubane, *Apartheid,* p. 103.
140. Quoted in H. Strauss, "South Africa 1960–66: Underground African Politics," *Collected Seminar Papers on the Societies of Southern Africa in the 19th and 20th Centuries* (University of London: Institute of Commonwealth Studies, October 1971–June 1972).
141. Gerhart, *Black Power in South Africa,* p. 262.
142. See Strauss, "South Africa," pp. 132ff.; Benson, *Struggle for a Birthright,* pp. 241-42.
143. See Chapter 1, above.
144. See Benson, *Struggle for a Birthright,* pp. 243-44; Gerhart, *Black Power in South Africa,* p. 253; Strauss, "South Africa," pp. 136ff.
145. See Strauss, "South Africa," pp. 137, 140.
146. Benson, *Struggle for a Birthright,* pp. 244, 250.

CHAPTER 3: ALLIANCES OF THE 1980S

1. *Survey of Race Relations in South Africa 1978* (Johannesburg: South African Institute of Race Relations, 1979), p. 33. Each year's survey is published in the year following. Hereafter each will be referred to by *Survey* and the year.

2. *Survey 1979,* p. 50.

3. *Work in Progress* 35 (1985): 16. Hereafter referred to as *WIP*.

4. "Terror" Lekota, interview in *WIP* 30 (1984): 8.

5. *Survey 1983,* p. 54.

6. *South African Outlook,* October 1983, p. 151. Hereafter referred to as *SAO*.

7. *Weekly Mail,* May 2-8, 1986.

8. Ish Mkhabela, interview in *WIP* 35 (1985): 12.

9. *Africa Contemporary Record* (1984–1985): B757. Hereafter referred to as *ACR*.

10. Saths Cooper and L. Ntloko, interview in *WIP* 42 (1986): 20.

11. See Howard Barrell, "The United Democratic Front and the National Forum: Their Emergence, Composition and Trends," *South African Review 2* (Johannesburg: Ravan Press, 1985), p. 67.

12. Allan A. Boesak, *Black and Reformed: Apartheid, Liberation, and the Calvinist Tradition,* ed. Leonard Sweetman (Maryknoll, N.Y.: Orbis Books, 1984), p. 118.

13. Ibid., pp. 160-61.

14. Ibid., p. 155.

15. Ibid., p. 115.

16. *Survey 1983,* p. 59.

17. *ACR,* B751.

18. Lekota in *WIP* 35, p. 13.

19. Ibid., p. 14.

20. Trevor Manuel, interview in *WIP* 35, p. 15.

21. "Ameen Akhalwaya on Black Political Organizations," *Frontline 6* (December–January 1986): 25-26.

22. Cooper, in *WIP* 42, p. 23.

23. Neville Alexander, "Nation and Ethnicity in South Africa," *SAO,* October 1983, p. 152.

24. Cooper, in *WIP* 42, p. 22.

25. *ACR,* B756.

26. *Survey 1983,* p. 60.

27. Ibid., p. 57.

28. Lekota, interview in *WIP* 30 (1984): 4.

29. *SAO,* October 1983, p. 152.

30. Ibid., p. 154.

31. Ibid.

32. Cooper, in *Weekly Mail,* May 2-8, 1986.

33. Ibid.

34. Alexander, "Nation," p. 153.

35. Cooper, in *Weekly Mail,* May 2-8, 1986.

36. Boesak, *Black and Reformed,* p. 159.

37. Ibid.; also *SAO,* October 1983, p. 158.

38. Matthew Morobe, in *UDF Up Front* 3 (March 1986): 6.

39. *UDF Up Front* 2 (October 1985): 7.

40. Ibid.

41. *Survey 1981*, p. 29; *Weekly Mail*, April 4-10, 1986.

42. *SAO*, April 1986, p. 42.

43. Mkhabela, in *WIP* 35, p. 15.

44. *ACR*, B757.

45. Mkhabela, in *WIP* 35, p. 15.

46. Ibid.

47. *Survey 1979*, p. 51.

48. *Survey 1980*, p. 57.

49. *Survey 1983*, p. 48.

50. Alexander, "Nation," p. 152.

51. *ACR*, B757.

52. *SAO*, April 1986, p. 40.

53. Ibid., p. 42.

54. See Jo-Anne Collinge, "The United Democratic Front," *South African Review 3*, ed. and comp. South African Research Services (Johannesburg: Ravan Press, 1986), p. 254.

55. See Lekota, interview in *WIP* 30 (1984): 5.

56. *Survey 1979*, p. 51.

57. *Africa Report 31* (November–December 1986): 48.

58. Alexander, "Nation," p. 153.

59. Lekota, in *WIP* 30, p. 5.

60. Alexander, "Nation," p. 153.

61. Ibid.

62. *SAO*, April 1986, p. 41.

63. Author's informal discussion with Ish Mkhabela and others.

64. See Collinge, "The UDF," p. 256.

65. *Survey 1981*, p. 29.

66. *ACR*, B752.

67. *UDF Up Front* 2, p. 1.

68. *SAO*, April 1986, p. 41.

69. Cooper, in *Weekly Mail*, May 2-8, 1986.

70. Ibid.; also *SAO*, April 1986, p. 41.

71. Cooper, *Weekly Mail*, May 2-8, 1986.

72. *Survey 1980*.

73. *Survey 1981*, p. 29.

74. *Diary of Liberation* (Johannesburg: Skotaville, 1986).

75. Mkhabela, in *WIP* 35, p. 15.

76. Matthew Morobe, interview in *Weekly Mail*, August 22-28, 1986.

77. Frank Chikane, quoted by Collinge in "The UDF," p. 254.

78. *Survey 1983*, p. 49.

79. See Na-Iem Dollie, "The National Forum," *South African Review* 3, p. 271.

80. Cooper, in *WIP* 42, p. 22.

81. Ibid.

82. See *Survey 1979*, p. 51.

83. Cooper, in *WIP* 42, p. 22.

84. *Survey 1983*, p. 61.

85. Collinge, "The UDF," p. 252.

86. *Survey 1985,* p. 38.

87. Collinge, "The UDF," p. 248.

88. *Weekly Mail,* October 3-8, 1986.

89. Ish Mkhabela, quoted in *Sowetan,* 14 October 1983.

90. Mkhabela, in *WIP* 35, p. 16.

91. *Survey 1983,* p. 49.

92. Mkhabela, in *WIP* 35, p. 16.

93. *SAO,* April 1986, p. 42.

94. Ibid., p. 41.

95. *WIP* 42, p. 20.

96. *Survey 1983,* p. 58.

97. Barrell, *South African Review* 2, p. 8.

98. Cf. *ACR,* B752; *WIP* 30, p. 8.

99. *ACR,* B752.

100. Lekota, quoted by Collinge, "The UDF," p. 259.

101. *Survey 1983,* p. 60.

102. *UDF Up Front* 3, p. 6.

103. *UDF Up Front* 2, p. 7.

104. *UDF Up Front* 3, p. 6.

105. *UDF Up Front* 2, p. 7.

106. Lekota, interview in *Africa Report* 29 (1984): 48.

107. See *Survey 1980,* p. 157.

108. Lybon Mabasa, cited by *Survey 1983,* p. 54.

109. Alexander, quoted by Dollie in "The National Forum," p. 268.

110. Quoted in Barrell, *South African Review* 2, p. 8.

111. Cooper, in *Weekly Mail,* May 2-8, 1986.

112. See Barrell, *South African Review* 2, p. 10.

113. Cf. *Survey 1983,* p. 55.

114. *ACR,* B753.

115. Ibid.

116. *Survey 1985,* p. 41.

117. See *Africa Report* 30 (1985): 50.

118. Mkhabela, cited in *Survey 1985,* p. 12.

119. Joe Tlholoe, interview in *Africa Report* 31 (November–December 1986): 63-66.

120. "Ameen Akhalwaya," *Frontline* 6, p. 26.

121. John L. Sebidi, interviewed by Margaret A. Novieki in *Africa Report* 30 (1985): 70.

122. Mkhabela, quoted in *Survey 1985,* p. 12.

123. *The Star: International Airmail Weekly,* January 3, 1987.

124. See *Surveys 1980–1982.*

125. See Coleman and Webster, "Repression and Detentions in South Africa," *South African Review* 3.

126. *Survey 1983,* p. 49.

127. See *ACR,* B754.

128. *Africa Report* 30, p. 47.

129. Lawyers Committee for Civil Rights Under Law, "Briefing on the UDF Treason Trial," August 1985, p. 57.

130. *Weekly Mail,* January 24-30, 1986.

131. *New York Times,* June 24, 1986.

132. *Weekly Mail,* February 28–March 6, 1986; Collinge, "The UDF," p. 249.

133. *Weekly Mail,* March 14-20, 1986.

134. *Weekly Mail,* August 22-28, 1986.

135. Ibid.

136. *Africa Report* 32 (1987): 45.

137. *The Star* (International), October 11, 1986.

138. Ibid.

139. *UDF Up Front* 3, p. 7.

140. *The Star* (International), September 2, 1985.

141. See *Survey 1985,* p. 40.

CHAPTER 4:
PHILOSOPHICAL AND THEOLOGICAL ETHICS

1. Those interested in pursuing this type of study further are referred to the original dissertation: "The Theory and Practice of Black Resistance to Apartheid," Boston University, 1980.

2. This was confirmed in an interview with Muelder on two occasions, the last on September 24, 1979. L. Harold DeWolf discusses such parallels in his book *Responsible Freedom* (New York: Harper and Row, 1971).

3. Walter G. Muelder, *Moral Law in Christian Social Ethics* (Richmond, Va.: John Knox, 1966), p. 153; Paul K. Deats, "The Quest for a Social Ethic," in *Toward a Discipline of Social Ethics* (Boston: Boston University Press, 1972), p. 33.

4. Muelder, *Moral Law,* p. 155.

5. Ibid., pp. 149-50.

6. Ibid., p. 149.

7. Ibid.

8. Ibid., pp. 10, 11-13, 15-16.

9. Ibid., pp. 10, 48, 50.

10. For a detailed account of the moral laws see Muelder's *Moral Law,* chaps. 4-7. See also DeWolf, *Responsible Freedom,* pp. 149ff. for other parallels.

11. Muelder, *Moral Law,* pp. 51, 65-66, 72-73.

12. Ibid., pp. 77, 80, 82.

13. Ibid., pp. 83-84.

14. Ibid., p. 94.

15. Ibid., pp. 97-100.

16. Ibid., pp. 101-2.

17. Ibid., pp. 52, 102-4.

18. See ibid., pp. 106-9; Immanuel Kant, *The Fundamental Principles of the Metaphysic of Ethics* (New York: Appleton-Century-Crofts, n.d.), p. 47.

19. Muelder, *Moral Law,* pp. 109-12.

20. Jean-Jacques Rousseau, *The Social Contract,* trans. Maurice Cranston (Harmondsworth: Penguin Books, 1968), p. 61.

21. Cf. Muelder, *Moral Law,* pp. 53-54.

22. Ralph B. Potter, Jr., "The Logic of Moral Argument," in Deats, ed., *Toward a Discipline,* pp. 93-114; Oliva Blanchette, "Law and Morality," in *Nexus* 30 (May, 1967): 12, 35-39.

23. See Deats, *Toward a Discipline,* pp. 31-32, 304-5.

CHAPTER 5: THE MORAL SIGNIFICANCE OF THE SOUTH AFRICAN STRUGGLE

1. See Anton C. Pegis, ed., *Introduction to St. Thomas Aquinas* (New York: The Modern Library, 1945, 1948), pp. 560ff.

2. Paul Deats, Jr., "Protestant Social Ethics and Pacifism," manuscript, p. 30. Italics mine.

3. See Walter G. Muelder, *Foundations of the Responsible Society* (New York: Abingdon Press, 1959). Cf. Muelder's comments in Chapter 4, above.

4. J. Philip Wogaman, *A Christian Method of Moral Judgment* (Philadelphia: Westminster Press, 1976).

5. See Chapter 2 above.

6. Not to be equated with exclusive black rule.

7. See Chapter 2 under "Freedom Charter."

8. Cf. pp. 40, 78, and 108 above.

9. Wogaman, *Christian Method,* pp. 200-202.

10. See above, pp. 19, 41.

11. Cf. p. 108.

12. Cf. Wogaman, *Christian Method,* p. 202.

13. Pope John XXIII, *Pacem in Terris,* p. 12.

14. From *American Inquisitors* (New York: Macmillan, 1928), pp. 21-22, cited by Paul Deats, Jr., in "Social Change and Moral Values," in Moral Man series (n.p., n.d.), p. 8.

15. Michael Walzer, *Obligations: Essays on Disobedience, War, and Citizenship* (Cambridge, Mass.: Harvard University Press, 1970), p. ix.

16. In the case of the ANC, though, the transition from military resistance to peaceful, political negotiation began as early as 1882. See Chapter 1 above.

17. Thomas Merton, *Faith and Violence: Christian Teaching and Christian Practice* (Notre Dame: University of Notre Dame Press, 1968), p. 12; Walter G. Muelder, "Critical Reflections on 'Violence, Non-Violence, and the Struggle for Justice,'" American Society of Christian Ethics: Selected Papers, 1976, p. 13.

18. Gene Sharp, *Exploring Nonviolent Alternatives* (Boston: Extending Horizons Book, 1970), p. 26.

19. See the following section.

20. Gene Sharp, "Problems of Violent and Nonviolent Struggle," *Peace News,* June 28, 1963.

21. See the last section of the next chapter.

22. This term, if defined in the popular manner, is not quite accurate in reference to the PAC. According to Walzer, civil disobedience is often "described as non-revolutionary encounter with the state. A man breaks the law, but does so in ways which do not challenge the legitimacy of the legal or political system" (*Obligations,* p. 24). As we have seen, the PAC wanted revolutionary change.

23. See Sidney Hook, "Social Protest and Civil Disobedience," in *Moral Problems in Contemporary Society,* ed. Paul Kurtz (Englewood Cliffs, N.J.: Prentice-Hall, 1969), pp. 184ff. That civil disobedience is by its nature nonviolent is hardly consensual, however. Walzer questions it as follows: "The insistence on the absolute nonviolence of civil disobedience is . . . a little disingenuous, as it disregards, first, the coercive impact disobedience often has on innocent bystanders, and second, the actual violence it provokes . . . especially from the police" (*Obligations,* p. 25).

24. See below.

25. Sharp, *Nonviolent Alternatives,* p. 33.

26. See Mohandas K. Gandhi, "*Ahisma* or the Way of Non-violence," in *Nonviolence: A Reader in the Ethics of Action,* ed. George Estey and Doris Hunter (Waltham, Mass: Xerox College Publishing, 1971), pp. 88-89; Martin Luther King, Jr., "Letter from Birmingham [Ala.] Jail," in ibid., p. 120.

27. Walzer, *Obligations,* p. 17.

28. Ibid., p. 57.

29. Muelder, *Moral Law in Christian Social Ethics* (Richmond, Va.: John Knox Press, 1966), pp. 53-54.

30. Ibid., p. 54.

31. Muelder's comment.

32. See Muelder, *Moral Law,* pp. 54-55.

33. Chapter 4 above; cf. ibid., pp. 56, 58.

34. Ibid., p. 54.

35. Denis Goulet, *The Cruel Choice: A New Concept in the Theory of Development* (New York: Atheneum, 1975), p. 303.

36. This was after 1960. See also note 16, above.

37. Gandhi, "*Ahisma*"; Martin Luther King, Jr., *Stride Toward Freedom: the Montgomery Story* (New York: Harper and Row, 1958), p. 179.

38. Robert McAfee Brown, *Religion and Violence: A Primer For White Americans* (Philadelphia: Westminster Press, 1973), p. xiii, also p. xv.

39. Muelder, "Critical Reflections," pp. 10-11.

40. Ibid., p. 9.

41. See note 31, above. Also Goulet's quotation on pp. 149-50.

42. Wogaman, *Christian Method,* pp. 85, 128.

43. Brown, *Religion and Violence,* p. 88; italics mine.

44. Deats, "Protestant Social Ethics," p. 15.

45. *Webster's New International Dictionary of the English Language,* 2d ed. (1953).

46. Sharp, *Nonviolent Alternatives,* p. 33.

47. Richard Shaull, "The End of the Road and a New Beginning," in

Marxism and Radical Religion, ed. John C. Raines and Thomas Dean (Philadelphia: Temple University Press, 1970), p. 33.

48. J. Deotis Roberts, *Liberation and Reconciliation: A Black Theology* (Philadelphia: Westminster Press, 1971), p. 191.

49. See pp. 150-51 above.

50. Further investigation of the question of sanctions in general follows in the next chapter.

51. Cf. Desmond Tutu, *Ecunews Bulletin* 20 (July 6, 1979): 6.

52. See *The Boston Globe,* October 7, 1977.

53. Lucy Mvubelo, *VOA News,* November 19, 1979.

54. See comment of the British Council of Churches in the next chapter, section dealing with economic sanctions.

55. Interviewed in *Voice of America News,* January 29, 1980.

56. Heribert Adam, *Modernizing Racial Domination* (Berkeley: University of California Press, 1971), p. 153.

57. Gandhi, *"Ahisma,"* p. 87.

58. William A. Hance, "Efforts to Alter the Future: Economic Action," in *Apartheid and the United Nations Collective Measures: An Analysis,* ed. Amelia C. Leiss (New York: Carnegie Endowment for International Peace, 1965), p. 121.

59. In a recent work, Ann and Neva Seidman have noted that although South Africa now "supplies 80% of its own industrial plant," its economy "has become increasingly dependent on the import of capital and capital goods imports." In spite of the returns it receives for its gold exports, it "still has almost chronic balance of payments deficit" (*South Africa and U.S. Multinational Corporations* [Westport, Conn.: Lawrence Hill and Co., 1977], pp. 17, 58-59). The London *Economist* of June 1978 further observed that the South African economy—which requires an estimated growth rate of 5.5 percent in order to provide jobs for most of its inhabitants—will not grow without foreign loans (*ICCR Brief,* May 1979, p. 3C). From this it follows that those criticisms of collective economic measures against South Africa that still emphasize its low dependence on foreign capital have become outdated.

60. Hance, "Efforts to Alter the Future," p. 121.

61. Ibid.

62. Deats, "Social Change," p. 26.

CHAPTER 6: FUTURE ACTION: HOW VIABLE?

1. Lawrence Schlemmer, "Future Political Implications of Present Trends," in *Directions of Change in South African Politics,* ed. Peter Randall (Johannesburg: SPROCAS, 1971), p. 27.

2. Ben Marais, *The Two Faces of Africa* (Pietermaritzburg: Shutter and Shooter, 1964), p. 62.

3. Schlemmer, "Future Implications," p. 22.

4. *African Perspectives on South Africa,* ed. Hendrik W. van der Merwe et al. (Stanford: Hoover Institution Press, 1978).

5. Ibid., p. xiii.

6. K. D. Matanzima, "Separate Development," in *African Perspectives,* pp. 404, 407.

7. Lucas Mangope, "The Political Future of the Homelands," in *African Perspectives,* p. 65.

8. Alan Paton, "Some Thoughts on the Common Society," in *Directions of Change,* p. 46.

9. Ibid., pp. 49, 50.

10. M. Gatsha Buthelezi, "White and Black Nationalism: Ethnicity and the Future of the Homelands," The Alfred and Winifred Hoernle Memorial Lecture, 1974 (Johannesburg: South African Institute of Race Relations, 1974), pp. 11-13.

11. Ibid., p. 14.

12. Ibid., p. 15.

13. Denis Worrall, "The Plural State System as a Direction of Change," in *Directions of Change,* p. 70.

14. Horst Kleinschmidt, ed., *White Liberation* (Johannesburg: SPRO-CAS 2, 1972), p. 3.

15. Clive Nettleton, "The White Problem," in ibid., p. 8.

16. Rich Turner, "The Relevance of Contemporary Radical Thought," in *Directions of Change,* p. 79.

17. M. Motlhabi, "Black Theology: A Personal View," in *Black Theology: The South African Voice,* ed. Basil Moore (London: C. Hurst and Co., 1973), p. 79.

18. Paul Deats and Herbert E. Stotts, *Methodism and Society: Guidelines for Strategy* (New York: Abingdon Press, 1962), pp. 64, 43f.

19. Larry Coppard and Barbara J. Steinwachs, "Guidelines for Community Action," in *White Liberation,* p. 42.

20. Dom Helder Camara, *Revolution Through Peace,* trans. Amparo McLean (New York: Harper Colophon Books, 1971), pp. 34, 37.

21. Richard Shaull, "A Theological Perspective on Human Liberation," in *When All Else Fails,* ed. IDOC (Philadelphia: Pilgrim Press, 1970), p. 62.

22. Richard Shaull, "The End of the Road and a New Beginning," in *Marxism and Radical Religion,* ed. J. C. Raines and T. Dean (Philadelphia: Temple University Press, 1970), p. 37; Camara, *Revolution,* p. 37.

23. Arthur G. Gish, *The New Left and Christian Radicalism* (Grand Rapids: Eerdmans, 1970), pp. 123, 125ff.

24. Coppard and Steinwachs, "Guidelines," p. 42.

25. See note 18, above.

26. Coppard and Steinwachs, "Guidelines," p. 112.

27. Ibid., p. 117.

28. Ibid., p. 301.

29. Ibid., pp. 306-8.

30. Ibid., p. 119.

31. Ibid., pp. 295, 296, 124, 128.

32. Ibid., p. 121.

33. Ibid., p. 69.

34. Ibid., p. 71.

35. Ibid., pp. 74-76.

36. Ibid., p. 298.

37. Ibid., p. 115.

38. Ibid., p. 116, quoting C. E. Rothwell.

39. Ibid., pp. 295-96.

40. Ibid., p. 113.

41. Ibid., p. 300.

42. Ibid., p. 114.

43. Ibid., p. 134.

44. Ibid., p. 38.

45. Ibid., p. 135.

46. Ibid.

47. Ibid., p. 308.

48. Ibid., p. 305.

49. See Luthuli on this, Chapter 2.

50. Phillip Mayer, "Urban Africans and Bantustans," The Alfred and Winifred Hoernle Memorial Lecture, 1972 (Johannesburg: SAIRR, 1972), p. 7.

51. Heribert Adam, "The South African Power-Elite," in *South Africa: Sociological Perspectives* (London: Oxford University Press, 1971), p. 91.

52. Steve Biko, "Let's Talk About Bantustans," in *I Write What I Like,* ed. Aelred Stubbs (San Francisco: Harper and Row, 1978), pp. 82-83.

53. *The Future of South Africa: A Study by British Christians* (London: SCM Press, 1965), p. 18.

54. Quoted in ibid., p. 16.

55. Adam, "Power-Elite," p. 92.

56. Ibid.

57. Joe Slovo, "The Armed Struggle Spreads," in *Guerrilla Warfare: South African Studies 1* (London: ANC Information Bureau, 1970), p. 40.

58. Robert Moss, "Urban Guerilla Warfare," in *Adelphi Papers,* No. 79 (August, 1971), p. 1.

59. Ibid., pp. 3, 13.

60. Heribert Adam, *Modernizing Racial Domination* (Berkeley: University of California Press, 1971), p. 123.

61. "Development of the South African Revolution," Proceedings from the Consultative Conference of the ANC, Morogoro, Tanzania, May 1960, in *Guerrilla Warfare,* pp. 47, 52.

62. Ibid., p. 52.

63. Martin Oppenheimer, *Urban Guerrilla* (Harmondsworth: Penguin Books, 1970), p. 42.

64. Moss, "Urban Guerrilla," p. 7.

65. Ibid., p. 13.

66. Ibid., p. 9.

67. Ibid., p. 16.

68. Slovo, "Armed Struggle," p. 36.

69. Ibid., p. 2.

70. Carlos Marighella, "Minimanual of the Urban Guerrilla," appendix to *Adelphi Papers,* No. 79, p. 20.

71. Moss, "Urban Guerrilla," pp. 4, 9.

72. Marighella, "Minimanual," p. 25.

73. Slovo, "Armed Struggle," p. 41.

74. Marighella, "Minimanual," p. 33.

75. Ibid., pp. 20, 22, 25, 21.

76. Andrew M. Scott et al., *Insurgency* (Chapel Hill: University of North Carolina Press, 1970), p. 92.

77. See Chapter 5.

78. *From Shantytown to Forest: Story of Norman Duka,* ed. Denis and Ginger Mercer (Oakland, Ca.: LCM, n.d.), esp. chaps. 7 and 10.

79. Marighella, "Minimanual," p. 29 (italics mine).

80. William A. Hance, "Efforts to Alter the Future: Economic Action," in *Apartheid and the United Nations Collective Measures: An Analysis,* ed. Amelia C. Leiss (New York: Carnegie Endowment for International Peace, 1965), p. 99.

81. Ibid., p. 95.

82. BCC, *The Future of South Africa,* p. 22.

83. Ibid., pp. 20, 19.

84. A. Maizels, "Economic Sanctions and South Africa's Trade," in *Sanctions Against South Africa,* ed. Ronald Segal (Harmondsworth: Penguin Books, 1964), pp. 124, 126.

85. Brian Lapping, "Oil Sanctions Against South Africa," in ibid., p. 137.

86. Ibid., pp. 136, 139.

87. Adam, *Modernizing Racial Domination,* p. 134.

88. Maizels, "Economic Sanctions," pp. 124, 131ff.; Lapping, "Oil Sanctions," p. 142.

89. See Hance, "Efforts to Alter Future," p. 101.

90. J. D. Marvin, "Sanctions Against South Africa: The Impact and the Aftermath," in *Sanctions Against South Africa,* p. 241.

91. Ibid., p. 243.

92. Hance, "Efforts to Alter Future," p. 125.

93. Amelia Leiss, "The United Nations: The Instrumentality," in *Apartheid and United Nations,* pp. 73-74.

94. *Peace News,* August 30, 1963.

95. Amelia Leiss and Vernon McKay, "The Issues after Two Decades," in *Apartheid and United Nations,* pp. 1, 6.

96. See ibid., p. 9; Gen. Assembly Res. 1598 (XV), 13 April 1961.

97. Hance, "Efforts to Alter Future," p. 99; Leiss, "Issues," pp. 10-11.

98. Amelia Leiss, "Diplomatic and Political Actions," in *Apartheid and United Nations,* p. 90.

99. Peter Calvocoressi, "The Politics of Sanctions: The League and the United Nations," in *Sanctions Against South Africa,* p. 61.

100. Leiss, "Issues," p. 15.

101. Amelia Leiss, "A Summation," in *Apartheid and United Nations,* p. 163.

102. Hance, "Efforts to Alter Future," pp. 98-99.

103. Leiss, "Summation," p. 163.

104. John de Gruchy, *The Church Struggle in South Africa* (Grand Rapids: Eerdmans, 1979), p. 47.

105. African theology is generally understood as a theology indigenous to Africa, whereas black theology is both indigenous and contextual.

106. J. G. Davis, *Christians, Politics and Violent Revolution* (Maryknoll, N.Y.: Orbis Books, 1976), pp. 111, 101.

107. Gustavo Gutierrez, quoted by R. M. Brown, *Religion and Violence* (Philadelphia: Westminster Press, 1973), p. 77.

108. Quoted by Paul Deats, Jr., "Social Change and Moral Values," in Moral Man series, p. 21.

109. On December 17, 1979. *Ecunews Bulletin* 40 (December 17, 1979): 1.

110. Paul Deats, Jr., "Protestant Social Ethics and Pacifism," manuscript, p. 30.

111. Davis, *Violent Revolution,* p. 98.

112. John C. Bennett, "Christian Responsibility in a Time that Calls For Revolutionary Change," in *Marxism and Radical Religion,* p. 66.

113. Gail M. Gerhart, *Black Power in South Africa: The Evolution of an Ideology* (Berkeley: University of California Press, 1979), p. 302.

114. Gene Sharp, *Exploring Nonviolent Alternatives* (Boston: Extending Horizons Book, 1970), p. 33. Sharp writes "nonviolent coercion" rather than simply "coercion."

115. Sharp, "Can Nonviolence Work in South Africa?" *Peace News,* June 21, 1963.

116. Ibid.

117. Sharp, *Nonviolent Alternatives,* pp. 29, 32.

118. Ibid., pp. 38, 35.

119. Sharp, "Strategic Problems of the South African Resistance," *Peace News,* July 5, 1963, p. 10.

120. Ibid.

AFTERWORD

1. See previous chapter.

2. Cf. Chapter 2 above.

3. Ibid.

4. See previous chapter.

5. See *A Survey of Race Relations in South Africa: 1976* (Johannesburg: South African Institute of Race Relations, 1977), pp. 53ff., 51.

6. Ibid., p. 25.

7. *Survey 1977,* pp. 159-64; also Chapter 1 above.

8. *NBC News,* 27 July 1979.

9. *Survey 1977,* pp. 159-64.

10. *Diary of Liberation* (Johannesburg: Skotaville, 1987).

Index

Adam, Heribert, 160, 184, 186, 188
Affirmative Action Program, 138, 139, 140
African Claims, 26
African Independent Churches Association (AICA), 43
African Resistance Movement, 19, 35
African Socialism, 56
African Students Association, 42
African Students Union of South Africa, 42
Afrikaanse Studente Bond, 19
Akhalwaya, Ameen, 111
Alexander, Neville, 95, 96
All African Convention, 26, 59, 61
All-in African National Action Council, 73
Amnesty International, 34
Anglo-Boer War, 25
Aquinas, Saint Thomas, 119
Association for Educational and Cultural Advancement of Africans (ASSECA), 43
AZACTU (Azanian Council of Trade Unions), 95
AZASM (Azanian Students Movement), 110
AZASO (Azanian Students Organization), 94

Baasskap, 13
Bambata, 7; rebellion, 25
Bantu, 14
Bantu Administration and Development, Department of, 58
Bantu Authorities Act, 53
Bantu Education Act, 27, 52, 57, 58, 213
Bantu Self-Government Bill, 14
Barrell, Howard, 83
Bennett, John C., 202
Bertocci, Peter, 129, 148
Biko, Steve, 4, 12, 34, 37, 49, 67, 71-72, 157, 184, 205, 212, 213, 215
Black Community Development Bill, 81
Black Community Programs, 56, 66, 71
Black Consciousness, 68
Black Allied Workers Union, 56, 71
Black Education Charter, 93
Black Local Authorities Bill, 81, 102
Black Parents Association, 172
Black People's Convention, 27, 33, 38, 43, 52-54, 57, 62, 67-68, 71-72
Black Sash, 104, 113
Black Theology Project, 27, 71
Black Viewpoint/Black Review, 66

Black Workers Project, 56, 66
Blanchette, Oliva, S. J., 130
Bochenski, Joseph, 51
Boesak, Allan, 81, 83-84, 89, 90, 96, 104, 115
Botha, General, 11
Botha, P. W., 15, 17
Brightman, Edgar S., 127
Brink, Andre, 16
British Council of Churches, 193
Broederbond, 139
Brown, Robert McAfee, 151, 154
Buthelezi, Mangosuthu Gatsha, 9, 28-29, 98, 107-8, 170-71

Caledon, Earl of, 12
Camara, Dom Helder, 175-76, 202
Cape Action League, 108
Cardiff Consultation, 154
Carstens, Kenneth, 25
Castro, Fidel, 188
Categorical Imperative, 124-25
Catholic Church, 22-23
Christian Action, 199, 207
Christian Institute of South Africa, 24-25, 33, 72, 114, 175
Church of the Province of South Africa, 22-23
Communist Party, South African, 18-19, 30, 61, 68, 87, 113
Congress Alliance, 8, 41, 48, 50-51, 55, 62-63, 85, 156
Congress of Democrats, 19, 35, 50, 62
Congress of the People, 69
Congress of South African Students (COSAS), 94, 101, 110
Congress of South African Trade Unions, 95, 105, 211
Congress Youth League, 40, 61, 76-77, 135-38, 141
Convention Alliance, 98, 108
Cooper, Saths, 98-99
Coppard, Larry, 174, 176
Cottesloe Consultation, 21, 25
Covenant of Justice, Equity, and Racial Harmony, 200

Craddock, Governor S. F., 10
Criminal Law Amendment Act, 30, 69
Criminal Law Procedure Act, 31
CUSA (Confederation of Unions of South Africa), 95

Davis, J. G., 200
Deats, Paul, Jr., 130, 134, 139, 149, 153-54, 163, 174, 177, 179, 181-82
Defiance Campaign, 27, 48, 59-60, 63, 68-69, 77, 99, 117, 141, 143-44, 212
deGruchy, John, 199
Desmond, Cosmas, 16
Detainee Parents Support Committee (DPSC), 113
de Toqueville, 189
DeWolf, L. Harold, 125
Dinizulu, Chief, 9, 28
Disinvestment, 96-97
Drum (magazine), 21
Dube, Rev. John, 26, 76
Duff, Patrick, 123
Dutch Council of Policy, 10
Dutch Reformed churches, 20, 21, 25

Ecumenical movement, 120
End Conscription Campaign, 104

Fauntroy, Walter, 115
Federation of South African Trade Unions (FOSATU), 95
Franchise and Ballot Act, 18
Freedom Charter, 8, 19, 26-27, 41, 44, 48, 50, 54, 69, 85, 88, 107, 109, 117
Gandhi, Mohandas, 144-46, 151, 161
Gardner, C., 24
General Law Amendment Act, 31-33, 75, 76
General Motors, 159, 161
Gerhart, Gail, 76, 202
Gish, Arthur, 176

Goulet, Denis, 149, 191
Graaf, Sir deVilliers, 18
Great Trek, 12
Group Areas, 90, 92

Hance, William, 198
Hertzog, J. M. B., 11
Hitler, Adolf, 151-52
Horrell, Muriel, 16, 41
Huddleston, Trevor, 22-23
Hurley, Dennis, 23

Imvo Zabantsundu, 7
Indaba, Natal-KwaZulu, 171
Inkatha, 9, 28-29, 98, 107-8
Interdenominational African Ministers Association of South Africa, 43, 201
Internal Security Act, 30, 32-34, 214
Investments, foreign, 56, 159, 161

Jabavu, John Tengo, 7, 18, 26
Jim Crow, 92-93
John XXIII, 139
John Vorster Square, 201

Kaffir Wars, 3, 7
Kant, Emmanuel, 124-25, 127
Kennedy, Sen. Edward, 96-97, 102, 104, 109, 111
Kgosana, Philip, 65
Khopung, Ethel, 45
King, Martin Luther, Jr., 144-46, 151
Kleinschmidt, Horst, 172
Koinonia ethic, 132
"Koornhof Bills," 90, 101
Kruger, Jimmy, 9, 214
Kuper, Leo, 63

Land Act, 1913, 11-12, 18, 26
League of Nations, 26, 197
Leballo, Potlako, 51, 75
LeGrange, Louis, 112
Legum, Colin, 89
Leiss, Amelia, 198

Lekota, Terror, 86
Lelyveld, Joseph, 79
Liberal Party, 18-19, 62
Lippman, Walter, 139
Luthuli, Albert, 44, 50, 52, 61

McCartney, Earl of, 10
Maizels, A., 194
Majority rule, 136-37, 140
Malan, D. F., 13, 21
Mampuru, 7
Mandela, Nelson, 17, 37, 44, 69, 72, 74, 105, 167
Mandela, Zinzi, 104
Mangope, Lucas, 169
Manifesto of the People of Azania, 88, 89
Marais, Ben, 166, 171
Marighella, Carlos, 189-91, 193
Marvin, J. D., 196
Matanzima, Kaizer D., 168
Matthews, Z. K., 44, 61
Meer, Fatima, 63
Mayer, Phillip, 184-86
Merton, Thomas, 142
"Message to the People of South Africa," 24
Methodist Church of Southern Africa, 21, 23
Mkhabela, Ishmail, 92, 97, 111
Modisane, Bloke, 20
Moore, Basil, 71
Moral Laws, 125-29
Morobe, Matthew, 90
Moss, Robert, 188-90
Motsoaledi, Elias, 74
Muelder, Walter G., 119-20, 122-32, 134, 142, 148-49, 153-54, 162
Multiracialism, 137-38
Mvubelo, Lucy, 160

Natal Indian Congress, 26, 109
National Action Committee, 50
National Convention, 20
National Education Crisis Committee (NECC), 4, 94, 96, 105

National Education Union of
   South Africa, 94
National Party, 1, 3, 9, 13, 15, 20,
   27, 30, 35, 53, 166
National Union of South African
   Students (NUSAS), 19, 42-43,
   71, 94, 114
Natives (Abolition of Passes and
   Coordination of Documents
   Act), 53
Native Administration Act, 33
Native Affairs, 11
Native Representative Council, 26
Natives Resettlement Act, 54
Native (Urban Areas) Act, 54
Natural Law, 120, 123
Naude, Beyers, 24-25
Neame, L. E., 11
Nederduitse Gereformeerde Kerk,
   20, 25
New Republic Party, 18
Nonracialism, 138
Ntsanwisi, H., 168
Ntwasa, Sabelo, 27, 71
Nyanga (township), 65

Orderly Movement and Settlement
   of Black Persons Bill, 81

Paton, Alan, 169
Paul, Saint, 140
Peterson, Hector, 213
Plato, 134
Poqo, 19, 75, 76
Port Elizabeth Youth Congress
   (PEYCO), 110
Positive Action Campaign, 63-64,
   74, 76, 141-44, 146
Potter, Ralph, Jr., 130
Presbyterian Church, 24
Pro Veritate, 72
Program of Action, 44, 47-48, 51,
   59, 63, 98, 117, 141
Progressive Federal Party, 18, 98
Progressive Party, 18, 25, 171
Promotion of Bantu Self-Govern-
   ment Act, 54

Public Safety Act, 30, 60

Rawles, Wann, 197
Reagan, Ronald, 101
Reeves, Ambrose, 22
Regina Mundi Church, 110-11
Representation of Natives Bill, 26
Revolution, French, 189
Rights, Bill of, 26
Rivonia Trial, 70, 73
Robben Island, 31, 69
Roberts, J. Deotis, 158
Rose Inns, James, 18
Rousseau, Jean Jaques, 129
Rubusana, Rev., 26

Sabotage Act, 32, 70
SACHED (South African Com-
   mittee for Higher Education), 94
Sampson, H. W., 11
Samuel, John, 94
Sanctions, economic, 193
SASOL (South African Coal, Oil
   and Gas Corporation), 194
Sauer, J. W., 18
Schlebusch Commission; Schle-
   busch/LeGrange Commission, 24
Schlemmer, Lawrence, 9, 18, 166,
   171
Scott, Michael, 22
Sebidi, John, 111
Seme, Pixley ka Isaka, 39, 76
Separate development, 10
Separate Representation of Voters
   Act, 53
Sharp, Gene, 143, 154, 167, 203-
   206
Sharpeville, 4, 31, 69-70, 188, 211-
   15
Shaull, Richard, 157, 175
Shepstone, Theophilus, 10
Sisulu, Walter, 69
Slabbert, van Zyl, 98, 107
Smuts, Jan Christiaan, 11
Sobukwe, Mangaliso Robert, 31,
   37, 41, 45, 65, 70, 75, 91, 158

Social Contract, 129
Social Gospel, 119
South Africa Act, 45
South Africa Constitution Bill, 90
South African Colored Peoples Organization (SACPO), 19, 50
South African Council of Churches, 24, 105, 175, 209, 211
South African Council of Trade Unions (SACTU), 62, 113
South African Indian Congress, 30, 48, 50, 53, 63, 68, 83, 109
South African Native Convention, 25
South African Native National Congress, 26, 39
South African Students Organization (SASO), 19, 27, 28, 33, 38, 42-43, 48, 52, 54, 57, 62, 66-67, 71
Southern African Catholic Bishops Conference, 23
Soweto Action Committee, 172
Soweto Committee of Ten, 172
Soweto Uprising, 4, 68, 71, 172, 188, 212-14
Steinwachs, Barbara, 174, 176
Stotts, Herbert, 174, 177, 179, 181-82
Strijdom, J. G., 13-14
Sullivan, Leon, 159-60
Suppression of Communism Act, 30, 32-33, 68, 70

Terrorism Act, 31-32, 67
Thesalonica Report, 200
Thoreau, Henry, 144
Tiro, Onkgopotse Ramothibi, 66
Tonnie, Ferdinand, 128
TransAfrica, 115
Transvaal Indian Congress, 26, 109
Treaty of Vereeniging, 16
Troup, Freda, 15

Tsolo, Nyakane, 65
Tsongas, Sen. Paul, 160
Tupamaro, 189
Tutu, Desmond, 94, 96-97, 102, 104, 115

UDF Declaration, 89, 100
Umkhonto We Sizwe, 19, 73-74
Union of South Africa, 39
United Nations, 102, 161, 165, 185, 193, 195-99, 207, 212
United Nations Charter, 197-98, 212
United Party, 16, 18, 169-70
Universal Declaration of Human Rights, 53
University Christian Movement, 19, 42, 71
Unlawful Organizations Act, 31, 69
Urban Guerilla Warfare, 187

Vaal Civic Association, 113
Vaal rent boycotts, 101
Van Riebeeck Day, 63
Verwoerd, Hendrik, 13-14, 17, 57
Viva Frelimo rallies, 63, 72, 144-46
Voice of America, 160
Vorster, John, 14-15, 17, 75, 151, 173

Waltzer, Michael, 140, 147, 149
Walshe, Peter, 171
Wilgespruit Fellowship Center, 211
Wogaman, Philip, 134, 136, 149, 153
World Alliance of Reformed Churches, 115
World Council of Churches (WCC), 21, 154, 200
Worrall, Denis, 171

YMCA, 43

Zanempilo Clinic, 66